CHAPTER 1

MANTRA: CLEANER OF MIND

All the movements of our body are direct result of electrical energy. Generation of this electrical energy happens in our brain. When this electrical energy, known as brain impulses, passes through our nervous system towards intended organ or faculty, then the act manifests. These electrical impulses emanating from our brain are called as orders or commands of our brain to all the organs and faculties of our body. Force of life or Prana is the medium through which we exist as living being or as an animate organism. At the same time all the five sense faculties of ours are also information gathering centers and these centers when stimulated send the information and impressions to our brain through the same nerves that starts from our brain. In a sense our nervous system is the same channel through which our brain send commands as well as receive data from our sense faculties.

Our mind is one of the faculties of our brain but as yet it is not pinpointed as to which specific part of our brain can be deemed as our mind. So in general it has to be accepted that as a whole our brain is the organ where our mind is or our total brain is our mind. Most of the impulses generated in our brain are registered on our mind, but there are some impulses which by-pass our conscious mind and can still be felt by us after they reach their intended site. Beating of our heart is directly regulated and related to our brain and continuous electrical supply from our brain is the reason our heart keeps beating. Similarly our brain also regulates our breathing. These functions of ours are called as involuntary functions of our body and up to some extent we do not have any conscious control over them. At the same time powerful emotions or emotional turmoil manifesting in our mind definitely effect changes in our heartbeat as well as in our breathing pattern and this phenomenon is proof enough that faculty of our mind has potentials to change even non-voluntary functions of our brain.

All of us know that around our body there is an energy circle that is known as our aura. This aura is the same electrical charge emanating from our brain, which not only reach all the nooks and crannies of our inner body but also spills out of our body. This aura is like halogenic glow we can see around the flame of the candle and its intensity as well as color keeps on changing as per the changes occur in the chemical composition of our brain and by the changes happening in our mind. Tibetan lamas learning medicine are said to be masters in reading aura of any person and can accurately place the personality traits as well as any illness the said person is going to face in near future well before its manifestation.

In Vedic culture much importance is given to the concept of mantras and its potential to change human mind and body. Any mantra is collection of some words in specific order and is to be pronounced or invoked in prescribed manner of posture and at certain times only. Any mantra when incanted generate effects of percussion on the seven chakaras existing in our body, of which the first chakra is at the base of our spinal chord near our faculty of regeneration or our sexual faculty and the last i.e. seventh, chakra is situated at the top of our head. The effect of percussion generates waves and the same waves flow in widening circles in our body. Similarly all the chakaras are deemed as power or energy points of our body and are deemed to regulate and control the functioning of all the internal organs of our body including our brain and mind. All the waves generated by incantation of the mantra accelerate the flow of energy present in our body as well as any blockage in the way of the flow is

TOWARDS AWARENESS

TOWARDS AWARENESS

By

Hemant Chopda

MD PUBLICATIONS PVT LTD
NEW DELHI

Published by

MD Publications Pvt Ltd

B/231-E, Greater Kailash - I

New Delhi-110048.

E-mail : contact@mdppl.com

Website : www.mdppl.com

Showroom

"MD House"

11, Darya Ganj

New Delhi-110002

Tel. : +91-11-23268645, 23271378

Fax : +91-11-29235450

ISBN : 81-7533-097-X

Printed by

Times Press

910, Jatwara Street, Darya Ganj

New Delhi-110002.

CONTENTS

GRATEFUL ACKNOWLEDGEMENTS

At the outset I would like to thank I.B.M.S. for providing me an opportunity for presentation of my views in this present form as project work for 2nd year M.S. degree course. Since long it was my intention to let people know that religioin is not mere concept or hypothesis, to be discussed as intelligent exercise but its practice should be integral part of our life. I have taken liberty to present my views about a form of Cognititve-Behavioral Psychotherapy, concepts of which are known and are available to all of us as Doctrine of Jainism.

I would like to thank following people without whose assistence and help this task would never have been completed; Prof. M.S.Bora, M.A. helped me as project guide and has published various papers related to the doctrine under discussions. Dr.M.K.Godbole M.B.B.S., D.C.H. our family physician, more than a elder brother and master of living arts. His insight in the matters related to medical science and its apllication in everyday life caused more awareness in me and the same is mentioned in succeding discussions at appropriate places. Dr.S.S.Akhegaonkar M.D. Consulting Psychiatrist is a renouned practitioner, who helped me from time to time to understand about clinical and theraupatic aspects of causes and reasons of human behavior and psychology. What I am today is the direct result of my association with Shri. Abasaheb V.Panse, Captain Indian Army, whose academic qualifications are M.Sc., L.L.B. but whose esoteric reach and experiences are beyond acedemia. I do not know what potential has he seen in me, but none the less he has taken me under his wings and tried to shape me as the person I am today. My elder brother, my wife, son and daughter are the most harsh critiques of me, their cooperation in my task made it possible for me to conclude the job satisfacterily. Writings of Shri Acharya Rajaneesh about Mahaveer and his theosophy about living, and material concerned with Yogic Sutras of Patanjali is the material which helped me develop my insight in matters related to religion.

I am humbly grateful to all of these people.

INTRODUCTION

Advent and existence of religious concepts as well as doctrine related to religion have not manifested accidentally. Our unawareness about its importance in everyday life has caused untold miseries to human race, and psychological as well as behavioral abnormalities are one of the personal miseries we are experiencing today. We as human are result of evolutionary process of the known existence but at the same time we are not the end product of evolution. Total existence known to man and man as part and parcel of the known existence are ever changing. Religion is considered as super-science compared to all the sciences developed by human, as it is directly related to human being.

We are meant to be happy and joyous people, as every animate in this existence do exist in joyous manner. But this phenomenon do not seems to be happening in case of human even though we are bestowed with superior intelligence and an equally superior mind. In a sense, because of our intelligence and superior mind, religion emerged as code of conduct for human being. No animate in this existence requires practicing any religion, because all animates are behaving in the manner intended by the nature.

Since long, to be religious and to practice any aspects of religion are considered as behavior of orthodox people. Emergence of this opinion happens due to reason that very few people understand and know, as to why they are going through the process and how they are going to benefit in the end. Similarly rituals and its practice are followed in traditional manner or in the manner practiced by our forefathers without knowing as to why they are to be practiced. As most of the doctrines are laid down long past and as the conditions at the time of their emergence are no more, the doctrine looses the meaning and its applicability in current time frame. It is believed that to be religious cause profound tranquility and peace in the life and existence of the practitioner, but this phenomenon do not appear to be happening in the being of practitioner or is not perceptible to the others who are around the practitioner.

Industrial revolution and various scientific innovations are meant to be for betterment of mankind. Similarly medical science is also developing in rapid rate for the betterment of human race. Logically all these advancement should have made all the people more contented and happy as there is nothing that is out of reach of human. But it seems that the more advanced we are becoming then in the direct proportion we are drifting further away from our basic being or self. And at this juncture religion can play its decisive part.

To be religious and its practice is the way of life where our awareness increases about our self and about our surrounding, and for the first time we start to understand as to what we really are and how everything in this existence is related to us or not. As human, are we always meant to expect, anticipate or desire from others and are we destined to always experience disappointments and disillusions? Why we do not experience eternal joy, happiness and contentment even after much coveted achievement, for which we have gone through many efforts? There are many questions and there are many answers to every question, but no answer remains exactly correct or apt for long, and again the same questions start to haunt us. The doctrine discussed in the succeeding chapters is an effort to make us understand where we can change and how this change can integrate our personality. Similarly, as any change towards positive growth primarily happens through our mind, then to be religious is a means that helps us to discover ourselves as to what we really are and what potentials we have. In this light we do not have to invent new ways to solve our problems as whatever we will invent will be applied from the outside, as whatever is applied from the outside will be a support or a prop and thus the invention and the invented will not help integrate our being in the longer run.

In religious parlance realization of self-means, experiencing our self in its natural form and realization of potentials means our capacity to excel in our chosen field. But the manner in which this doctrine is to be understood and applied is intended to be used to realize our potentials by way of our achievement, and the achievement can be religious or of such a nature whereby the person will be considered as unique in his chosen field.

It is believed that behavioral abnormalities and various psychoses occur due to core beliefs of a person. Core beliefs are strong beliefs that we may hold about our self and other people or objects. We do not question these beliefs, but they are simply assumed to be true and are not always obvious and most of the times we may not be aware about their being. However, as they are very powerful, when our thoughts or emotions appear to be extremely negative, stagnant and overwhelming, it is likely that such beliefs are dominating the very core of our being. At the same time the nature of these core beliefs do not correspond with the accepted norms prevalent in the society in which the said person is living. Similarly the said person do not accept the proof that the way in which he behaves is not according to accepted social or familial norms, but on the contrary due to his core beliefs the said proof is altered or distorted in the manner that is nearer to his core belief. Intention of this thesis is to show that before the consolidation of core beliefs and its manifestation happens, by birth we inherit some inclination towards certain beliefs and assumptions and certain personality traits that are passed on to us at the time of our conception by our parents as well as by our forefathers. In this regard we take birth with some of beliefs of our parents genetically. Practice of religious doctrine known as austerity is intended to acquaint us with our basic nature or natural form or our self, so that when we become totally aware about our self then our perception, beliefs and assumptions will change and our understanding will become more clear.

In these discussions our senses are termed as faculties and the way they are expressed are termed as attitudes. Our overall behavior is considered as conditioned behaviors for the reason that till we do not know as to why we are behaving in the manner we are behaving. Our mind is also considered as one of the faculties and how to use it as faculty and not as central to our being is also clarified.

To my understanding the statement that religion is eternal and appears to take new form from person to person and from time to time is factual statement. So based on this fact, it is my personal belief that Doctrine of Jainism in practice since long is not bearing spectacular results only because its practice is happening in traditional manner due to which its true essence is not understood and practiced in proper perspective in relation to current environment. In this light the practitioner of the doctrine seems to be religious person but in reality is not reaching anywhere. In no way this writing is to be considered as criticism of the doctrine or the current practitioner, but from purely psychological view point it is my intention to clarify the reader that behind any act or behavior the thought, the mindset, beliefs and the assumptions of any person is the driving force because of which our behavior pattern emerges. And so the elaboration of the concepts appearing in the subsequent chapters is my honest effort to let the reader verify on his own whether his beliefs and assumptions are on the mark or are they to be altered, changed or to be cast away. To my limited experience, difference between religious and non-religious person happens at the level of mind but should not be measured by mere acts alone. It is my firm belief that every religious doctrine is meant to make changes in the mind of the practitioner and when these changes takes place then the acts and behavior of the person also changes and then such a person starts to become religious which is nothing but gradual increase in his awareness, maturity and wisdom.

removed which ultimately stimulates all the faculties of ours and infuse the same with more energy.

Any person practicing incantation of mantra is suggested to instill pious thoughts in the mind at the time of incantation. In this manner our faculty of regeneration gets stimulated, our breathing become deep and heart throbs in regulated but powerful manner. Deep breathing cause calming and tranquilizing effect on our mind and our heart throbbing in powerful manner carries oxygen and nourishment to all the parts of our body including our brain. Till the incantation is going on all the faculties of ours function as one integrated system and overall we experience the feeling of wholesome being. And this integrated and peaceful state of mind is the window period when we can instill positive and creative thoughts in our mind and can pursue the same upto satisfactory conclusion.

Most of the times it is our ego that causes hindrance in the development in positive and creative manner. And for this reason mantra is the tool to dissolve our ego for some length of time in which we get the chance to set our mind in right way. In Hindu philosophy "Aum" as basic mantra is in use since long and various other mantras are also developed placing Aum at their start. Many practitioners and masters are of the opinion that even Aum as basic mantra has potentials to generate energizing and tranquilizing effects on our mind.

Potentials of mantra is considered as a tool of ground breaking to our otherwise conditioned and rigid mind. Once this practice is applied for some time our mind become mellow and flexible; then this flexibility is used to start the journey towards austerity, which we adapt in the manner as to how we can use our mind to our best advantage in creative and positive manner and realize our full potentials.

Mahaveer was the 24th and last known Tirthnkara of Jaini culture, & the discussions we are going to have are incorporated in the doctrine known as Doctrine of Jainism. In this doctrine it is shown that how as human beings we think and behave keeping our mind as central to our existence, how erroneous our belief is and what we really are in reality. All the concepts are based on very scientific manner and can be applied and verified in our day-to-day existence. In a nutshell the doctrine is nothing but the model way of living for all the human beings in fulfilling and creative manner, and ultimately realize our full potentials.

Mantra and its meaning as laid down by Mahaveer, is as follows-

Namo Arihantanam; I bow to the enlightened souls. Namo Siddhanam; I bow to the liberated souls. Namo Ayariyanam; I bow to religious leaders. Namo Uvajjayanam; I bow to the religious masters. Namo Loe Savva Sahunam; I bow to all the monks and nuns of the world. Eso Panch Namukkaro; these five salutations are capable of, Savva Pava Panasano; destroying all the illusions and sins and this is, Mangalanch Savvesin; the first happiness among all forms, Padhamam Havai Mangalam; of all happiness.

In the above mantra Jaini practitioners do not ask for any favors or material benefits from any of the godly persons like Tirthankaras or monks or nuns. But by saluting such persons Jaini receive the inspiration from the above-mentioned five benevolent for the right path of true happiness and total freedom from the miseries of life as well as realization of the self.

In all there are five salutations in this mantra. The meaning of the word Arihanta is the person who no more has any enmity, conflicts or negative emotions against which he has to struggle. The person known as Arihanta is the being who stay in non-conflict that in other words is to exist in pure awareness. To be Arihanta is peak after which there does not remain anything to achieve. It is the destination after which there are no more journeys. In this state nothing remains to be done, nothing to achieve, nothing to live for; there is total end to any and every act. What remains is pure existence till the body parts from the force of life, Prana or spirit. And this being or stage is called as Arihanta.

The concept is very novel in the sense that no specific person or deity is mentioned in this maha-mantra, not even Jaini culture is mentioned. The reason being, Jain culture accepts the fact that Arihanta not only happens in Jaini following but in other cultures also. It is accepted that this phenomenon can and may happen in which this state can be reached by other doctrines also, and all those persons are appreciated; that to be pure being is sufficient in itself to bow in front of by way of salutation.

In our present times there are various religious practices and doctrines in vogue but this kind of all encompassing maha-mantra is one and only, where pioneers from other religions are also appreciated and accepted. This mantra is dedicated to those who have realized the ultimate of their potentials and it is dedicated to goal and not to any person. By way of definition of language, word Arihanta is negative in the meaning; what they have achieved is not mentioned but what they have castaway is told. As there is no limit in negativity and as our language is limit bound, word Arihanta is used in abstract fashion.

In the second salutation a positive word is applied i.e. Namo Siddanam. Meaning of the Siddha is the person who is totally liberated from all the thoughts, emotions, acts, desires in worldly parlance. This state of Siddha being is equal to Arihanta in the sense that even Siddha is on the way to be Arihanta. In Vedic culture, to be Siddha is to be ready to go into oblivion where Arihanta has reached.

Third salutation is Namo Ayariyanam. Meaning of the word Ayariya is Acharya state of being. Acharya is the person whose acharana i.e. behavior is as per his thoughts and what he achieves is in accordance to his thoughts. This state is the sign of total integration of the intelligence, mind and body of the person. In other words his being in behavior is in correspondence to his achievement. We as common people can look at the behavior of Acharya and can appreciate his being as to what he talks he does and his talking and doing is as per his thoughts and intentions. But in comparison, behavior of Arihanta & Siddha is beyond our comprehension as in their liberated state they may behave or not behave at all in worldly manner. More or less the same dilemma has to be faced in case of Acharya also; we do not know what his achievement is going to be but his behavior correspondences to the day-to-day behavior that we can comprehend and understand. As the way of behavior and motive behind it cannot be perceived easily by our conditioned nature, in the end we have to accept the person and bow in front of him on the premise that whoever behaves as per his achievement is Acharya.

Fourth salutation is Namo Uvajjayanam. Meaning of the word Uvajjaya is Uppadhyay; not only thought, not only corresponding behavior, not only achievement but also his way of talking is in correspondence with his basic thought. A person who has achieved knowledge and who behaves as per his knowledge and who talks as per his acquired knowledge is accepted as Uppadhyay.

Fifth and last salutation is towards those who are so simple and straightforward that we may think about them as mere ordinary or average person's, who practice religion with total faith without any inclination for recognizance. And such people are termed as Monks and Nuns. At this stage it should be understood that these salutations are not going to make any difference to all the above persons of achievement, even though they are directed towards them but are going to make us aware about our self and induce us to be like them. This mantra is just a cause to make us bow in front of them and our bowing is the key to make us flexible towards change that will help us grow in positive and creative manner.

Mahaveer is of the opinion that no mantra is useful till the practitioner is ready to accept its potentials for self-growth. Even if we go to temple, mosque or church and bow in front of the idol or deity with the emotion that our supplication is going to benefit the idol, then we exist under false notion. All the places of devotion are places where we have to forget about our image and ego, what we are in worldly manner, but we should have understanding that there is one place where we may bow with the feelings that we have still not reached where others known as pioneers has reached. Bowing is the cause that makes us humble, because till we are not humble we are not going to change. When any one is ready to bow his ego starts to dissolve and this dissolution of ego is the cause that opens our heart and mind towards awareness about self and our surrounding.

Basic importance of any mantra is to develop receptivity in our self and this receptivity generates faith in us.

CHAPTER 2

WHAT IS SUPERIOR AND SACRED?

Mahaveer says that what we have to become we have to think on the same theme. Reason being that we could achieve only that, about which we positively know or can imagine about. On the contrary what we have not seen or imagined, we can't be. We can only achieve anything, about which we positively expect to happen by heart and mind.

It is not only blood that flows through our veins or not electrical current that courses through our nervous system, but third and important flow of prana-urja (Force of Life / Vital Force) also flow through our body. Chinese healing therapy known as Acupuncture Therapy is also based on this third flow known as prana-urja. There are around 700 points on our body from which our prana-urja can be influenced by way acupuncture needle pricks. Practitioners of Acupuncture therapy are of the opinion that blockage in the flow of our prana-urja is the reason we have to face various illnesses and in this therapy this blocked or interrupted flow is regulated and then the patient regains health.

We have to understand that our belief about anything reinforces our thought and such reinforced thought literally manifests and takes tangible form. The thought thus reinforced becomes consolidated and it merges in our force of life or prana-urja. Once its merger happens with our force of life, the thought works like initiator or as driving force and we start to behave in the manner by which the thought starts to take form of actual act.

According to Mahaveer our mind is like magnetic tape, once any thought emerges and when the thought seems to be worth pursuing we start to contemplate, brood and go on thinking on the basic thought. Further Mahaveer is of the opinion that everything and anything happens due to our thought (dharna). Here dharna is to be understood as our state of mind and once we start to pay conscious attention to any thought our mind molds itself accordingly. There is a saying that as you sow, so shall you reap.

Any person who is desirous to be a creative person, and any person who has to start the journey towards realization of the self, has to consciously install good thoughts in his mind. Any mantra is the tool and its incantation is the source that helps to install holy and sacred thoughts in our mind. It is to be understood that core of every human is naturally good and creative. Why good, pious or sacred thoughts are given this much importance? In Hindu culture pious or sacred has a synonymous word i.e. Mangalam. By birth we are habitual to think in the manner that is advantageous to us, so we learn and adopt this kind of thinking process by following members of our family and other acquaintances. All this thinking process is self-centered without regards for any other object or person. And in this manner we behave in conditioned manner. So most of the times our behavior in conditioned manner brings back results that are not as per our expectations and we feel or experience unhappiness or sorrow. To break our mold of conditioned behaving person who has to experience sorrow and miseries all his life, we have to analyze our mind, remold it in creative manner by installing good thoughts in our mind consciously. And this changing of our old thoughts to new and good one is possible, provided we are ready to change.

According to Mahaveer our Chetana- force of life is infinite, and with our will we can make it move as per our intentions. At the same time it is without any basic source, because any source, however powerful it may be or however in abundance its generating potentials may be, is bound to dry-up now or later. And this is the reason Mahaveer has denied the concept of God as creator of existence as well as human being. Mahaveer says that our soul is selfsame and its vehicle that is our body, because of which we are recognized as humans, behave and act according to the setup of our mind and intelligence. We have to understand that our mind is the catalyst, which can be changed and molded in desired manner. This declaration of Mahaveer gave primary importance to individual and made humans responsible for himself, who may exist in average manner or can change in creative ways and realize his full potentials.

It is our soul that turns into super soul at the time of realization and this state is termed as Paramatman, where for the first time it is perceived in its original form. Our soul is selfsame, self illuminating, it do not receive power from any one as it is powerful in itself, it is not created by anyone and no one has potentials to destroy it nor it is dependent on anyone or at the mercy of anyone.

Realization of the soul in its original form is the state of Arihanta or Arihanta being. And Jaini culture accepts this happening in all and any religious following. Mahaveer asks as to what is superior in this existence; to be Arihanta, to be Siddha & to be Acharya are superior. Every human has potentials to achieve any of this states and this achievement should be the goal of every human being.

What is the meaning of to be religious? Different people will give various opinions about this subject and every known religious doctrine has its own opinions. But Mahaveer defines religion in very different manner; to be in self is to be religious; when everything and everyone exist in its characteristic nature, animate or inanimate, is religious. And every person, when he/she remains in his/her basic nature without getting influenced by anyone or anything, and behaves as per his/her nature is to be understood as religious person. According to doctrine of Jainism when any person tries to influence any thing or anyone outside of his nature is considered as violent person or whoever can be influenced by anything or anyone is to be recognized as bonded person. This concept can be understood by the example that, when fire is burning in its purest form there does not materialize any smoke. But as per a saying, when there is smoke there has to be fire, is erroneous, because smoke materializes only when there are impurities in the fuel or water is present in the fuel.

As per Mahaveer every thing in this nature exists as per its characteristic nature and potentialities. To get out of our original characteristic nature is to exist in non-religious existence and trying to sought after or achieve that which is not in the bounds of our potentials is the cause of misery and unhappiness. So to be religious is to analyze our capabilities and to consciously strive to reach the realization of our potentials has to be our goal or aim.

As per the renowned theosopher Shreiwetzer what is worth achieving to any human being is- to be more and more, to be deep and deep, to be in and in, and constantly turning into something more and more. But we can achieve more and more only that of which we have any glimpse or know about. And Mahaveer suggests that to be Arihanta, Siddha & Acharya are the peaks of human potentials and these states are superior in human existence and are worth achieving.

About human mind, Mahaveer and all the pioneers of all the religions as well as great thinkers, philosophers and psychologists have stated that, to be a contended human being we have to consciously analyze our mind, regimen it under the guidance of our inherent intelligence and acquired wisdom, change it where necessary, then use it as an instrument but do not let it wander aimlessly as if it is master of our being and existence. In this regard even Freud is of the opinion that human beings are nothing but bunch of desires, but according to Mahaveer, at this junction religion can be helpful to us.

In the book written by Acharya Rajneesh on the doctrine of Mahaveer, western psychologists are severely criticized; these psychologists are not helping people to leave aside their sacrilegious behavior, but on the contrary are analyzing the same as a natural aspect of human being. Today, if we look at western culture and the way in which those people exist and behave, then the major responsibility goes to such psychologists because they are stating that ignoble aspect of human behavior is inherent in every human. It seems that they are not aware of importance of religious side to human existence or are interpreting the doctrine in erroneous manner. As every human has potentials to exist in higher states and we as psychotherapists have responsibility to make people aware in this context, that there is a way by which we can come out of our present predicament; and the way is to practice any religious doctrine of their choice.

Its a common practice all over the world, that just by taking birth in any family that is following any religion, the newborn has to inherit the same religion. When this type of acceptance happens due to inheritance, people start to loose meaning of the religion, as they have to behave as per the norms specified and secondly it is not their own choice. Whatever we inherit by way of succession without doing anything on our part as our own achievement then such inheritance cause boredom and apathy towards inherited. For this reason people should have open choice to follow and accept any doctrine of religion of their choice, irrespective of following of the family. Otherwise there do not seems to be any spark left in the human being to assert himself or do anything on his own or test the inherited doctrine on his own.

CHAPTER 3

ABOUT SURRENDER AND ITS REASON

What is the difference between all the religious pioneers and people like us? All the pioneers exist beyond the realities perceived and experienced by mind or through the mind, but we people singularly exist through mind only. And this distinction happens only because we are not totally aware as to what we really are but pioneers have realized as to what they really are.

Association of our basic and original self with our mind is the cause that makes us believe that our body is our basic self and we do not have any other identity except our bodily existence. Intervention of our mind has become our second nature, which is nothing but conditioned nature and existence. As our mind is one of the faculties of our brain and our force of life or Prana is altogether different force, religion is the scientific process whose application makes us aware as to what we really are.

Surrender has completely different meaning when it is applied in the context of religion. To surrender is state of mind as ego is. Further it should be understood that both surrender and ego are emotions that are two sides of the same state of mind. There is very fine distinction between surrender and acceptance of surrender. In surrender the act or completion of total surrender may happen after some time, and to arrive at this state may happen after too much vacillation or we may turn back and regain the prior state. This vacillation can be termed as deliberation, as to are we really going to surrender, why we want to surrender etc. But to accept to surrender happens when our experience teaches us and shows us that till now whatever we have thought and expected is not happening, and as a last resort we have to surrender. In this context we arrive at the decision to accept the surrender after all the due deliberation and this acceptance is the sudden jump from egoistic being to surrendered being. And this accepting to surrender, as a state of mind, is considered as dissolution or death of ego, after which we can start on the journey of religiousness.

Bhagwan Krishna asked Arjuna to leave aside all the doubts and deliberations, and to surrender to me i.e. Krishna. That period was of total faith and the tenet was acceptable because people were simple and straightforward. But at the time of Mahaveer the period was of logical thinking. Similarly Mahaveer was of the opinion that to suggest something to someone, even though the suggestion is going to be beneficial to that someone, is transgression on the free will of the other, and was considered as very subtle form of violence. On the contrary to ask anyone to surrender to me was treated as egoistic on the part of the asking person as well as challenging the will of the other person. As per Mahaveer's doctrine, acceptance of surrender should happen with surrender's free will, without influence or suggestion of any other person.

Religion is nothing but way of living in concert with the vast existence and surrounding, peacefully and joyously. Similarly religion is to be treated as code of conduct for human beings or it may be considered as art of living or science of living. Till the practice of religion does not make us realize as to what we really are, it is a scientific way of living and once we come to know our real identity then the same religion takes the form of art of living and existence. Religion as code of conduct is applicable to humans, developed by humans for humans only, because of existence of our powerful mind and matching intelligence. All the animals in this existence do not require any religion for the simple reason that they exist and behave as per their intended nature, but only human being has potentials either to be a super or model human being or can exist and behave in the manner lower than animal.

To be religious is the last resort for human being to understand his true potentials in relation to the existence, apply them in proper manner and become free from all the heartbreak, miseries, unhappiness and sorrow. When we become disillusioned that whatever we have desired and expected do not happen, or is not happening, whatever we have achieved turns to ashes, whatever achievements we have made is not capable to make us satisfied forever; then religion becomes the mainstay to our being. This is the stage where we come to know that till now we have existed under the dictates of our mind and we experienced nothing but illusions of happiness and joy; from now on we are going to analyze our self and in this analysis, for the first time we come face to face with our ego, and understand that our ego is the key because of which we were experiencing illusions. This first encounter with our ego is the stage when we start to be critical about our egoistic state and this awareness is the pivotal point when our ego starts to dissolve and becomes surrender. This happening is called as surrender to the religion and we start to become religious, and this surrender is the foundation on which religion stands firmly.

It is the opinion of the people who are studying the phases of evolutionary process, that human started to develop intelligently when he started to stand on his two legs, and also at this stage his ego also started to develop. Any upright person is not standing straight physically, but he also becomes more opinionated and rigid about his beliefs and principles. And this is the reason that when we go to mandir, mosque, church or places of religious congregations, that we have to prostrate or sit on our keens in front of the deity or altar. Process of surrender or dissolution of ego primarily starts with our body.

Dr. Lawrenzove of Institute of Suggestology of Bulgaria has done lots of research in the field of radical teaching & learning technology. According to him Vedic practice of Shawasana is closely related to the concept of surrender. In Shawasana we lay down on the earth or on a mat laid on the ground, and the moment we lay down we start to relax not only physically but mentally also. In our laying down we leave all the bodily defenses, which do not happen when we are standing. At the same time to defend while standing our mind also remain alert, and this constant alertness cause stress and tension in our mind. So when we lay down first our muscles relaxes and when our mind appreciates this relaxation of our body, then it also shifts from alertness to relaxation. The same phenomenon occurs when we sleep parallel to earth in the night and feel freshness in the morning. In supine position our defenses as well as our will to resist also relaxes, this is the reason why psychiatrist ask his patient to lay down on the coach before he starts to talk about his problems.

Acceptance of surrender is an emotion or state of mind, which causes the feelings like floating weightlessly or like jumping into a flowing river without any resistance or to let ourselves go as the current carries us. To be egoistic is to be fearful; no one wants to show his fear of loosing control or how helpless or how uncertain he is, so ego becomes our camouflage.

Acceptance of surrender changes our mental geometry and enhances the flow of our force of life or prana. The surrendering person does not have to fight with the general rules of existence but transcends them, which otherwise cause mental bondages. Surrender cause opening of our mind on all the levels, so that positive changes can be made easily.

About religion Jesus Christ has made a very enlightening statement; "Those who will try to save themselves will be no more, but those who are willing to be no more, no might has strength to destroy him."

CHAPTER 4

RELIGION: THE ART TO BE IN THE SELF

According to Mahaveer to exist in eternal joy and happiness as well as total freedom happens when we are religious. And to be religious happens only when we exist in our nature as a human being. Feeling the emotions of sorrow and unhappiness is the indicator that we have deviated from our basic nature and are not in concert with our self.

Whenever we try to attach ourselves with the other and whenever the said other is not compatible to our nature then this association becomes the cause of discord with our nature which results in friction between our self and the other. This friction is the cause of sorrow and unhappiness. When we try to save the other that is out of bound of our nature, then irrespective of all the toils and efforts the other cannot be saved at all and it will be lost. Experience of frustration is the direct result of those efforts, which are made to maintain the association between the other that is not in accordance with our nature and loosing the other make us realize how fruitless our endeavor was, so when our efforts thus become empty gesture then this futility becomes the cause of frustration.

Since after birth we are conditioned and this conditioning gets reinforced when we start to realize that not only we, but also all the people of our family as well as all the people of the society behave as we are behaving. This general pattern of behavior takes the form of norm of our existence. Then as per this accepted norm, we also start to expect from our self that which we want to be and from the others, that they should act and behave which will help us to realize our expectations from the others. In this manner we never look into our self, as to are we capable to achieve what we are expecting, or do we have the capability or potentials to fulfill our expectations? In a sense we reject our self without understanding our basic nature and start to behave in the manner the others are behaving. There are very few people who accept themselves as they are; because of which they live without stress and frustrations.

Without understanding about ourselves, when we try to become someone or the other as our ideal or role model, or when we covet the position we think is ideal for us, then this motivational behavior remain as mirage only, but we do not get the expected or reach anywhere. This non-fulfillment of our expectations or not reaching the ultimate goal we have set for our self, become cause of illusion and ultimately we become disillusioned.

For this kind of behavior Mahaveer has coined a very apt term, he says that we are other oriented people. Mahaveer says that ultimately we can achieve only that which is well within our potentials i.e. our self and nothing else. We can strive, make more efforts, hope to achieve, may dream about achieving and sometimes may have illusion that we are going to achieve the expected, but in the end we do not reach or get what we have anticipated to get.

Sartre made a statement that the other is hell. But according to Mahaveer the statement is only half-truth, he says that the other may be hell but emphasis should not be on the other as hell, but should be on the self as heaven. Mahaveer went still further and denied the other as hell only to show that as there are expectations from the other, then the non-fulfillment of the expectations from the other is perceived as hell. When we perceive heaven in the other who is going to fulfill our expectations and when fulfillment do not manifest, then by the law of our conditioned nature the other become hell. The other may happen in the form of wife, husband, son, daughter, friend, riches, position or anything, and is called as delusional expectations. If we do not expect from the other, then there is no cause of sorrow. If we correctly understand the concept of Mahaveer then it becomes perfectly clear that other is never hell, but our expectations from the others and to believe that the other is heaven, creates hell.

It is a fact that we never or very rarely learn from our past acts or performance. Either we blame the circumstances or blame the other, but to us we are never at fault. And in this manner we remain under illusions or create new illusions, which in reality is not the case or which is not going to happen as we anticipate. We willfully fantasize where truth is something altogether different. And cause of all this manifestation is our conditioned mindset. How illusive we want to be depends on our sustaining power, but now or later the illusion is bound to break our belief. What we have to do is start to check our self, analyze our self and stop finding substitutes to blame, which we have perceived as our wish or expectation fulfilling agents. We have to try to pinpoint and learn from our experience, that are we making the same mistakes again and again, as this phenomena is the cause of frustration.

Mahaveer says religion is sacred, but which religion is sacred? The religion of non-violence (Ahimsa), tranquility (Sayyam) and austerity (Tapa) is sacred, but no further explanation is given. To go into experience there is no necessity of any reasons, explanations or formulas; but our own logic is sufficient. If we have to check experience we have to go through the process of experiencing but for logical formulas logical explanation is adequate. People like Mahaveer or Einstein make statements. If we ask Einstein why water is combination of oxygen and hydrogen, then Einstein will say what is the meaning of – why? It is so. Science makes statements about other and religion makes statements about self, science is about objective and religion is about subjective. For scientific verifications we have to go into laboratories and with the same token, for subjective verifications we have to go into self that is religion. At the same time what is considered as sin or sacrilegious by general population is- to act or behave against religious doctrines is sin, but this belief is totally erroneous according to Mahaveer.

Have we at any time thought that whenever sorrow or unhappiness is experienced by us, the cause seems to be other and not our self? We are always ready to blame for our failures and the blame always lies with circumstances, shortage of money, spouse, friends, shaky business or others who are not capable to understand us, but we never blame ourselves. And this phenomenon happens due to our belief that we always expect joy and happiness from the other, and this belief of ours is the root cause of all the unhappiness. So Mahaveer says that, if we have to experience true joy and happiness at all, then we have to verify our above-mentioned belief and start to analyze our self. Because when we expect something from someone, then we forget that that someone expects the same of us, in the same manner. And this is how illusions come into being.

Our mindset entrenched in conditioned manner is very intricate and it do not function retrospectively. In our relationship with others, we expect something to manifest that we anticipate and up to certain extent our expectations seems to be materializing, but what we have basically anticipated do not manifest or we believe that if not immediately, then at some future date it will manifest. And for this reason Mahaveer labels us as future oriented people, we do not want to live or exist in present. This characteristic of our mind to exist in hope, which is going to realize in future, is the key that creates illusions. Mahaveer says that if all the expectations of all the people come to fruition immediately and as expected, then people will become mad or may commit suicide. Unless and until we start to live in present, hope of good future is the only mainstay for the people, which give them sustaining power to endure present. People from materialistically advanced society experience more emptiness and stress, for the simple reason that they do not experience any privations, and very few anticipations remain to be realized in future. In such a case, to experience the thrill of living they have to take resort in use of various drugs or have to project and express their desires and expectations in bizarre manner.

Why we feel sorrow in our existence when we do anything? The reason is we have lost the capacity to live in present, to extract maximum out of present circumstances, with the notion that in future circumstances will be more favorable. We say that in present we are laying the foundation because of which our future will be more secured and rewarding. In this manner we loose the opportunities presented as of now, as our sight is set on our future, but we forget that our present is the key that is creating our future. We have to change our beliefs that our future may or may not be rewarding and joyous, but if we do not exploit our present to the fullest, then there are chances that we may not have any future at all. As the existence in which we are living is ever changing, where circumstances change regularly, where people with whom we interact also change as per the circumstances; so if we do not change as per the demands of time then we will be left behind to flounder in our self created whirlpool. Similarly what we have experienced in past and what we are experiencing now, can help us to understand ourselves as to whether we are correct in our assumptions or not. But when we intend to go through any experience in future in the set manner of our past performance, then it becomes reality that what we have anticipated will very rarely happen and the experience we were anticipating will not manifest, as our future is still long way from happening. To experience is characteristic feature of present only and we can only expect and anticipate from future, but cannot be sure about its manifestation.

Practice of religion or to be religious, is nothing but self-appointed cognitive therapy that teaches us to be aware of what we really are in relation to circumstances and how to be more productive and happy in our present. We have gone through countless experiences and are still going through many and most of the experiences have taught us that they are not worth repeating again even in future also. But it seems that our conscious attention span is very weak, our memory retention is very short term and this is the reason why we go through similar situations in the same manner as we had gone through in our past. We very rarely look at our performance in contemplative manner and our existence and being in this manner is termed by Mahaveer as unconscious being or unconscious existence.

As far as memory of repetitive behavior is concerned we behave in the manner like we are in trance or in a state of hypnosis. We look at any object on display, which appeal to us and then we think that having that object is going to make radical change in our being. But when we have that much-coveted object in our possession, there do not happen any change in us or in our surrounding, nothing of novelty is felt by us but on the contrary we feel the same as we were used to feel before the possession of the object. In this manner we behave like automatons, irrespective of having potentials to consider pros or cons of any behavior and its aftereffects. In our conditioned nature, as far as day-to-day existence is concerned, we are used to fall in the same ditch again and again. To save our selves from this predicament we change the ways, but again we found new ditches and fall into it. It is not fault of the way or the ditch, but our unconscious being is the cause due to which we fall again and again. Till we are ready to consciously take stock of our self and change in proper manner, the fall is inevitable.

Why to be non-religious is termed as sinful? According to Mahaveer, desire to expect joy and happiness from any other without being aware of our true nature,

is to be considered as sin. For sin Mahaveer uses the word deviation; according to him sin is state of mind, and is the learned and conditioned belief of our mind. To deviate from our true being is the cause of sorrow and unhappiness, and to exist in this manner is to exist in sin or to be non-religious. Even our physical body is not ours; in future it will be full of diseases and illness, it will age and become old, infirm, and it will be taken away from us when death happens. So when our own body that is so near us is going to cause us pain, betray us & ultimately desert us, then others are more far away. Not understanding this phenomenon and not accepting its inevitability is deviation from our self, and is the cause of all the sorrow and unhappiness. Mahaveer says that our body is not ours and what we are is not our body, to understand and appreciate this phenomenon is the intention of religion. Whenever we feel pain, sorrow or disillusions, understand and look at where this experience is felt, and to differentiate this happening is called as to be religious.

The reason we do not exist in joyous or happier manner is we neglect our self and expect joy and happiness from other; the other may be animate or inanimate. In this case if the other is a human being then we forget that he has also his own agenda to be fulfilled, his own expectations to be realized, his own desires to be met, considering all this, is he going to give priority to our expectations from him? The same happens with inanimate objects, inanimate objects exist in the existence with certain characteristic limitations, but if we expect more from the same that is not possible as our expectations are out of bounds of the nature of the object, then we feel sorrow. And this dependency of ours on the others make us object oriented. Then at the end we either feel sorrow for non-fulfillment of our expectations or has to fantasize that we are going to get what we want, this is illusion. The doctrine we are discussing is to make us aware as to how we can exist in joyous state of being, because to be joyous is not our right but our destiny also.

By conditioning and imposition of acquired habits on our basic nature, we have become extroverts. Purpose of religious practice is the procedure to redirect our attention from objective to subjective i.e. to alter the psyche. According to Mahaveer, meaning of the word religion is twofold; to be religious is to exist in self, and the doctrine is the set of processes or procedures, practice of which helps us to direct our focus towards self. Ahimsa or non-violence is considered as soul of religion, Tapa or austerity is circumference of the religion and Sayyam or tranquility is bridge between center and circumference. In other words Ahimsa is soul, Sayyam is physical body and Tapa is breath. So if breathing stops, soul will exist and body will also exist but we will be no more. Similarly if tranquility breaks, then austerity is possible and non-violence can be practiced but no religion will manifest.

As per Mahaveer non-violence or Ahimsa do not denote what we understand and accept in conventional manner. Mahaveer's concept of Ahimsa is somewhat similar to Buddha's Tathata i.e. total acceptability. To Mahaveer Ahimsa is; on my part I will not transgress or encroach anywhere, will not be hurdle to anyone, will go on my own way in such a manner that no one will perceive my passing as cause or reason to change his intended course or experience inconvenience, I will exist in such a manner that no one will experience my existence. My being will be of such nature that no one will feel my presence or perceive my existence.

As understood and accepted by general population as well as perceived by Jaini's, meaning of the word Ahimsa to them is: do not harm anyone, do not be cause of sorrow or hardship to anyone or do not kill or be cause of anyone to be killed. This understanding is very surface understanding and is in direct contradiction to Mahaveer's basic concept of to be religious. To Mahaveer, to be religious is to exist in self and when anyone exists in this fashion then being of others looses any significance to the religious person. Similarly Mahaveer says that even though you are willing and ready to cause sorrow to anyone, but if the other is not willing and ready to accept the sorrow caused by you, then you could not pass sorrow or unhappiness to anyone. In the same manner it is absolute illusion of ours that we can make anyone happy if the other is not ready and willing to be happy or joyous.

All of us are perfectly aware that till now we have tried to be happy in various circumstances and by various means, but at the end we come to know that what we expect, very rarely happens. Then we shift our attention willingly from to be happy towards unhappiness, with the notion that as every time we have tried to be happy caused unhappiness, now we are going to create unhappiness, at the end of which we will become happy. In both the instances our aim is to achieve happiness, but now we are going into exercise in reverse manner. According to Mahaveer, in both the instances we shift from one extreme to other. And it is law of nature, that whenever we exist in any extreme we have to experience stress and tension, and this cause further sorrow and unhappiness.

For example, if some one is used to praise us continuously but all of a sudden he insults us, then the amount of sorrow we feel become so profound that we become gloomy and we forget his praiseworthy remarks made in the past. Considering quantitative praise over extended period of time, one incidence of insulting remark should not be considered as stinging. But as we have become conditioned due to constant praising remarks from the others, we become over sensitive and become emotionally vulnerable with the false notion that in reality we are praiseworthy so no one should criticize us.

If we look at all the sorrows and unhappiness we have experienced till now in honest manner and try to analyze them, then we will realize that 99% of the times these sorrows or unhappiness are self created due to our erroneous notions about our self and our worth. Many people who are acquainted with us tell us about their difficulties and how manfully they have weathered the crisis. If we observe the manner in which they talk, the emotions they show, how in detail they explain every thing and how they exaggerate, the impression they are trying to make is so transparent that even pinprick is perceived as wound of sword. It is a general psychological fact that people crave attention of the others in any way or at any cost in positive or negative manner, but very rarely accepts indifference. Even Mark Twain has stated that, " either you praise me or insult me but do not be indifferent to me". In either praise or insult we feel that we have some substance, people are at least counting us for good reasons or at least for our nuisance value, which boost our ego. On the contrary indifference directly strike our ego or our image about our self and make us feel that we have no value or we are not going to be counted anywhere. Most of the times a person of egoistic nature take very subtle form of revenge of the person who shows indifference. Nitsze implored Jesus that, "please does not present the other cheek if someone slaps you, because it shows how insignificant we are and we feel that we are mortally wounded, for this reason we have to crucify you".

All of us are trying to project our presence and identity to the others; even an infant is neither out of this race nor a very old person. All are striving by any means to make their existence felt by the others. And to Mahaveer, this effort to make our presence felt by others is also a kind of violence. Domination of wife by husband, of the husband by wife, of father by his children and of children by their father is nothing but assertion on each and everyone's part, to let others know that we are also present and count me as an individual identity. And in this phenomenon the asserting person is not only projecting his identity, but at the same time he is rejecting presence of the others and this rejection of others to project our self is considered as violence by Mahaveer. Our insistence to project our existence, our identity, our being at any cost and by whatever means is called as violent existence.

Exactly opposite existence is non-violent existence; as to why I have taken birth in this world is not known to me and as this vast environment is sustaining me without any bias, with the same token all the others are existing and as I do not know for what reason they are living and existing, I do not have any right to envy their being in this environment. They have as much right to remain in this existence as I have. This understanding on the part of ours makes our being in this existence as non-violent existence. Egoistic behavior that I am something special or outstanding and all the others are nothing compared to me, but to act and behave to reinforce this belief is the cause of violence. At the same time to be non-egoistic is considered as non-violent existence by Mahaveer.

Human psychology in general accepts the concept that every individual strives to project his unique identity in front of the others, with the notion that acceptance accorded in this manner makes the individual secure in the belief that he is part of the surrounding and is equal to others. It is called as assertion of personality. But when others do not accept any individual in normal manner, then the said individual takes resort of such behavioral patterns, which in ordinary circumstances is deemed as bizarre behavior. Mahaveer says that first of all try to understand what capacities and capabilities we have, how we are going to utilize them to reach our goal, do not ever compare our self with any one as the other may seems to be doing the same things we are doing or intend to do. Because in such a manner outside acts may tally but end result will not be according to our expectations, as every individual is unique and his potentials are also unique.

How egocentric person behaves in childish manner to appease his ego, Mahaveer has given a fitting example; a person all of a sudden declares that he is going to renounce family life and going to be a monk. This declaration may happen due to distorted ideas about self or to prove to others that nothing is impossible and he can do it. This happens in similar circumstances where members of the family, friends and acquaintances tries to dissuade such a person from his decision, but then conflict between personalities manifests and the renouncing person become more adamant and insistent. Mahaveer says, make him totally aware as to what may happen once the decision is finalized and leave him to his own devices, but do not try to dissuade him again and again or do not try to be curious as to why all of a sudden he wants to renounce the family life. Nine times out of ten the person starts to reconsider his decision and backs down. When such people understand that no one is ready to stroke his ego then their resolve punctures like hot air out of balloon and he land on terra firma again. People behave in this manner due to inflated ego or to run away from personal responsibilities, or to escape from faulty or erroneous decisions, which are of their own making. Such incidence make people sober and much more attuned to the stark reality.

Tathata of Buddha and Ahimsa of Mahaveer is mostly identical concepts. Literally meaning of the Tathata is total acceptance of circumstances, environment and others as it is, and Ahimsa means no efforts on our part to transform or to change the existence, environment, objects or people; which most of the times is beyond our capacity to change, but to understand the difference and to change our self accordingly, or be sanguine enough where change is not possible to accept that what has happened is all right, what is happening and will happen will also be all right.

Due to our conditioned and unconscious nature we do not accept what reality is but anticipate that expected should happen. So whenever changes are sought where any change is not possible, violence ensues. When human start to expect more he becomes violent. Whatever measures we apply to fulfill our desires that are out of bound of nature, causes more violence. Any person who has more expectations and anticipates more as well tries to change the others more, deviates from his basic nature and become more violent. These are some pointers that show how violence manifests.

CHAPTER 5

AHIMSA/NON-VIOLENCE: END OF LUST FOR LIFE

Why violence happens? As per Mahaveer lust for life causes violence.

Lust for life means to live and to live at any cost even though when the life seems to be empty, without any purpose or without any positive achievement. But still we like to live. If the option is given to us that we would live forever but in that case all the others will have to die then we will accept the former alternative. Till the time of death, we hope that somehow death could be evaded or postponed. This powerful eccentricity to live at any cost is called the lust for life and insistence to go on living in this manner is the cause of violence.

According to Mahaveer this lust for life do not save our existence but in this process the cause to end other lives starts. And ultimately death ensues. Before us many has tried to live forever but those have failed. When anyone willingly forsakes lust for life only then he can achieve the attitude of non-violence. When we leave the insistence to be alive at any cost, then we accept the premise that we would not harm the others. But this should be remembered that forsaking the lust for life does not mean desire to die, nor it is suicidal.

Even Freud has explained two basic desires of human beings. One is lust for life and other is lust for death. To the former he has given the name as Erose and the later is named as Thanatose. According to him when lust for life becomes diseased then lust for death becomes prominent and at this stage people commit suicide. But Mahaveer is not for suicide and he will not agree to this concept. To Mahaveer to be suicidal is nothing but distorted presentation of lust for life.

Generally we see people who attempt to commit or commit suicide, only because they are willing to live only if their conditions to live in certain manner are met which are according to their beliefs, standards or assumptions. A person is in love with some one else and that person rejects them. Sometimes people expect to be appointed at prestigious post due to which his social status and monitory gains are going to be enhanced. But when they are bypassed or superseded then out of frustration they go for suicide. But if the rejecting person agrees to accept the former and if the bypassed person is rewarded the post, then they do not commit suicide. Now what happens is they are so persistent about their anticipations and demands that they are ready to live only if there certain conditions are fulfilled, otherwise they are willing to die. This persistency is so deep and subtle that they are ready to go against themselves and are willing to die, but this does not mean that they have discarded lust for life. It is something like reversals of symptoms but that do not mean that there is no disease.

Mahaveer allowed a process called Santhara i.e. willful death. But this sanction is awarded on certain premises- such a person in all his honesty should feel that there is no lust for life, and then he should stop taking food and water. It is ascertained that average healthy person can live for 90 days without food or water. So if the person has any semblance of lust for life then he will return from his decision. But if this in not the case then he will wait for 90 days or till death intervenes.

Whenever suicides are attempted the decision to die arrives in a fit of passion. So if intervention happens at a proper time or if the critical moment is passed, then no suicide happens. What happens is, insistent intensity of madness to die, passes away when the critical moment is averted.

90 days is quite a long period. We have experienced as to how our mind works and we know that our mind do not remain static, steady or in the same emotion for extended period of time, even for 90 seconds. It is not easy and this is the reason that Mahaveer has granted the option of santhara but he is not suicidal. In reality lust for death is nothing but the lust for life in disguise. It is like opposite polarities. When we deny any polarity willingly or otherwise, the other remains with it. As we accept in psychology, as happens in law of physics, for every action there is reaction. Santhara or willful death should be defined as- decrease in lust for life to such an extent that a person enters in to void.

But today what is happening is, due to this sanction by Mahaveer many mentally misguided people are following this doctrine not due to understanding but due to selective acceptance of the concept, which seems to be tailor-made to their expectations. These people are masochists by nature.

Violence happens in two ways; one is other oriented and the other is self-oriented. If we try to hurt any other in any way then chances are we would be arrested by the police and could be tried in the court of law and there is possibility of punishment. But if the process is self-oriented then 99% of the time such person will be treated as sage or holy person. He will be perceived as higher being and will be treated accordingly. The reason behind this phenomenon is unawareness of our true being, as well as to believe that we are nothing but flesh and blood.

Behavior of masochist nature on the body of the self is also treated as violence. Because as presented in Jainism, the real you is nothing but our soul and the physical body is vessel, which is the configuration of 5 basic elements present in the environments and are independent from our force of life or prana. This concept is very subtle. What happens in death? We can see the physical body lying on the ground but the prana or force of life as real you is departed, but sans animation our body seems to be same and without any change. In this way the person who is trying to harm himself is also treated as violent person only because the body is the configuration of basic elements and these elements are always independent of our force of life, as are others. But as there is no provision in the law, no third party can intervene in self-harm. Similarly due to erroneous understanding of the concepts of religious practice it is believed that when any one denies himself from any pleasurable experience, such person is holy person but not as a violent person.

This behavior of self-harm according to Mahaveer is nothing but assertion of ownership or feeling of superiority. We know that what we perceive as life or living could not be saved at any cost, because by birth the process of death also starts and the natural end of life happens due to death. So by way of behaving in negative way under the false hope of enriching the existence causes nothing but violence. It has to be understood that powerful lust for life shows denial of death, which is going to happen now or later, as it is law of nature.

Lust for death comes into being when due to abnormal expectations lust for life is threatened. Acceptance of death happens when lust for life becomes weak. Mahaveer accepts death and this acceptance happens due to inevitability of the incidence, happening now or in future. And this thought is helpful to become non-violent. Denial of death in itself is violence. Due to depraved belief of not accepting my own death I expect others to die. But when I accept my death then I accept lives of the others. And when we accept that whatever happens death is going to happen to all the others and me also, then the madness to hurt the others, to be violent losses the momentum.

So Mahaveer says that, importance of death is proportionate to the importance of life. When life becomes precious, then death also becomes more threatening. How acceptance of the death happens? When we come to understand that life, as we know is not life as precious because no matter what but still we are going to die- then in retrospection death also looses its meaning and importance.

When we say that we have to live at any cost then at the same time we say that we are not ready to die at any cost. But when anyone accepts the inevitability of both the incidences, then such person could not remain violent. Violence creates fear in the others, which works like a barrier to prevent others from encroaching the space around and near us.

One other thought is of considerable value that when our lust for life is stronger then in the same way we try to save other things around us. This lust for life widens upto our materialistic possession, which increases our concept of "mine", "I", personal ego. If any thing damages, not only the object become damaged, but we also get hurt. This attitude of materialistic possession also becomes means of violence.

CHAPTER 6

SAYYAM/ TRANQUILITY: TO BE ON THE MIDDLE PATH

Pioneers like Mahaveer do not think in the manner as good or bad, but their thoughts and perceptions are based on degrees like good, better or best, and totally evil or lesser evil. Thinking in terms of extremes is our way of thinking and this causes contradiction. When we think of good and evil, our thinking depends on our perceptive and understanding, which do not necessarily mean that others should also think in the same manner and at the same time our labeling happens to be totally good or totally bad. But pioneers like Mahaveer exist in the gray areas as far as thoughts and perceptions is concerned.

When we have to exist and exist with lust for life, then even if we accept or not, we remain violent. But we could get out of this, by leaving lust for life and become non-violent. Try to understand that lust for life creates violence, which happens due to our persistence of thought. Even Mahaveer was in existence for forty years after he attained the state of enlightenment. Do we think that in those remaining 40 years there was no violence? But the way in which he maintained his existence was so low-key i.e. existence in tranquility was so all encompassing that only those acts, which were necessary for basic sustenance, were practiced. Secondly he has no lust for life. It could be understood in this way; he left himself totally at the mercy of the nature and surrounding, with the understanding that –I am ready to live or die here and now, from this instant onwards nature will decide as to my existence or extinction, no efforts or aggression will be perpetuated on my behalf in any way for either option. When any person starts to live in this way and manner, then as mentioned above, if any violence at all seems to be happening, then it has to be categorized as barely evil in relation to the every day efforts we have to make that are considered as violent means.

Further incidence of violent nature as stated in other details are that human being is the only specie on this planet, that when he is totally well off and when he becomes bored due to lack of thrills, he goes on hunting expedition. The term well off is used to show "not lacking anything and having sufficient for his sustenance". This hunting expedition is considered as adventurous sport or a special quality. But on the contrary when any animal kills the human, it is considered as untimely death of the human and termed as murder. But we have to keep in mind that any animal, domestic or wild, does not attack or kill indiscriminately till it is not hungry or till its existence is not threatened. In this sense animals are more tame and civilized than humans. Only human is the species that goes for hunting when he is full as compared to other animal that goes for hunting when he is hungry.

When our attitude is- I am the center of universe and to prove this exaggerated egoistic idea or attitude, I am willing to hurt all and sundry or will remain neutral in such cases where there is no harm to me. What is our definition of rape or aggression? Most of the time we commit rape and this word is used not considering the specific meaning but as form of aggression. This concept is specifically directed towards male of human species. How many times we commit cohabitation with our wife, with her prior consent? Because in the court of law sexual act committed with any women without her consent or willingness is called rape. Now no wife, except who is independent in thinking and assertive will oppose her husband. This happens because of her psychological make up as a female, who are generally taught that the place of the wife is secondary in the family and should consider the happiness of her husband as her primary duty, as he is the bread winner and leader of the family.

All of us are so conditioned that without the consent or willingness of the other we take everything for granted and do not behave as we wish. Deep down we all are somewhat sadistic because the process of breaking the resistance of the others or using the force to achieve something somehow appeases our ego.

Concepts of criminal psychology are based on the premise that any person can become habitual criminal when his conduct goes unchecked by society at large and people are afraid to fend themselves in front of criminal. This attitude of general population to avoid the criminal at any cost reinforces the belief of the antisocial person that fear is the key and this belief cause the thrill to dominate others with the assumption that he is someone of unique nature. This understanding about self as someone special drives him towards more atrocities and he will become hardened and habitual criminal. Habitual molester of opposite sex also assumes the same. Till women are of the belief that they are weaker than the molester as well are hesitant to let others know that what they have gone through, with the erroneous belief that they are going to be criticized and not the perpetrator, then the molester become immune to the norms of the society and goes on committing same acts again and again. If you are a boxer or a wrestler and if you accept defeat without serious efforts, then the winner loses the thrill of winning. It is to be understood that winning becomes thrilling victory, only when the opponent resist fiercely and we have to overcome the resistance with more efforts.

To be egoistic, is state of mind and to fulfill or to satisfy our ego we have to struggle more, as others are also same as we are. To win and win at any cost is the cause of violent behavior. The more we win then more inflated our ego becomes, and as our ego can be boosted to any limit, we go on behaving in the same manner whereby ultimately we become more competitive and violent as well as egoistic. And this phenomenon happens in every walk of life.

Male of the human species are more direct in their behavior, but female in general adopt more subtle form of behavior and at the end it is male who is held responsible. A book written by Kirkguard by the name of A Diary of A Seducer shows how subtle the ways of female are. The person depicted as main character of the book is shown as an amoral person and this character tells the reader, that it was his belief that his charm was so irresistible that every conquest was his own achievement. But ultimately he realized that it was very subtle encouragement on the part of female because of which he was driven and they seduced him. It is the characteristic ways of female mind that they induce the male to propose and in a very subtle manner show that they are ready to accept the proposal.

How do we predict behavior? How we predict about people, as to how will they behave, react in general or in any specific situations. The less aware people, the less understanding they have about surrounding and environment, from any cultural group, ethnic group, caste, creed- we can generally map all their behavior in general or in specific situation. Non-developed sense of understanding about the self makes it possible that the person can be predicted.

Very interesting concepts has been presented about predictability of Mahaveer or any other person who is of similarly enlightened state. If a murder is in process and if Mahaveer is present at that time, the reactions of the Mahaveer would be very interesting and may be out of our understanding. Mahaveer will say that I was witness to the murder in progress and my body intervened and in this process he will be out of act that will not bind him to any karma. By thought, desire, expectations, impressions or cause, acts done under above feelings brings out karmic binding and the binding bears fruit in the way of any outcome or reactions. But when all acts happen in the void i.e. as witnesses, then these acts are not binding.

We are very much curious as to what Mahaveer will do in certain circumstances. This happens to confirm that such and such act can be followed in certain circumstances, which are behavior pattern approved by the master. And here problem starts. Any act by any person, in given circumstances could not be labeled as pattern of behavior, as the thought behind the act, perception to act happen in such a way, as well the persons personality also plays unique role as every person is unique in itself. Our thoughts, perceptions and personality are different than any other. So following of any act could be inadequate or wrong in our case.

So the followers of the Mahaveer, as well as any person who follows the act of any other, would very definitely make mistakes. What we are doing is following on the act and not the process behind the act i.e. thoughts and emotions. Following Mahaveer, act by act may cause distortion, pain and misery because you are just doing what you are seeing without due process of the background. The only way is to become Mahaveer; an enlightened being and this is the only alternative. Repetitions of the act are nothing but the habits born due to the ritual.

Something happens in fasting, which seems to be carrying much significance in Jaini followers. Fasting on the part of Mahaveer happened only due to his total immersion in deep meditation, in which case feelings of bodily demands were not experienced as relationship with the body was at the lowest ebb. On the other hand his followers, when practice fasting were experiencing the existence of the body due to empty stomach with redoubled force or are thinking of food to be consumed after the fasting. But this was not the reason or intention of Mahaveer to incorporate fasting as the process towards self-awareness.

But in all the cultures this is happening, there are followers who like rituals, just goes on repeating acts without understanding the process behind acts. And this following by way of followers create conflicts between various cultures. Followers of Jesus will not accept Mahaveer or Krishna, as they do not act as Jesus used to and vice-versa. For every one of those enlightened beings circumstances were different, period in relation to time were different and there own background was also different.

Our barometer of measuring gyana or enlightenment is based on the acts alone. But we have to keep in mind that acts originate out of enlightenment or awareness and this happening is very special and very different than acts itself.

It is very unfortunate that whenever creator of any doctrine or culture passes away, due to blind following the same culture disintegrates after sometime. Even if Mahaveer takes birth today, it would be foolish to expect that the same acts will happen again as circumstances are changed, values of life have changed, and everything is different than what it was in existence 2500 years back. The only way open to us is to follow the doctrine but at our own risk, at the cost of loosing everything in the process. The blue print is still available. But to undertake this job is very monumental and risky as we do not know that if we would ever reach where Mahaveer has reached. We have to be very patient and most of the time has to learn by trial and error method, which require endurance, will power and faith. But as we are people who accept set routes, we do not feel it is necessary to go into depth of anything as to follow the doctrine and its rituals is easier. But any following cause uncertainty only because the expected or end result do not match with the experiences explained. And this is the reason that the acts happened by Mahaveer or other pioneers are called as happening.

Life is very dynamic and ever changing. Clinging to acts is like collecting and counting the leaves, which have fallen down in winter and to claim that we have acquired the knowledge of the whole tree, is erroneous. Falling of leaves is a passing phase; because once a leaf falls new leaves are in process of sprouting.

What is the meaning of the word sayyam or tranquility; to exist without extreme is the meaning of Mahaveer. To understand the applicability of this state of being, we have to understand our common attitudes that we know very well. Loosely we will define this concept as patience. Patience can be experienced by other person's behavior only. By observing acts of others we arrive at conclusion that the person is very patient. But this patience, which we perceive, can be false or can be shown as restrain in any behavior. Because to be patient or to restrain oneself is an inner process which manifests as patience or restrain on the outside.

Generally what we mean and understand is that, Sayyam or tranquility is practice of repression, control or restrain. Any person who stops himself from behaving, restrain his faculties and feelings from expressing, keeps absolute control, the person is perceived as the person of patience or sayyami. But these definitions and the meaning of the word sayyam as perceived, is very negative approach. We are not aware of its positive aspects, which in itself is a power to change the total perspective of everyday life as well as religious life. All the life processes are positive. But due to our misunderstanding, faulty interpretation and blind following, we are aware of only its negative aspects. Mahaveer's approach towards and about Sayyam is very live and positive.

So, if as per our negative definition, we practice Sayyam then it will bring out only pathological results. Practitioner of this concept will seem to be living under pressure, will look burdened; will loose the virtue of spontaneity. Sayyam in its real form will enrich our life and we will be always fresh, with the dynamic flow of life forces at their peak. But as per our understanding nothing like this happens. Another popular misconception regarding practice of sayyam is its practice is meant for those people who has renounced this world and are following the path of sanyasa. All of us are practicing sayyam in lesser or greater degrees in our everyday life. To stop ourselves from taking any action, to follow any doctrine without going into its depth, to restrain ourselves in certain circumstances –we call this behavior as sayyam. But if we are honest with ourselves, then we will agree that whatever act we have done, the expression do not happens to its fullest extent. There is the feeling that something has remained to be done. And this residual balance of suppression accumulates over the period of time and cause mental illness or pathological behavior. What we mean by stress, depression and fatigue, is nothing but the half-hearted expressions on our part; we stop either due to social norm or constrain, or are not sure about our self.

Every creative aspect of life is positive way of growth and most of the negative restrains cause suppression. In this regard, the proper way of sayyam can be understood .To our way of thinking practitioner of sayyam is the person who is fighting with his faculties, attitudes or feelings and has to balance his acts constantly. But as per Mahaveer, Sayyam is the virtue of a person who accepts everything in its totality. Practice of sayyam is to be master of our faculties and its related attitudes. Most of the time we have to balance the attitudes of which we are not master as they are more powerful than us. Then we have to control them. But if we are masters then we do not have to control them or fight against them, but they fall under our will to be useful as we wish. If we are weak we have to stand against them, but when we are strong they do not stand against us. So in our weakness, we go on balancing the acts all the time, with the fear that the moment we loose the control, we are going to fall down. But now or later this is going to happen, and when the continual restrain snaps, what has to happen happens in grotesque form, which is called as mental illness or pathological existence. When we understand our mind, what kind of thoughts we are thinking about, how we can realize our thoughts, feelings and emotions in practical ways, then there are chances that we can be integrated and powerful from within and then the same power of our mind, which when remains unchecked and cause stress or tension, can be exploited in creative manner.

So the sayyam as told by Mahaveer is our basic self which is dwelling in its own power and this power makes all the faculties docile and well under our control. The same power helps practice celibacy, help practice ahimsa and the self that resides in this power is called as sayyami. The person who is sayyami in this manner is tranquil person. Basic characteristic of tranquility are non-vacillating mind, without existing in any extremes, without tremors and established in itself.

Now it is very easy to understand our general state of mind, which is always vacillating, to be in the state of one extreme or the other, trembling state of mind can be termed as non-tranquil mind or non-sayyami mind. We experience our mind only when it is in either extreme. And this is the characteristic of human mind, which happens only because of our imposition of habit nature and conditioned way of thinking. When we are healthy we do not feel our body, for the reason that all the bodily functions are synchronized as intended. But the moment any disease develops we experience its presence due to pain or dysfunction. The same applies to mind, till it is in neither extreme we do not experience our mind. When we as per our thoughts, direct the bodily function towards the task, then we fulfill the same in fully concentrated state of mind. But the moment any contradictory thoughts occur we loose our concentration. In this state, tug of war starts when we try to finish the task started, but at the same time contradictory thoughts also strives to focus the concentration on itself. And in this state, mental turmoil starts, which cause discontinuity in our concentration and in this state only we experience the existence of mind. So when this mental turmoil is related to any of our basic sense faculties and its related attitudes, then pull and push between both the extremes in thoughts cause dissipation of the energy of the faculty. Any basic faculty taxed under mental upheaval is the cause of psychosomatic symptoms.

In today's Jaini culture the practice of fasting is on rise. This is not happening due to proper understanding of Mahaveer's doctrine. Average Jaini is generally overfed. Any type of extreme creates boredom, stress and tension in mind as well as in the body. To break this boredom under the guise of fasting, this concept of Mahaveer is practiced under misguided notions, which has very different psychological and applicable meanings, which are presented in the further chapter. But the misguided concept of fasting, as religious practice is the belief of erroneous nature, because at the same time after the completion of fasting the same person goes into bing eating. The cause is very biological. The effect of fasting invigorates digestive system, purges the body of its toxins, which in turn increases the hunger, which in turn cause more consumption of food. And the same cycle of fasting and rejuvenated hunger goes on as a vicious circle. Mind in any extremity is like pendulum and when the association between mind and body is firm, then the effects on the mind and body are expressed in bizarre manner. While moving in any direction, the pendulum is gathering the momentum to return to other direction. Tranquility or sayyam is, to be in the middle and very less perceptible movement in either direction.

Quantitative food intake is one extreme and fasting without any food is another extreme. When we eat; what generally happens is either we feel the very full stomach or we eat less and feel the hunger. Balanced diet, not in the sense of qualitative or in caloric values, but in moderate quantity should be taken. And in this case due to moderate intake we neither feel distension of stomach or pang of hunger. And the same principle is applicable in every faculty and its related attitudes.

Mahaveer has stated that "mind" in itself means tension or stress. It is the pre-requisite of mind that it is felt when it is in any extreme, because till it is not in any extreme, we do not appreciate its existence. So when we are in the middle then no type of tension or stress exists.

True tranquility only happens when there are no more minds. And Mahaveer and Zen Buddhist monks accept the same concept, that to be tranquil is cessation of mind. And this is how purest sayyam and tranquility happens.

Practice of meditation when applied in proper way causes the feeling of imminent death in the mind of practitioner. This happens only due to cessation of mind and nothing else. There is no possibility of death in meditation, as since birth we are used to the association of mind and body as our real existence, and we feel alive only because of our association with our mind. What happens in meditation is, we elevate our consciousness towards higher peaks where there is no use of mind. By this technique it becomes easy to release tension, stress, feeling of fatigue. And this is the reason why people feel refreshed and re-invigorated after meditation.

When opposing extremities of any faculty or attitude stands in front of each other, they start dissolving and the person feels free. When greed and sacrifice, lust and celibacy as states of mind stand in front of each other, they become null and void. Emotions of any extremities are nothing but reflection of the same but other extremity. All human attitudes related to all faculties are nothing but the personality traits of the human being and they are but two sides of the same coin. Basically all the emotions are singular but due to our existence in duality and conflict, we are used to experience them as individual emotions when they are experienced in extremes.

When we breathe we breath with effort. In reality any involvement in breathing on our part is not warranted or natural, because biologically and naturally breathing is the non-voluntary process and we do not have to think, decide or choose how to breathe. But in this very natural process also we frequently intervene which is very abnormal. When we are aroused like in anger, grief, aggression or passion, these emotions of arousal not only disturb our bodily functions but as integral part of our being our mind is also affected. Either we breathe more or less than necessary, which harms our body and mind. Hyperventilation happens, barring asthmatic attack or due to blockage in air track, due to mental disturbances in majority of the cases.

Breathing in its natural form can be experienced in meditation. When we go deep in process of meditation the breathing becomes so deep and so spaced out that we think that the breathing is stopped. When mind is very calm and quite it works on bare minimum. Its like an attuned scale, both sides are so balanced that no movement is happening and this is how total tranquility can be glimpsed.

Only because of the nature of our mind, to be in any extreme, that we feel our existence. And all of our thoughts and actions happen in the same way. Without physical and mental stress or tension, we do not think that we are a living being. Our ego is the motivational force, which induces us to live in extremes. And this state of our being causes violence. And the more violent we are then our personality portrays itself more forcefully.

In Emilio Jolla's memories he has written that if all the people in this world become good people, concepts of story writing will not be possible. There do not happen any thing worth writing in the life of good people. There is very little known about the life of Jesus. Birth of the Jesus is known, then at the end of five years he was seen in a temple. Then again at the age of thirty years people saw him. And at the age of thirty-three, people saw him, while he was crucified, and here the story ends. Events of the intervening thirty years are not known. And the only cause of not knowing was because there were no events worth mentioning in his life. Last incidence of crucifixion was the event happened in the life of onlookers, and not in the life of Jesus. The statement made by Jesus at that time is proof enough, as to what dies and what never dies. "O God forgive them, they do not know what they are doing." Jesus, in his compassionate way says that what the crucifiers are trying to do is killing the body under the misguided notion that mere killing of Jesus will eradicate his teaching. But Jesus, being enlightened soul knows that separation of the body from the soul is death of body only. But all the people who were for for the crucifixion, are going to carry the burden of their being cause to the death of Jesus, till they die.

We only do those acts or things, which attracts the attention of the others. And this happens only to project our identity and personality. Psychologically also it seems correct, that if we become successful in creating the society where every good virtue of any person is recognized, in correspondence to the anti-social behavior of the others, then the anti-social elements will have to change towards goodness. Misguided or anti-social behavior happens only to assert the identity and personality of the person who is behaving anti-social manner.

We feel alive only when we behave or act. And to feel alive in this fashion, we have to exist in stress and tension i.e. at the extreme. Then we have to be angry, aggressive, passionate or sacrificing. But in this manner when we form friendship enmity also comes into being. For every action, there is reaction. Because in our existence, either we have to balance, or nature balances on its own. We could not be friend only to any one, till we are ready to denounce or identify non-friendly as our enemy. The moment we choose any one or anything, the opposite automatically stands. To go out of selection of either, we have to be tranquil. And tranquility as a virtue happens only when we are in the middle or remain willfully out of selection.

CHAPTER 7

TRANQUILITY: TO BE A CREATIVE BEING

For most of the humans, to live or to exist as we are and just to go through every day routine at any cost is considered as living, and this manner of our being is always accepted as better bargain than death or dying. Most of the humans exist in this manner till they die. But the way in which we live without being creative in any way, is nothing but living till death. And this happens only due to blind following of any cultural or religious doctrine

In general, meaning of the word sayyam is accepted and understood, as to control or to restrain. To shrink, no amount of awakening is necessary. But to be creative, we have to rekindle all our energies, which only happens by way of positive efforts on our part. But as we are conditioned and taught since birth about the set ways of living as our forefathers has lived, we accept it as the way of life. So like all our ancestors, we walk in their footprints, which is very easy. Accepted values since long become our second nature, which corresponds to our surrounding also. So to shrink we do not have to do anything, but only have to leave aside or cast away those attitudes that are not in correspondence to the existing society. But what happens when we abandon the troublesome attitudes? There remains nothing to go on, which makes us restless and creates void only. Then what we do is create some new attitudes, which most of the times are nothing new, but the new versions of the old ones only.

But life is not like that. To live in a creative way, we have to understand and re-group our inner powers that help us to be more creative. Once we become aware of such power and tap the source, then we do not have to abandon any attitudes, but only due to our creative way of life what we acquire becomes creative.

In any following, people follow those idols to whom they are following by way of acts happened by the idols. Acts happened by Mahaveer were directly connected with his thoughts and experiences. But the main difficulties faced by any follower is that, he goes on repeating the same acts, without going into the due process And we know that any act, without ' why' as to its meaning, looses its significance and creates boredom. Every repetition causes boredom. Most of the acts seems to be pointless and are not related to the changed environment. But as happens in any religious following, which most of the times happens without thought or the manner in which the tradition are adhered to, its adaptation becomes easy only because to follow anyone or anything, do not tax our intelligence. But when challenged about its importance and significance, no one can answer satisfactorily about it. Then in seemingly balanced society, these acts are perceived as bizarre behavior and the person following them is ridiculed. Why we are so much interested in following? As stated above, following on the part of the follower do not demand any efforts. Secondly the follower can see the other followers are treated with much reverence by the society. Which works as reinforcers to act in the same manner. When there is well-defined path available, then no one likes to pave new path for the same destination. Because to pave the new way, many efforts are required, about which very few are willing enough, and further there is doubt, as to are we going to reach the intended destination? This phenomena happens due to lack of will power, attitude to leave aside the intended endeavor in the mid stream, stress and tension in psyche as well as body becomes unbearable, journey seems to be uphill, as well as criticism by the society is perceived as eminent. So all these factors induce the people to just follow the idol or traditions.

But if positive and creative changes are to be achieved, then efforts are must. Guts and will power is necessary so that we would not deviate from the chosen path. We have to bear in mind that most of the times journey itself and not destination, is more fulfilling and enlightening. What happens in the process, while journeying, we learn much more and become mature. We come to know that what used to cause much more trepidation was just notion of ours. And when we knowingly undertake this type of exercise and when positive or desired goal materializes, the process of growing starts to gather momentum.

Jesus, Mahaveer and Buddha started from within and corresponding acts happened on the outside. So whenever we start from within and understand the significance of the inner process, then whatever we have accepted as significant from the outside becomes insignificant. When we accept anything by due process of understanding and experience, we just leave aside, but do not reject- just leave aside, which till yesterday was of considerable importance to us. So when we achieve any thing of significance, do we think that now we will cling to something trivial? When we have gems and diamonds in our hand, then are we going to cling to stones and pebbles of ordinary nature? No, to give place to higher goal or achievement, we have to break the old mold, have to reshuffle our priorities and make room for the creative aspect of our being. This dynamic process of struggle for further improvement goes on till we are on the peak. And this is the way of positive and mature personality growth. So when anyone just goes on leaving aside anything or everything, without thought but considering the acts of the others, will not achieve anything. On the contrary, the said person in turn will become just empty, pathological and sick person.

Attachment of any value to any thing is relative. Attaching greater value to any thigh trivial is pointless, until more valuable is achieved in its place. Because till we know that something more valuable is available and is well within our reach, then and only then, we will strive to get the same and in this process the less valuable looses its significance. So if what we have is considered as valuable, then it remains valuable only till we get much more valuable to replace the former.

Only because of our attitudes we could not leave inferior and by the same token we do not get acquainted with the superior. Any force on our part to separate from inferior is not tranquility or sayyam. At the most it will save us from further deterioration, but as we are not acquiring any thing of substance in this place then it will cause stagnation. Restrain, as tranquility is negative approach. At the most it will disguise the thorns pricking our mind. When we start to believe that restrain or control is tranquility, then it will weigh us down, our existence will be without joy, there would not be any spring in our steps, our smile will not be spontaneous. This list of contra indication is quite long. All the above traits show that we are still not tranquil in true sense, but are still living in extremities. Any restrain on the mind cause conflict, unless and until we know the way our mind works, it cause tension. And this restrain and its resultant tension sap our energy continuously. We do not know what to restrain, why to restrain. Because as mentioned above, the moment we are in conflict the other and opposite remain as it was. Any thought or emotion comes in to being with their counter parts. And this is the basic nature of human mind as well as the balancing act on the part of the existence. We the people always remain in conflict and duality, and this is the root-cause of tension and stress. So when any emotion or thought remains as persistent, but when we willfully behave against such thought, then our mind becomes divided and fragmented. So when all these fragments start to clamors for our attention, then conflict starts. And in this conflict we loose mental peace, loose our energy and become pathological. So any person who fights with his self, will not win till he understands his basic nature.

But creative mind do not come into being without positive rein forcers. We believe in the belief, that to win is to fight. But as far as mental state is concerned, with whom we are fighting? No one else, no outside elements are present, but with our self-only. Like, if we induce both our hands to fight with each other, then it is no-win situation, because behind each, our energy is the only power that will fight. And in this process our self gets devastated. We become fragmented and disintegration happens.

An enlightened being like Mahaveer will never lead towards negative aspects. According to him, the necessity of the process of tranquility / sayyam is towards total and integrated personality.

When we lie or steal, we disintegrate. Portions of our mind always remain separated. However we appear to others, we could not accept the act happened by us in totality. But whenever we are truthful it becomes our merit, and this merit keeps us integrated.

According to Mahaveer, those thoughts or actions, which help us to remain integrated, are called as merits (Punya), and those acts and thoughts which divide us, is called as sin or sinful existence.

The process of tranquility, as shown by Mahaveer could be acquired not by fighting against anything. Tranquility has to be instilled, but the ways are radically different. No fight against faculties, attitudes or against any one else. But we have to delve in our psyche as the source of conflict. And once we tap this source, what is important, what causes stress or tension, will be understood. So when we understand the cause or reason of the conflict, then the same cease to exist, only because now we come to know our basic nature. Before this process starts we were used to be outwardly oriented for the causes and reasons of misery, tension, anger etc. Any problem, difficulty or hurdle remains as an enigma, only till it is not faced squarely.

Suppose a person is very much interested in any kind of food and the specific food is constantly causing temptation to have it and have it at any cost, then how could he be tranquil? He will start avoiding one kind of food today and another kind on tomorrow and something else afterwards. Now the question is, is he going to be successful in his endeavor? Not probably. What he is doing is avoiding the actual food but not the obsession or interest in food as such, which is causing obsession. In other words it seems like he is sacrificing certain type of food, but at the same time what about his interest, which is very much mental attitude that basically causes attachment with certain food, is the cause of obsessive consumption. In this fashion what we see is he is behaving in restraining manner by avoiding the food, but at the same time his old mental process is still very much attached to the specific food, and is obsessively thinking about the same. To Mahaveer this is not sayyam; it is plain and simple suppression. This suppression causes mental obsession, which will make his personality suppressive and this will make him fearful about all the food. Proper approach is to understand about obsessive thoughts regarding food, which when realized on mental level will free him from obsessive food fixation and normalcy can be regained. To understand, how and why our mind attaches our faculties to any thing is the way towards tranquility.

Mahaveer says that all the five sense organs are not only related to outside world, but in reality they are bridges which also connects us to our inner being. Similarly these senses are much more potent than those which are connected to outer world. Organ of taste, organ of sight, organ of hearing, organ of smell and organ of sensations are all connected to our inner self also. So tranquility is the process and practice, as to how to redirect these organs towards our inner self.

Generally any sense organ of ours becomes cause of unease or trepidation. It becomes much more powerful in the sense, very subtle cue or slight stimulation activates the faculty and the emotion to satisfy the demand become insistent. Like specific food activates the hunger, even though our stomach is full. Or the organ of sensation is much more active. Their activation in overdrive causes unease and embracement i.e. they are active to the limit of obsession. But don't fight with them because the same organ due to which we are driven to act and act in spite of our will, are the organs, which are the bridges through which, we could go back towards our self. These bridges are useful and can be traveled in both the directions. We can use this facility to start the return journey. People due to misunderstanding demolish such connecting links and succumb to suppression and related diseases. So do not destroy or neglect them, because the most potent on the outside is equally potent in the inside also.

Indulge them to the fullest and then stop the process of fulfillment. Now, try to feel the same feelings within your self. Whenever you get some spare time try this technique with total attention and in a very short period we could experience the same feelings in more vivid details that will be more alive than outside experiences. Once we became capable of applying this process to any organ then we can manipulate all the sense organs in the same fashion. We have to understand that we do not get distracted due to organs or faculty but because of involvement of our mind as the medium of experience due to which creation of conceited attitudes are formed. So to punish the faculty and its related organ, we apply restrain, which cause destruction of the link. As mentioned earlier, no one but our self becomes attached and attracted because of the intervention of our mind, which cause relevant organs to respond. But when we do not get anticipated results we punish the organ with restrain and suppression. Conscious restrain or suppression is also one of the extremes, and behind every extreme the power working is ours only. So before we think about any punishment to be inflicted on any organ, we must analyze our self and try to understand as to why we are behaving in this manner. Any sense organ is just instrument at our disposal, so to punish the instrument is foolhardy.

To understand our sense organs, how they function, how our mind due to its conditioned nature drives the organs towards repeated acts, is the key towards the process of achieving creative tranquility/sayyam.

Mahaveer also explains one more aspect. All the sense organs do exist in the form of physical appendages which are known as external organs i.e. eye, nose, ears, mouth and skin. There are three types of souls- one is outer soul, which is operating through external organs. Second is inner soul, which is operating through the sense organs in inner direction. The third is supreme/ super soul, which do not differentiate between outer and inner souls. Where outer or inner is no more but it just IS, then it is our true form. To be established in self is called Param Atma by Mahaveer. Mahaveer presents this Para-psychological concept and this concept is described in detail, where cause or reason of behavioral psychology can be understood and its positive application can be used as psychotherapy. This concept is not mythical, but it is purely scientific analysis and its application helps us towards higher awareness. Most of the times religious beliefs and doctrines are considered as one and the same. But it is to be understood that beliefs are personal experiences and cannot be accepted with the same intensity by others of the same following. On the contrary doctrine is to be understood in the light of current environment, considering current values and should be applied with flexibility. The intention of this writing is to show that religious doctrines are nothing but code of conduct expected to be understood, adhered to and applied, by every human being in his everyday life by which he can live and exist as human being with perpetual joy and sagacity, as well can be used as psychotherapy.

In Moscow University, there is a separate department called Psycho-Tronics, where handpicked scientists are given grants and provided facilities for the research about traits of mind under the sub-heads as Psycho power & Psycho energy. In the loose form Mahaveer explained the same concept 2500 years back.

Tranquility considered as sayyam is practiced in negative form because of surface and superficial understanding of the concept. In this manner people loose everything without any creativity or without any positive achievement. Sacrifice of any thing, by way of blind following and without knowing as to why we are sacrificing, makes us empty and pathetic. At the same time loss of energy and of potentials of the sense organs also manifests.

Due to traditions and traditional behavior, negative aspects of existence are experienced because tradition shows only that which has been left aside, but not the inner process of the mind as to why something is cast away or abandoned. We not only inherit religion by birth but traditions also. According to Mahaveer, this inheritance is acceptance of somewhat dead concepts, in the sense that what we are given is not earned by us, and whatever we have got is given to us without any choice on our part for which we do not have to make any conscious efforts or without verifying its applicable values in relation to its inheritors. Materialistic inheritance and conceptual inheritance are two different aspects as far as inheritance is concerned, because materialistic inheritance is tangible but on the contrary conceptual inheritance may suffocate the inheritor if the concept do not correspond with the inheritors basic nature.

The most unfortunate part in today's social system is, that by birth alone we are awarded a readymade religion and tradition.

Root cause of whatever unrest & upheaval we are experiencing since long is the acceptance of religion by birth, which give people belief that they are superior or inferior by birth alone, and this notion gives them sanction to think and behave as per the accepted norms inherent in such religion and tradition.

So when we could not break the mold of inherited religion, then due to lack of any other alternative we behave in aggressive manner. And this happens due to ego also. Because when we are part of leading religious pack, then our aggressive behavior earns us accolade and people start to follow us. Competitions for supremacy between various religions goad us towards more aggressive behavior, which cause nothing but atrocities, violence, compulsory conversion and domination, which in turn causes much of the violence.

To be religious happens on the individual level only, where society at large has no meaning as far as religion is concerned. In which religion-following family you are born is also of no significance. We our self has to choose and strive for any religion as per our temperament and liking. It is not and should not be a family heirloom handed down from generation to generation. And in this regards basically all the religions and its doctrines are of the same nature. Only difference happens to be in its way of practice and the language in which it is laid down. As mentioned above, if it is shown to us that Mohammad, Mahaveer, Buddha and Jesus, all the enlightened beings are dwelling at the same place after the ultimate achievement, then the revelation would be a stunning blow to the individual and society, as well as will be a rude awakening.

We would be acknowledged as really religious people, only when we will allow every individual the freedom to choose the religion as per his choice and not by birth. Even today's practitioners of psychology are interested to know from which religion you are, what following you are adopting and why? Even when we know that all the individuals are basically same physically, but it is also accepted that different religions and its following makes major changes in practitioners psyche because of which people have different beliefs and behave accordingly. At the same time some beliefs are considered as outdated by others or society, and at the same time behavior happening due to such beliefs is also considered as abnormal and bizarre. Similarly when any behavior is considered as accepted behavior in the follower's religious context, then the possibility of considering the same behavior as taboo in other following also happens.

It is possible to be religious by nature, for all the people, only if they are free to choose as per their understanding, liking and willingness to practice. The concept of any one society or group of people having the same religion is childish and bizarre. But on the other hand, if they are individually religious, then this concept as religious society can happen in reality. Deeply religious people of various practices, who understand the meaning of religion as well as are aware enough, can form the society irrespective of their beliefs, even though they are diametrically different in their belief from each other and are mature enough to accept the same. In such a case there is possibility of peace and prosperity for one and all, which will eradicate most of the mental disturbances.

On the other hand, religious ascendancy by birth is just a formality for which we do not have to do anything. But in such a case chances are that even though such people are not religious in true sense, they are branded forever. And this label creates void and frustration because our behavior contrary to this belief causes criticism. On the contrary an atheist is more powerful than the so-called religious person, only because to be an atheist is his own choice and his decision. In such a case we could not win any argument in front of the atheist, because if he says that there is no God, then how we are going to prove that there is God, about whom we do not have any experience, as we have been given the bounty of God by birth alone.

So any choice on our part is called merit. And the moment we choose, we choose at our own free will. And this process makes us more mature. In this way whatever is the out come, we are ready to accept the responsibility.

Practice tranquility with understanding. Try to understand who we are, why we are here. Why we are doing what we are doing. Let us stop for some time and analyze our self. Then afterwards we start to live the life, we have to live. Do not be more insistent about results, because whatever they will be, they will be according to our own choosing. We have to check our inclination, what makes us tick, which direction is easy for us, in which way we could realize our full potentials. We do not have to follow the idol of our family's, only because it was decision of our ancestors, and we may not have the same inclination. So when we follow our own dictates, after due consideration, miracles starts to happen. And we exist easily, without strain, stress and tension. In this regards, there is fresh dawn for us.

Have we ever thought that whatever mistakes we made, we make the same mistakes again and again. This happens in every day life and seems to be our general attitude. We call this happening as habits. But most of these habits show how dense we are. If we honestly look in to our behavior and criticize our selves, then we will come to know that we are repeating the same 10 to 15 mistakes regularly. It seems that by this behavior of ours, we do not learn anything. We rationalize that every time circumstances were different, we were not aware as to what we are doing. But have we ever thought that whatever the circumstances, the common factor is always the same i.e. we, our self was the same element. And so the person who is not ready to learn from past experience will find it very hard to be tranquil. What experience teaches us is that whatever the circumstances, we should not have to react. We should have to be calm. Because last time also we have reacted in the same fashion and has repented afterwards. So when and if, we are ready to learn from past experience, then we can acquire tranquility. We do not have to be so weak, that any outside cue or stimulation should cause us to deviate. Tranquility means; now I come to know that certain experiences due to which I experienced pain, sorrow, mental and physical unrest, which happens only due to my attitudes, so hereinafter I will not behave in the same fashion.

What is the difference between reasoning and rationalization? In reason, we honestly find that whatever is going on around us is going to happen again and again. If we have capacity to change the surrounding, then we will try to change it. But if the change is not within our reach, then we will change our self. But in rationalization, we justify our behavior, irrespective of circumstances and show how weak we are. In childhood or in advanced age the mistakes remain the same and most of the attitudes also remain the same. But children are not well acquainted with the surrounding and to them attitudes are still to be learned, so their mistakes can be caught easily. But in advanced age, we become clever and can camouflage our behavior. At the same time experience has taught us that to be caught red handed is very embarrassing, so we become subtle in our behavior. And this subtlety saves us from getting caught. But basically in both the cases the attitude remains to be the same.

Non-tranquility happens only due to our conditioning. Because since long we are following the same pattern and it has become our second nature. This conditioned behavior makes us feel alive. To us, Sayyam/tranquility is akin to restrain, suppression or control and all this collectively makes our attitudes negative. This negativity ingrained in our psyche, is the root cause of our not being tranquil. What we have to do is, to stop rationalizing our acts and look at the reasons as to why we are behaving in the way we are behaving. We do not have to be cavalier that we will cast away this, this and this. No, we do not have to leave anything, but at the same time we have to remain open and flexible, and while going along the way, we will concentrate on the experience. In this experiment, whichever is not worth considering or repeating, will automatically be left aside, and what will remain will be worth pursuing and creative. Then the most interesting thing will start to happen, that we will not feel any void or emptiness after the completion of the process. Because once the process of pursuing the superior starts, then the inferior drops down automatically, as we do not have to leave anything on our own which is inferior. This experiment is definitely going to make us more contented and fulfilled.

So once we start applying the process on any attitude of any faculty, the same process automatically applies to all the other attitudes of remaining faculties. It is we, who are concerned about any one attitude of any one faculty, but biologically they are linked together. This fact is clinically proven as well as psychology also accepts the same. Any organic dysfunction not only affects the specific organ but also affects the total system as whole. All systems are integrated. When we go to any doctor for any illness, he asks about all the symptoms by ways of feelings, history, and only then prescribes. Most of the time we think that prescription is not properly drawn, but the doctor with his training ascertains the cause and prescribes accordingly. Then the regaining of the health seems miraculous. The same applies to the tranquility. This is the basic treatment, which when we apply to our mind, then its soothing effects are experienced in whole of our body. Only one barrier of negativity requires being demolished by way of self-analysis then the remaining barriers fall down automatically, like sympathetic detonation.

When a psychiatrist is approached by anyone with mental disturbance, then primarily he inquires about the behavioral patterns of the other family members also. Most of the times illness happens due to cumulative effect of behavior of the other family members. The intention behind this enquiry is, to ascertain whether the cause for the disturbance is arising out of the family ties or to determine if the affected person is mentally vulnerable. This concept can be stretched upto society, then nation and ultimately unto total existence also. But to change the whole world is not an easy task, so it is better to change our self. Considering all the eventualities, the concept of family therapy came into being.

We must remember that good is less good than better, and better is less good than the best. Even though best is appreciated the most, but it takes more time and efforts, so first let us start with good and along the way we will be best. Self-analysis is the key and tranquility is the process by which this change will happen. A journey of thousand kilometers starts with first step and this happens every time in all the circumstances. Any willing change towards positive aspect of life will direct us towards personality of positive traits. Just a ray of light will show us that darkness of any density as well as of chronic nature can be eradicated. Following any one may seems to be easy way out, but what the other is doing will be his choice and we have to understand that whatever the other is choosing, may not be good for us. A food of other may prove to be poison for us. When we start to follow any one, we think that we will reach with some more efforts, but this very rarely seems to happen. By doing more efforts we only spend our precious energy, but the chances of our reaching anywhere worth reaching remains low. This kind of following is called as blind following by Mahaveer and deviation from our basic nature also, but this is how we create illusions. To follow anyone, most of the times we follow the behavior or the acts of the significant other, but the driving force behind any behavior or acts happens due to thinking behind, about which we always remain in the dark. What we have to do is analyze our self for which we have to be ready for trial and error method. We may start with any thing that seems to be way for us, but at the same time we do not have to be too insistent about any path we are adapting, but on the contrary we have to be open and ready to improvise along the way and we very definitely will reach. No one can judge anyone, but we can judge our self, as we know what we are doing. Then, if we succeed the satisfaction is ours and if we fail, then no one is to be blamed but only us. In this trial and error method even if we do not reach our goal then we are not going to be disappointed as we are going to be more mature than before, wise than before as well as for the first time we will be encountering our true potentials. This is the formula of positive growth and enlightenment.

Today we see persistence of following the others who are successful, only because we have to reach certain destination, but we are not ready to undertake the process of self-analysis. No one is ready to do this on his own, only because every one wants to have ready-made answers to their problems and are not sure that they on their own will reach anywhere. But as mentioned earlier, existence is very intricate, and unless and until we are ready to change as per our original nature, nothing is going to help us to reach upto our desired goal. Most of the time the process itself is more pleasurable and educational than the actual goal. We have to accept our self as we are, have to refocus our attention from any following to the self-analysis and then have to follow our own dictates arrived at by our intelligent deliberation. This is the way of tranquility and this is how we will exist in tranquility.

CHAPTER 8

AUSTERITY: WAY OF DIRECTING FORCE OF LIFE

We can define about any subject or concept only when we have some knowledge of the concerned subject. With the same token it is not possible to define about anything of which we have no understanding or knowledge. As far as non-violence (Ahimsa) and tranquility (Sayyam) is concerned; the way in which these concepts are understood and practiced is based on traditional understanding, which do not correspond with Mahaveer's way or definition. So in this manner when we define non-violence and tranquility, then such definitions also become erroneous. But as we are bound by traditional upbringing as well as following, even these erroneous definitions are also accepted and this acceptance created a false notion that we are not violent and are tranquil. To Mahaveer, practice of non-violence and tranquility happens only when our state of mind is attuned to the proper meaning of the concept, and based on this understanding we start to behave. As any change in our psyche happens when old concepts are discarded and new ones are installed, then such changes can be experienced by others, only when our behavior or acts start to manifest in altogether different form from the previous personality norm. In a sense conceptual change in our psyche can only become apparent when behavior and previous acts manifest in new ways

In Vedic culture meaning of the word austerity is Tapa Or Tapascharya i.e. style or mode of everyday living or being, based on the doctrine of the religion or the culture the person has accepted and is adopting. This type of behavior can be seen and followed by the others in everyday living. But in this case also, following of the doctrine happens in traditional manner and most of the times the rituals and customs are also adopted in the manner prescribed and mentioned in the doctrine without understanding their significance in our existence. But as mentioned before, all the religious and cultural doctrines are laid down so long ago, that the circumstances, atmosphere and natural conditions are not what they were at that time, but even people for whom these doctrines are laid down have also changed.

Basic purpose of austerity, as traditionally accepted by Hindu and all the related religious practices are concerned, is the belief that after going through the process, the practitioner is going to have a confirmed place or reserved slot in the heaven at the end of his natural life i.e. after his death. This existence after death in heaven is considered as happy and joyous existence or afterlife. To Mahaveer, the manner in which any religious doctrine is practiced with the preconceived notion of joy and happiness, is indication of future oriented achievement and in this notion, it is firmly believed that in our current existence we are not going to experience any joy or feeling of satisfaction as we are, because to take birth as human being is the only chance we are going to get, through which we are going to achieve ultimate salvation. But this belief is totally erroneous, because Mahaveer says that practice of any doctrine is to make our present being and existence joyous, satisfying and contented, and this is the intention of every religion. At the same time religion and practice of its doctrine is the only way for human to become aware about his self, what he can expect and achieve as well as what potentials we have as well as how to realize them to the fullest. On the contrary we do not have to bother about what is going to happen after our death, because how we exist in present is going to decide as to how we are going to be at the end of our life. Firm belief that whatever we are going through, whatever we are experiencing and whatever we are going to be, is beyond our reach and we have no power to change anything as we are destined to be just the way we are. When people start to believe in this notion, then to be religious seems to be last resort to create a future, where at least we can experience joy and happiness after our death, this is how people accept traditional meaning of religious practice. In reality when we expect joy, happiness and sensory pleasure, but instead ultimately we experience nothing but sorrow, unhappiness and depression, then in this light the meaning and the purpose of austerity, in traditional manner, start to become distorted. When we logically expect joy and happiness, but in its place experience the opposite, then we change our basic belief and start to believe that if we start to expect that, which we do not want to happen and experience i.e. instead of joy or happiness, we must voluntarily encounter and face sorrow and unhappiness in the first place, then ultimately we will experience joy and happiness. Logically and mathematically, this concept seems to be very straightforward equation, so this is accepted as the true form of austerity. So we start inventing ways, which are painful, sorrowing and denying everything that is pleasurable. To this process we call as Tapa i.e. ask for that, which we really do not want, but expect and get what we primarily desired in exchange. In psychology this is known as conditioned reflex.

In reality what happens is, basically at our core we remain as we are in spite of our changed belief. We anticipate joy and we get sorrow, so we go into reverse process and go into painful processes called misguided and misunderstood religious doctrine, with the new belief that ultimately we will experience anticipated joy. So, however we go into the process, the basic expectation of happiness remains as of paramount importance.

In traditionally accepted belief, when we talk about Tapa/Austerity, we define this concept as Sorrow + Expectation

= Austerity. But this definition is wrong because no one desires sorrow, unhappiness etc. However, when we manipulate the equation then it is bound to create chaos only. Because when in sorrow and pain also we feel pleasure, then the process make us pathological and we become masochist. This association happens due to completely diverse expectations and the cause is our conditioned nature due to wrong association, and we start to perceive and experience even pleasure in pain and sorrow, which ultimately turns into mere illusion.

In India, there is a cult which practice self-flagellation as the form of austerity, to cast away and to purge the mind from libidinous thoughts. The moment any practitioner feels that he is getting aroused, he will flagellate himself to purge his mind of the thought. But unfortunately what happens is, such a person looses the capacity to enjoy natural ecstasy manifesting out of personal relationship with the opposite sex, till he is not beaten beforehand. This is how our mind works, and this is how masochists come into beings. Continual practice of self-flagellation, removes the possibility of any normal sexual relationship, as the process itself becomes the ultimate act of intercourse.

But the people, who are spectators to this act and behavior, think that how extraordinary the person is and how much sayyami he is. But in reality nothing divine is happening, because the practitioner is totally immersed in the carnal pleasure, which has taken the form of auto-masturbation. When any pain or painful experience is associated with any act and when the act happens due to distortion of thought, but perceived as pleasurable, and when the emotion manifests in distorted manner with the perception that ultimately we are going to experience desired effect and repeated again and again in the same manner even with the distorted belief, is called as conditioned obsessive-compulsive behavior.

Same thing happens in the case of self-mutilation. Desire to beautify or adorn the body happens because other people may accept us or pay more attention towards us. But, when in spite of all the efforts we are neglected, then the obsession to beautify takes the form of other extreme and to disfigure the same body starts to happen. But the motive and intention to attract attention of the others remains to be the same. And in both the instances the medium is the same i.e. our body, and the motive also remains the same i.e. to attract attention of the others. This happens due to superficial conflicts in the form of attention provocation. When beautification fails the same body is perceived as enemy and then disfigurement starts. In all, this behavior is very pathological and nothing more than another extreme of the same basic concept of attracting the attention of the others.

Attitude of self-indulgence or attitudes of austerity, when practiced on surface are basically related to our physical body only. In indulgence we expect sensory pleasure and in our kind of austerity, we punish the body for the same reason, that the body is not fulfilling the expected experience of pleasure. It is one and the same thing, and is nothing but a form of revenge on the body, which basically is an instrument.

Mostly what happens is, the so-called austerite do not believe that any one can be happy or is capable of experiencing joy and satisfaction. His approach and thoughts are very self-centered. If I am not happy, then how can anyone else be? And most probably the concepts of hell, eternal damnation are the distorted fantasies of these so-called austrite's. He will experience all the happiness of heaven, for which he is torturing his body in this life. And with the same token we will have to be in hell, as we are not going through the same process as he is. In a nutshell this is nothing but the act of balancing. He is creating future for himself and at the same time creating and planning the hell for us in the future. Whatever happiness we are experiencing today, the same will materialize in much more magnified manner for him in the future. One more basic characteristic of the so-called hell is; we will be tortured forever without the respite of the death. Because if we die then we are not going to suffer forever and eternal damnation will not happen. As per the perceptions of the so-called austerite, all the condemned should suffer forever in the hell.

From whose fertile mind these ideas came? Because the true practitioner of austerity will never imagine sorrow and suffering for the self as well as others. Religious scriptures written by the so-called austerite's are filled with vivid descriptions about hell and torture or are understood by them with the intention to intimidate the masses that are following them with the intention to keep the masses under their control. And this is nothing but the product of perverted minds, minds which are so warped that they could not imagine or experience any joy, happiness or pleasure which, if not possible for and experienced by them, then to no one else has the right to them. What we have to remember as a psychological fact is, whatever we are fighting against the same manifests in distorted form around us. This is what the so-called austerite is projecting i.e. thoughts from his suppressed mind.

Whenever we are thinking of any attitude of ours, which is troublesome, then austerity, in the form of self-analysis is the proper process by which we can overcome such problems. First of all we do not have to stand against it, as it will cause suppression. We have to try to understand its significance as to our behavior pattern. We have to understand its cause or reason, as to why we go on repeating the same act again and again even though we are not experiencing the desired feelings. When we analyze the same in this new light we have to accept the thought as it is. When we accept anything in this manner, it looses its obsessive hold on our mind and we become tranquil. Acceptance after due deliberation of any thought, emotion or feeling saves us from its nuisance in the form of constant brooding and preoccupation. At the same time we save ourselves from reacting in any extreme manner, which again saves us from stress. Once we learn this technique in full, then we become able to keep our mind in balanced state.

Attitudes are like disputes between husband and wife. Dispute in this form is nothing but reverse form of love. We go into arguments with only those people who are of some value or significance to our being. But, when there is no love and so no dispute, then this type of relationship is nothing but mutual divorce or total indifference.

Even Freud states that when there is love, there is bound to be conflict. So freedom from conflict is freedom from love also. Further he also states that expression of sexuality and war are also connected but these events are also identical to love and conflict. Till we are sexually hyperactive, nature of warring will also go on. What happens in war happens in sex also i.e. more powerful dominates and weaker becomes receptive or passive.

According to Mahaveer if we have to leave inferior then at the same time we have to cast away superior also or on its own it will drop out. The same happens in the case of revulsion and attraction, friendship and enmity. Whenever we intentionally choose any one, then we start to exist in extreme and that state weigh heavily on our mind. When we fight against any thing, we are stuck with the thing or attitude. Our attitude to fight with or against anything, which is very common behavioral pattern, is in reality is nothing but unconscious acceptance on our part that the other is more powerful than us. But when this phenomenon happens, we unknowingly increase the strength of the other by paying more attention with the intention that the other should not overcome our defenses. We have to understand, that the more attention we give then more preoccupied we become with the thought to resist, and this is the manner in which the other starts to become stronger.

There are three basic characteristic features to the nature we exist in, which are attached to human being also along with every thing in this existence. To understand these characteristics is going to reveal how in conditioned manner humans behave and why.

First characteristic is termed as Typical Nature (Prakriti), which is basic and natural characteristic of human, to exist as intended by laws of nature. But when the human deviates from the natural laws, then he transgresses the basic laws of nature and goes into abnormality (Vikruti/sacrilegious act). Formation of society happens at that time, when human elevates himself by such acts and behavior that he transcends the laws of nature but do not deviate from the same or remain in the framework. This happening forms the society at large and is called as Culture (Sanskruti). Most of the times our behavioral pattern remains such that we do not exist within laws of nature or remain constant in deviated phase, but we keep oscillating between both. This is the main reason because of which every person has some eccentricities in his perceptions, understanding and behavior. Furthermore, when the deviation becomes profound, then the behavior of the person is labeled as abnormal behavior. As we very rarely happens to be in our natural state, the same is also true that we very rarely transcend the basic laws of our basic nature, but still we describe our self as cultured. So, if at all we have to become cultured then we have to adhere to the laws of nature and at the same time have to try to transcend the same and elevate our self.

So when we fight with our basic attitudes, which are nothing but the traits of the natural faculties, then we are fighting against our basic nature, where no matter what, transgression happens. This type of misguided, unaware or unconscious fighting and the resultant transgression is nothing but further deviation from the nature. What we should know and be aware of is, this type of behavior happens only in human beings. No species of animal is prone to mental disorders. And this fascinating phenomenon happens only because all the animals exist in their natural limits.

Exception happens in those animals, which are kept as pets, kept in the zoo or performing in circus, where their existence is controlled by humans. But even these animals again acquire their natural equilibrium once they are let loose from human control.

Only we humans are very special species, who are given the potentials to be super humans or lower than animals. Homosexuality is a behavior trait that is found in humans only. We are given the option where either we go beyond natural faculty, in which case sooner or later we are going to fall down, or understand the faculty and its creative power that will elevate us as cultured beings.

The meaning of the word transgression is – breaking of law, command or rules, which can be natural, legal, social or self inflicted. In relation to all kinds of laws, austerity is to be deemed as the process; going through the process means we transcend the laws or rules. To transcend is to go beyond the law of good or bad, to elevate above superior or inferior, or not going to accept or reject anything. In austerity we do not have to fight or stand against any thing or any attitude. We can and have to start the journey from wherever we are. And in this process we start to save whatever energy we have, because in acceptance also we have to spend some energy, as acceptance of anything also creates rejection at the same time. At the same time in this process of austerity whatever remains as leftover falls down automatically, because we elevate our self above anything as well as everything. Suppose we are at the bottom of a valley, where there is darkness but at the peak of the mountain there is still sunlight, which is visible to us. Now we only have to start climbing towards the peak where sunlight is. In this process of our climbing, we are not groping in the dark or resisting the dark, but we have changed the direction towards light i.e. we are transcending the darkness. In the same manner austerity can be applied. When we fight or resist any thing, we have to remain in the proximity of the element with whom we are fighting and in this way we have to remain where we are. But when we start to extricate ourselves from any situation, then we stand above the situation where we were and this is known as transcending. Most of the attitudes of ours are of such a nature that we move only in circles but reach no-where. There are various types of attitudes in us as well as all around us where we have to exist. And to overcome all this we have to undertake the task of analyzing them, which is time consuming and most of the times fruitless exercise. Austerity is the proper process by which we concentrate on the self as to how we will elevate our self above these attitudes.

As per Mahaveer, those who resist any attitudes are extrovert and those who try to understand their significance and alter their own perception by way of self-analysis is introvert. To Mahaveer extrovert is the person who is not aware that attitudes are specific characteristics of the mind or sense organs, but believes that outside stimulations and cues are the causes that lead us towards behavior or acts, on which we do not have conscious regulatory capacity to command the same. When this belief is strongly accepted, then the extrovert tries to change circumstances or situations, which most of the times are beyond our influence. The person existing by this erroneous notion, do not analyze his self as to whether his belief is true or false, is to be considered as extrovert. Whenever we concentrate on anything we increase the strength of the other, by focusing our attention. Extrovert tries to combat outer stimuli without understanding or looking into the self, as to why he is feeling influenced or stimulated. But we have to understand that anything that we cannot control or alter but is bound to exist, as may be it is the law of nature or existence, against which we are bound to loose. In introspection our focus is to be directed towards our inner working and we have to try to understand and adjust the self accordingly. In this exercise stimuli or cue remain as they are but by our increased awareness we become capable to transcend the same.

In every day life also we see lots of incidences of such behavior. When the attention of the others is focused on us we feel more full and rejuvenated. But the moment the focus shifts we become restless and disturbed. Psychology also accepts the fact that there are such patients who, when neglected show the symptoms of illness. All the clinical check-ups fail to show any organic dysfunction, but they are mentally ill and such illness falls under the category of psychosomatic symptoms. For such people cognitive therapy is suggested. Children are more prone to this type of illness and they understand this process more easily than adults. When wife becomes ill, the husband takes leave from the office and attends to her in which case, the wife regains the health miraculously. Why this type of behavior happens is, till the wife is hail and hearty no one was aware of her presence. So by way of illness she is desperately trying to attract the attention of her partner that she is also present, so kindly take note of her but do not take her for granted. But when this type of behavior repeatedly happens then it becomes habit as well as cause of rejection also.

It is a fact and is to be understood that whenever we have to attend any ill person we must attend him with the intention to help him regain his health, but should not pay constant attention towards him, as our constant attention may create interest in the mind of the patient and may prolong the illness. Such attention provokes in the patient the thought and feeling that till he is ill, it is advantageous to remain ill, as only in illness he is getting all the attention he is craving for. In such a case the patient draws erroneous inference and become interested in illness than in cure. This type of misunderstanding on the part of patient, cause condescension of the attitude, which results in pathological association between attention and illness.

When we project our attention on someone or something, we

become cause of increasing the power of the other. And the same happens in opposite condition. The same happens in the case of political leaders, actors and in the case of the persons wielding prominent positions. Till they are center of attention of the others, they remain active. But the moment they retire or step down from the exalted position, they start to run down and wither away. Even their life span seems to shorten. Attention is subtle kind of food also. It fills us. So whenever someone falls into love the person's food intake decreases, as food is replaced by love. So when any person is not loved sufficiently or if he thinks that he is not getting due attention, then he starts to eat more. He perceives in the food the substitute to fill the void or emptiness he is experiencing due to lack of love.

As mentioned earlier, focus of attention generates power and this power gets stored on the object or at the site of attitude towards which it is directed. In this manner the capacity of the attitude to function increases in the same proportion to the energy stored. So when we are doing any job, the attitude to work for the given job and the enhanced power makes it possible to do the job satisfactorily and with due concentration. So when the work is completed the attitude comes down to normal state, by spending the attention-generated energy. In this way the cycle becomes complete. Now let us take into account any troublesome attitude or thought of ours, which we are trying to get rid of. The same focus of attention happens, which generate and store the energy in the same manner as mentioned above. But in this instance we are trying to use the stored energy to suppress the attitude or thought. We have to understand that whatever we try to suppress, now or later it is going to come out in distorted form, which make us more pathetic. What naturally happens is, the stored energy looks for release, but when no release happens, then the stored energy due to continual pressure of suppression bursts out or releases itself at the weakest link and poison our total system. This spilling or release of suppressed energy causes mental disturbance and abnormal behavior. If we do not voluntarily release or give opportunity to release the suppressed pent-up emotions or feelings, then we find ourselves in a vicious circle where the said energy is again and again stored and it releases itself in the same manner. This phenomenon is to be understood as relapse or remission in most of the psychologically disturbed persons.

Austerity is the process that helps us to chanelize or to redirect our energy force known to us as Prana Urja. As our physical body is coalition of five basic elements existing in the nature, Prana Urja is also one of the elements in the form of Agni/fire. The basic characteristic feature of fire in any form is, it always travel's in upward direction.

Mahaveer asks the practitioner of austerity to create new centers on which we can focus our attention. In Vedic culture, it is accepted since long that in the human body there are seven centers, which are known as Chakras, on which austerite focus his attention at the time of meditation. In fact these Chakras are not organic in nature. But Yogic practice of the Hindu culture accepts their existence and all the postures or asana of the Yoga are instrumental in their activation. They start at our naval region and the last one is situated at the top of our head. Basic concept of austerity and its practice or the aim is to direct our Prana Urja or force of life and the practitioner is asked to concentrate at the top Chakra, by which the practitioner attains the state of Samadhi. In this process, all the attitudes as well as all the thoughts, good or otherwise, remain where they are, but at the same time we become very much tranquil and integrated. So once we start to practice this process and understand its advantages, then we have to just focus our attention on the required task, complete it, and shift to the mode of austerity again.

This mastery or skill of shifting the attention at will is the key to positive growth and creative personality. In this process we experience the satisfaction of doing the day-to-day work at par, without stress or tension and ultimately we become masters of our own.

As mentioned above, our force of life is also a form of Agni and its basic nature is to flow in upward direction. But when we do anything due to our habit nature which is nothing but transgression, as most of our habits are superimposed on our basic nature, we start to experience tension and unrest. Any transgression causes barriers in the upward flow of force of life, which cause stress and tension. Whatever difficulties and problems we face in our every day life happens due to habit nature. Since our birth we are taught to behave in the fashion which is the norm of our family and which corresponds with the society in which we have to exist. At the same time we are also taught to curb our basic instincts, which are nothing but natural attitudes. But this teaching and the learned way of behavior consolidate and become our habits and this habit bound behavior is accepted as cultured behavior as well as praise worthy or model existence. In this manner we are very strange people, that if we encounter any person who is guileless, simple and straightforward then we criticize and ridicule the same but we never think for a moment, that such a person could be basic form of human being and exists in natural manner.

Our habits are superimposed on our basic nature. And this superimposition cause oscillation in our general behavior, in which case we exist from extremes to extremes. So the more deep rooted the habits, then more oscillation happens and to overcome these habits become hard and tedious. Habit of smoking, taking alcohol, use of drugs, and assumed or believed sexual expressions are some acquired habits where total casting away from the habit do not happen but even moderate behavior happens after much struggle, waste of time and precious energy. Basically, most of the habits are acquired as substitutes for our natural inclination to be easy and relaxed. Most of the above habits are addictive unless and until we ascertain as to which natural faculties they are denoting or for what they are substituted as rein forcers. People take álcohol in joy as well as sorrow, and this happens only because their inability to express themselves in natural form, about which they are not sure that others in the surrounding will accept or appreciate. This happens generally with the people of sensitive nature who have to go through criticism for any act again and again. At the same time, the belief that any person under the influence of alcohol is to be tolerated, as he is drunk, causes the drinker to go on drinking with impunity. So the habitual drinker takes advantage of this belief and expresses himself freely while he is under the influence. Mostly what happens at the rehabilitation center is, that the person who has to kick the habit is allowed to express himself as he thinks fit. And when most of the participants voice the same theme, he becomes assured that what he is feeling and wants to express is nothing novel or abnormal but very common occurrence, then he becomes reassured. This reassurance and acceptance from the group helps him to kick the habit.

So-called austerite and average person behave in the same way. Both are facing difficulties due to attitudes. But so-called austerite seems much more eccentric in his behavior only because he concentrate more on the attitudes with the intention to cast them away. What we have to remember and as mentioned earlier that the more attention we pay towards any attitude, then more powerful they become, and we have to concentrate on them ceaselessly least they should not dominate us or pull us down. As now we have come to know that we have to accept all the attitudes and thoughts as they are. In this manner we stop to resist them as well as fight them. Then we have to go into the basic faculties of ours, ascertain as to what causes the existence of such attitudes, and when we get the reason as to why they developed in the first place, then we are in the position to overcome them. We will go into a simple exercise.

There are some painful incidents that happened in our life, about which we would like to forget as these memories are causing mental unrest. Now to forget about anything, we have to remember again and again as to what has to be forgotten. But this phenomenon of remembering to forget is causing most concentrated attention generating efforts, which in turn makes forgetting impossible. What we can do is we will accept the painful memory or incidence in its totality, and once this happens then the accepted becomes taken for granted and further anguish to forget stop bothering us as well as energy dissipation also stops and we regain peace.

Austerity is nothing but the most scientific way of assessment of our mental process and its' working. This is the process of self-analysis. But popular miss-conception that any thing religious is to be incorporated in our life at the advanced age is the hindrance. There are laws of physics, laws of chemistry, laws of nature and in the same manner religion is the law of human nature as well as intended code of conduct for the humans. So once we understand their significance in our everyday life and become aware with due understanding the way in which they work, then what we experience is tranquility and stress free existence.

Staunch followers of the religious doctrine believe in all the rituals as the proper practice of any religion. But when we follow the rituals in this manner the practice cause boredom and in most of the cases frustrations, because we do not experience any positive and creative change in our self as well as our surrounding. Then those who are somewhat bold, stop the practice and those who are not so bold, keep suffering. Cause of frustration happens because to discontinue in the mid-stream warrants criticism by the follower of the same practice as well as by the practitioner of the other practices. Adherence to peer following as well as criticism by the same peers, do not happen in school or colleges only, but in the following of any other form also. And the same happens in all the religions. This blind following without due understanding becomes cause of death of all that is positive and creative. When we accuse the young generation as irresponsible or non-religious people, then the accusation is baseless. Young ones are more open than us, at the same time they are more critical, only because they want to know as to why we are doing what we are doing. But as we also do not know about the same thing, we become mute and this silence on the part of elders is inferred as indifference or neglect by the younger generation, which in turn fuels rebellion.

Austerity is practiced in two ways. One is the proper way and the other is false or erroneous way. Practitioner of the later will become weaker, only because he is resisting the natural faculties about which no one can do anything. But in his resistance he will loose all the energies, which are more or less limited. The former will concentrate on the self as the creative aspect of his being, and will ignore all the trivial as meaningless. This elevated approach will generate upward surge of force of life, which is invigorating in it-self due to which energy conservation happens, and he will become stronger than before.

If a person is denied food for 30 days, his faculty of sexual function will become weak. But does this mean that he has achieved celibacy? The answer is no, but what happens is all his systems become weak due to starvation, which cause biological dysfunction. Further, starvation does not mean that his faculty has become null and void forever, and he will never function as before. Once he starts with his regular intake, then within a week's time he will start feeling sexual stirrings. If we take this person as so-called austerite who is trying to attain celibacy, then he will again become fearful about his arousal. In this case he will be on the guard forever about all the food and its effects, he will become hysterical and will wither away. So-called austerite will maintain him self on bare- minimum, as take lower intake and will go for higher activity, so nothing should remain as residual to cause him concern. But in such instances, he will exist fearfully.

Before starting the process and practice of austerity, we have to do one thing. We have to take stock of what cause us much disturbance, what motivates us to be extrovert, what cause deviation in us. All these may be thoughts, attitudes or stimulations, and then we have to keep in mind that these are our leakage points as well as starting points also. Now we are ready to go into creative aspect of Austerity.

CHAPTER 9
EXPERIENCING OUR ENERGY BODY

Religion in itself is a super science and any aspect of the doctrine of any religion is scientifically proven branch of the same science. Science gives us the information about any elements as to what it is made of and helps us to prove the same. Science is about tangible objects, and how any two elements of seemingly diverse properties can be merged. Similarly religion as super-science is the technique or probe, which not only touches the non-tangible but also helps us to govern and redirect our force of life. In this light our force of life can be manipulated in such a manner that verification of our beliefs and reciprocal behavior can also be tested and changed, which in turn helps us to experience our true identity.

Science informs us as to how and why any matter exists, by which process it comes into being, its formula and management. As per Mahaveer and likes of him who have reached, the meaning of the religion, as science is to experience the ultimate Truth with the help of which something can be done. Understanding the basic characteristic of Truth is the instrument, by which some radical change, something constructive and creative can be done. Practice of any religion is the process of total transformation in our being; a mutation. Austerity is the primary formula towards intended transformation and religious doctrine is the guideline on which this transformation happens.

Science has proved and accepted as fact that nothing in this existence is solid, stationary or static. Everything is dynamic and flowing. What we see or experience as solid or stationary happens only due to higher rate of flow. When something flows at higher speed, it is impossible to see the gap between the flow. In our primary school we have gone through a scientific experiment of a circle drawn on the white paper, on which colors of rainbow were drawn separately. This circle was mounted on a spindle, which when rotated at moderate speed was able to show individual colors. But the moment the spindle was rotated at higher speed, all the colors merge into each other and we can see the white circle rotating. Dose this mean that all the colors have vanished? No, the speed of rotation is of such higher rate that the basic color - white, is seen and perceived. And the same is happening all around us. Some forces are so dynamic that we perceive those things as solid. This phenomenon is nothing but an optical illusion.

Existence as we experience is multidimensional and continuously flows at predetermined pace. Out of which seven are accepted by every science known to mankind, only because it can be proved by scientific methods. But the eighth dimension is the human force of life, rather it should be stated that whatever is animate is called as eighth dimension. This happens only because animate can move on their own as per their will. The same force of life becomes ninth dimension in human for the reason that human conscious is much more developed and it can be moved in any desired direction. Religion as a science can be applied on this dimension and austerity is the process, which helps us to verify this concept.

In Vedic terms this ninth dimension mentioned above as force of life is also called as Energy Body or Prana, which is real 'I', real and natural form of every human being.

In the last chapter we have discussed about Chakras and the process of their activation. The last or top most Chakra is situated at the top of our head. Meditation as one of the process or branch of religious practice is related to these Chakras. So when we go into deep meditation, and when our force of life or Prana is elevated at the top most Chakra, then realization of the self as to what we really are, happens. Here at this Chakra we experience existence of our Energy Body/ force of life/Prana. In Vedic parlance this Chakra is known as Anahat Chakra. Arriving at this top most Chakra is the state of realization or understanding, that our physical body is separate entity than our true being.

Experience of this kind of phenomena permeates the being of the austerite with such warmth that at his core or center, he becomes cool and this happening is considered in religious parlance, as realization of the self. The reason behind this phenomenon is, by the way of practice of austerity, the practitioner activates all the centers in his body, which generate lot of heat and because of this generation of heat, the practitioner is known as Austerite (Tapaswi). Cooling of the core and heating of the exterior is nothing but the balancing act of the nature or existence. Even science has accepted that the Sun, which is very hot on the surface, is the coldest at its core. It is law of nature that what is perceived or directly experienced at the surface or exterior, exactly opposite is at the core or center, as without one the other will not exist, i.e. balancing happens only because of the opposite.

Some acts or rituals are considered as related to religious practices, about which some scientific explanation will make clear the above phenomenon and at the same time will show that they are based purely on scientific principles. Yogis and fakirs walk on burning coals and this act is taken as miracle. But in reality what happens is the walker wills the force of energy existing in the feet towards higher intensity, which happens to be more than the burning coals. So when the relative spot heat is more than the actual heat, then the actual heat is experienced as less hot. We only have to increase the inner energy out put of our feet. In this manner the exact reverse can also be experienced.

When a person is kept under the spell of hypnotism, his conscious mind comes under the control of the person giving suggestions. So if the hypnotist keeps a pebble in the hand of the person under the spell and suggests that a burning coal is placed on the hand, then the person under the spell will feel extreme burning sensation as well as his hand will be blistered as if really burned. In this exercise, the effort is to show that our firm belief as well as powerful suggestion can be used as driving or motivational force to shift or move our force of life. In hypnotism, the same force of life or energy body pulls back from the related organ by mere suggestion, as the same suggestion is perceived as threat to the well being of the body.

The reason behind all this explanation is to show that our energy force can be manipulated and at the same time intensity of its flow can also be increased or decreased, as per our will. Austerite understand and apply the same technique and directs the force of life in desired direction.

Loss of any limb due to accident or by way of amputation do not cause decrease in the force of life or in energy body. Most of the persons who have lost a limb, feel on physical level that at certain times they completely forget that they are not whole and try to use the limb that is no more part of their body, but they still experience whole body sensation. The same phenomena happen in old age, that ageing happens to the physical body but not to the energy body. The Chakras in our body are considered to be energy distribution points in our physical body and these points are deemed as the controlling outlets, which regulate the functions of the organs and faculties directly under their domain. So when the energy force pulls back or fluctuates at any point, the outlet of the energy also interrupts and we experience ill health or disease. Now-a-days transplant of the diseased or malfunctioning organ is common occurance. When a heart is transplanted the possibility of further ailments of the same organ should not happen, but still when the same person dies due to heart failure, then other cause than ailing heart is to be accepted. And this other cause is when the energy point or Chakra, controlling heart function oscillates or releases the energy in fluctuating manner then malfunction occurs in working of heart or heart-attacks occurs.

In austerity we knowingly or unknowingly work on and activate all these Chakras, and this is the reason proper austerite always enjoys good health. At the same time when no organic cause become apparent for the dysfunction of any system, it should be taken for granted that energy force is fluctuating and causing the illness.

In Chinese therapy of Acupuncture, there are 700 points in our body through which force of life/energy body can be probed as well as manipulated with the intention to regulate the flow or enhance the same. Chinese practitioners of acupuncture therapy accept the concept of flow of energy force as well as its fluctuation as cause of organic illness or dysfunction. In acupuncture, the insertion of a needle at specific point re-activates the flow by which health is regained. Ayurveda, the basic science of corrective and healing process of human illnesses and diseases, accepts the concept of existence of energy body and its flow is germane to the well being of human body. Yogic practice of various postures or asana is also one of the branches of the same Ayurveda, and its regular and scientific practice helps the person to maintain good health. Yogasana's activates all the Chakras in human body as well as regulate flow of energy and this same concept is accepted by Chinese acupuncture therapy also. In Yoga, a Chakra as a single energy point is worked upon whereas in acupuncture therapy 100 points adjacent to any Chakra is worked upon.

The energy that makes us capable to function sexually is generally taken for granted to be useful in reproduction only. The same is known as Oja or Urga. Similarly sporting events where use of physical prowess is of primary importance, also accepts the potentials of the same energy and its storage, to increase and maintain physical power. All these beliefs, as well as concepts on which these beliefs are based, are true. What we have to understand is that this is the only energy source we have, which ultimately helps us to achieve the realization of our self, known as self-enlightenment. This energy alone is the means, as well as its positive manipulation helps us to go into austerity. Because austerity is the process where use of sexual energy is used as vehicle towards higher awareness. Yogic asana's and postures are nothing but exercises to exert proper pressure on various energy points that activates the same as well as its related Chakras. At the same time energy from other points and Chakras is also redirected towards desired centers, that otherwise remain dormant.

In austerity, having faith and conviction in the belief, that we are going to achieve the set goal is very important. Any belief becomes firm and can be pursued wholeheartedly only when we have faith in the concept. In psychology belief is termed as motive, and faith as re-enforcer of the motive. To any practitioner of austerity, flowing thoughts are to be accepted repeatedly and are to be followed diligently.

First of all we have to accept that the physical form of ours is not real. We have to sever the association with the physical body i.e. our body is not our real self. It is to be understood, that any old belief could be negated only by new belief with firm faith.

We know what death is, even though we have not consciously experienced the happening or encountered the same. We have seen many dead bodies. What difference do we see? The body we have seen in live form is the same at the time of death also. The major difference we see is absence of animation, which happens due to partition of Prana or energy body from the physical body. This partition of Prana or energy body from the physical body is our real 'I', which is the driving force. So when we accept this reality consciously then above-mentioned explanation becomes nothing but truth. And the basic characteristic feature of truth is; our acceptance or rejection does not change it.

So while going into austerity we have to start with – I am not the physical body, but I am energy body/life force/ Prana/Chetana. And this rejection and acceptance, negative and positive has to happen at the same time. As we know that all the existence is balanced, then we have to balance our conviction, and faith in the conviction at the same time.

CHAPTER 10

WHY AND HOW ABOUT FASTING

Mahaveer divided various processes of doctrine, even though they are one continuous process of austerity. The division is done with the intention that in divided manner they can be understood in proper perspective and can be practiced easily. As human attention and concentration span is quite limited, we understand anything in segments only.

We have to start from where we really are. To Mahaveer austerity is the practice to increase our awareness about our self. We become aware about ourselves by going into self-analysis and this process happens in our inner realm or in our inner being. But as we are conditioned extrovert by habit nature, and as we are not acquainted with our inner being, we have to start from the outside. For instance, if the river that is flowing towards ocean, stops and return back, then it will arrive at its source. Hereinafter the procedures or processes, which are to be discussed, are of the same nature. By the law of nature and existence, we should exist in our nature, where we are destined to be. But because of our transgressions and way-ward behavior, we are far away from our original nature.

To the persons like Mahaveer and other enlightened persons, inner and outer is not different. According to them, what are inner, manifests on the outside. They perceive inner and outer as a whole and not as divided, as reality is. Divisions are meant for our convenience.

There are two types of orators, one speaks from that point

where he is and the other speaks on the level where we are. So Mahaveer, as compassionate, knows our difficulty of understanding and is speaking at the level where we are as listeners. To him inner is first and outer is secondary. But to us, who has lost the faculty to be in the self, outer is perceived as first and inner becomes secondary. To us, outer can be seen and experienced starkly, so it is to be understood initially. But in the outer also there are pitfalls, as following of any acts may happen blindly without understanding, and not knowing as to why we are doing what we are doing. As happens with the followers of Mahaveer, they start with the outer first, but as there are two sides to all the concepts, and unless and until both are understood and practiced simultaneously, nothing substantial happen. At the same time, if we decide to complete the outer processes first and then go for the inner processes, then what we desire to achieve will never happen. The reason is, that even though we differentiate between outer and inner processes the basic concept remains as one and the same. At the most, outer and inner can be considered as two sides of the same coin. In this regard, if we decide to complete outer processes first, then our whole lifespan is short to complete the task, and ultimately we are not going to achieve any thing as we have left the inner process, which have to be gone through simultaneously as the counter-part of the outer process. As happens in the cognitive therapy, we have to consider the schemas of the patient as the inner working along with outer circumstances or stimulations, which cause the abnormal behavior, as the outer stimuli. So it becomes our responsibility that we must understand all the concepts of any doctrine that appeals to us, and then go in to the process with the understanding that we have to simultaneously practice both the facets of the concepts even though we divide them for the purpose of understanding. Meaning of the word division is, more than one of the same. It is to be understood that until integration happens, the picture will never be complete, so the purpose of division is purely functional.

The motto of the medical science is, treat the patient and not the disease, is based on the fact that basically our immune system is weak and this weakness cause illness. Manifestation of the illness or malfunction happens at the site of any organ or faculty, only because the said organ or faculty due to overwork becomes vulnerable, and this vulnerability helps to mutate the disease or illness and in this manner the symptoms surface at the site of organ or faculty. But as all the organs and faculties are part of the whole body, they are integrated system as a whole and are connected with each other as well as are dependent on each other. In such a case to treat the symptoms is not going to cure us. So patient as a whole is to be treated, and then there are chances that the disease can be eradicated. The same concept is to be applied and followed in religious doctrine also.

Any explanation about any concept or thought becomes mono dimensional, only because of limitations of expression in any language. In such a case we have to understand and follow the concepts along with all its facets as a whole or as integrated concept, even though we divide them for our understanding. In clinical psychology a drug known as SSRI is prescribed for more than one symptom, which is combination of various compounds. Even though all the compounds are different from each other, they are complimentary to each other. They work at different sites and at various levels at the same time. Religious doctrine is to be treated and applied in the same manner, and only then we can experience the desired changes not only in our acts and behavior, but in our psyche also.

Now we will try to understand the various aspects of the doctrine laid down by Mahaveer, which are 2500 years old, but are still important and worth practicing in today's existence and environment.

First outer process of austerity is Fasting (Anashan). Generally accepted meaning by all the people, as well as followers of the Mahaveer, is avoidance of any dietary intake or food. But its esoteric meaning, which was of greater importance, is very different.

Our body has double mechanisms, of which we are aware of only one; but the other is not known to us. The other mechanism starts to work in emergency only. As per the type of work we are doing and the general routine, we take various type of food, which gives us energy and nourishment that help sustain us in every activity. The food after digestion helps to create blood, nutrients to bones and muscles. When any surplus energy and nourishment remains after overall demand of our body, then the remaining surplus turns into fat and is stored in the body.

So in case of emergency, when it becomes impossible to get food from the outside then to keep the body functioning, second mechanism kicks in. The surplus food, which was turned into fat and was deposited at various parts of the body, starts to disintegrate and is used as food supplement.

The basic importance of fasting, as first step in austerity is to experience and understand the gap, that occurs at the end of first mechanism and before the second mechanism becomes operational. Mahaveer asks us to concentrates on this gap and for this reason fasting is important. This gap between the two is our neutral position, where we exist with our self for some moments. This gap helps us to experience our original form or existence. This experiment must happen all of a sudden, at the spur of the moment, only then due to spontaneity we may experience the shift more vividly. So the repeated practice is not suggested, only because then we loose the perception of the gap due to routine. But 3 or 4 experiments with longer intervals in between with total awareness on our part will help us experience the gap.

The same gap happens between sleep and awakening, as the same mechanism works in this case also. So unless and until we are totally relaxed in body as well as in mind, sleep becomes illusive. This happens only because if we are preoccupied or if we are in the contemplative mode, then our conscious mind does not loose its hold on our body and mind, because of which we remain awake. The gap we are talking about happens, when mechanism of sleep starts to take over and mechanism to remain awake is slipping away. This state occurs and is experienced like we are in trance, after which we gradually slip in to natural sleep phase or cycles.

In sleep we do not experience hunger, because the same mechanism is working which was working at the time of fasting. It is very common experience of ours, that if we are mentally or physically exhausted then we go in to deep sleep that is very much like unconsciousness. This phenomenon happens due to our system's automatic avoidant or escape measure, which is trying to safeguard our mind, as our mind is not capable to function properly under intense pressure for longer duration. Similarly energy reservoirs of our body also deplete and to recoup the same energy our physical movements become slow to conserve the remaining energy. Going into sleep happens due to mental exhaustion as well as to save our sanity, and to give our body chance to rejuvenate. We talk about untold agonies or unbearable pain, but very rarely we go through the experience. Because till the pain threshold reaches the intolerable or acute level, we become unconscious. And this is the reason why most of the people die in unconscious state. Our belief, that we are body, cause intense pain at the time of death. The experience of energy recession from our physical body is experienced as rending and tearing sensations on the plane of our body, which causes pain. Unconsciousness is the occurrence that works like anesthetic in case of severe mental shock or in the case of total body exhaustion, to save us from major mental or physical damages.

As mentioned above, these double mechanisms are working all over our body and they are attached to all our faculties. The most important thing is, in emergency we do not have to voluntarily shift from basic to secondary, it happens automatically, as survival measure.

Sufi Mystics experiment on the same gap, but in opposite way that is called as Night Vigilance. They resist the onset of sleep to such an extent that mechanism of wakefulness becomes exhausted and stops working. So the moment it stops working and before the sleep mechanism takes over, the gap that occurs, is used for self-awareness.

In Tantra also the same techniques are followed on the above-mentioned lines. They experiment on breathing; inhalation and exhalation. The practitioner is asked to concentrate on inhalation, then observe, then on exhalation and again observe. So when there is no breath in the body and when the fresh breath is not taken as yet, the gap is where we are, where our self can be experienced.

But as breathing is non-voluntary process the same may happen in case of sleep also. On the contrary deprivation of sleep, as way of experiment cause serious disturbance in most of the people's psyche. So Mahaveer takes food and its intake as basic tool for experimentation. Food and its intake is everyday occurrence in every one's life, and the concept of fasting is known throughout the world for various reasons. At the same time intake as well as to abstain from taking any food is fully voluntary function, so if we think that we are going to be starved we can start with the intake at any time. What we have to remember is that the concept of fasting is not related to food or to fasting, but it is related to the gap and its perception or experience, as what we really are – physical body or energy body? The shift, from primary to secondary happens to everyone, but the only difference is the time, as intermission, required. In someone it will happen in two days, others will have to wait for more than two days. But generally the shift happens within three to five days. And when this happens, then we, for the first time come to know about our real being. And with this conscious experience, the process of austerity really starts.

To maintain the novelty of experience of any process, practice cause blunting. *But the so-called followers of Mahaveer are going on fasting spree, under the misguided notion that they are doing something sacred. Surface understanding & blind following cause distortion of worthwhile concepts & this is one of the examples.* Fasting is to be treated in the same manner as we will treat any scientific experiment, then what we can experience will be novel.

Zen Buddhists from Japan also use similar technique for relaxation. We also talk and think that we know the manner in which we can be relaxed. This relaxation of ours is concerned with our body only. But unless and until our mind is relaxed, no relaxation of body will happen. Zen Monk tells us to stretch our body to its limit from head to toe. He suggests us to use all our energy in this stretching experiment. In this experiment we will feel that something is going to snap or break in our body. And when we maintain this position for some time then he suggests us to let go, stop stretching. Then what relaxation we will experience will be total relaxation. And in this process also, the same gap appears, as appears in Mahaveer's concept of fasting.

As mentioned above why Mahaveer selected the concept of fasting? The reason being food is the basic necessity of our body and about dietary intake we are more aware. Outcome of the fasting experiment helps us to understand the relationship between body and food. We know and have experience, as to what hunger is and we take food to appease the same hunger. So when we are hungry and take food then whose hunger we are satisfying, body hunger or hunger of our self? Fasting is the separating and differentiating process by which we come to understand our true nature; that are we physical body or something else.

When we go on eating without being aware about our true nature, then our association with our body as our true self increases. At the same time more food in our stomach make us drowsier and according to Mahaveer, this drowsiness makes us more unconscious, in which we fail to see beyond our bodily existence. In sleep also not only our body sleeps but our mind also go to sleep. Every experiment presented by Mahaveer is based on to increase our awareness about our real self, as well as awareness about our mind and body. Because, unless and until our mind is razor sharp, we do not experience our intelligence potentials. When we are full of food, all our energy has to work to digest the food lying in our stomach. Even energy working in our brain shifts to our stomach and we experience lack of concentration in any intelligent work. Sufficient energy does not remain in our brain, even though if we resolutely try to concentrate, then our chain of thought gets interrupted. Those people who are engaged in more intelligence related work become less aware of food, only because they concentrate on mind as faculty of intelligence and not on the body.

Mahaveer is not against food or is not against hunger as a biological requirement of our body. This process of fasting is suggested only to make us aware of our true nature in this existence. Excess food cause division of energy, and in this regard very little energy remains with our brain. To realize our brain as pure intelligence, it requires more energy and this realization happens only when our stomach is empty. But at the same time it is not implied to remain without food forever, but as mentioned in the title of this chapter, we are moving towards moderation of food intake, as the real goal.

Since long, followers of Mahaveer has denounced non-veg. intake as the basic practice of non-violence towards animals. No doubt this understanding is true and correct, but this is not the basic objection presented by Mahaveer. Human body and its digestive system are very similar to those animals that are vegetarian by nature. The length of our intestine is long, compared to non-veg eating animals. Similarly intake of non-veg takes more time to digest in our body, so we have to spend more energy to digest the same. And Mahaveer is against needless expenditure of energy, for very scientific reasons.

According to Mahaveer our diet must be moderate in quantity as well as light in preparation, only then it becomes easy to digest which require minimum energy, after which the remaining energy can be directed towards our mind and intelligence, which will be used to increase our awareness.

This is the primary reason why fasting/Anashan is stated as the first concept of doctrine of austerity. As a people we are not only earth bound but are food bound also, and we are conditioned in this way since our birth. Most of the time we do not eat to survive but we survive to eat. Just any item of food, which is very much to our liking and in which we are more interested, sways us and we start eating like crazy.

When we abstain from anything, as happens in fasting, we go on contemplating about food in our mind. As to what we will eat once the fasting stops, how many times we will eat to even the loss we have incurred at the time of fasting etc. We know that food is directly related to our stomach and the allotted work of our mind is to contemplate about the matters that are related to intelligence e.g. decision making, course of action to be taken, evaluation of the circumstances, taking stock of our capabilities etc. What we are doing is, we are fantasizing about something that is not going to satisfy our natural hunger in any substantial way. But on the contrary we are increasing the burden on our mind, which is not its intended function in the first place. And in this way we are not being more aware, but are derailing other systems also. This abnormality of ours makes us more pathetic. By way of contemplation we are crating substitute stomach in our mind. So Mahaveer tells, that if contemplation is going to happen, then it is better to eat and let our mind be free for its intended work.

Experiment of fasting will be satisfactorily concluded only when mind is neither contemplating about food or about fasting.

As per Mahaveer, at the very bottom of our unconscious mind there are but two predominant thoughts as basic instincts, one is about food and the other is about expressions of our sexuality. Most of our basic thoughts or thoughts in any forms are but extension of either of these two instincts. Freud also ratifies this concept. To any libidinous behavior energy is required and this energy is generated by food intake only. So if any person is very much obsessed about food, then the possibility of the same person behaving in baser or in libidinous manner seems to be certainty.

Characteristic feature of human mind that behaves in conditioned manner is of wanderer, and this happens due to the reason that we are not aware as to how our mind works, and for the same reason we are not masters of our mind. Contemplation about anything happens due to wandering nature of our mind. Similarly contemplations most of the times create substitutes only. Psychologically substitutes are more interesting and novel than actual happenings. The reason of this phenomenon is, our mind has untold potentials to stretch the imagination, but it is a fact that by way of imagination, nothing substantial ever happens. Happening of any act after due consideration or proper contemplation frees the mind from wandering aimlessly. Psychotherapist and psychoanalyst are more interested in our beliefs, assumptions, perceptions and thoughts behind our behavior, as well as about what we dream, for the reason that what is fermenting in our subconscious mind causes our behavior. On the contrary, our conscious mind and behavior related to the same may become tainted with our ego and our image about our self, and this tainting may cause altered projection about our self that can be erroneous.

To contemplate about anything, is acquired habit and formation of this habit comes into being, either because what we expect to happen or get, is not going to happen or we are not going to get it, or what we intend to do is not going to happen as we have no capability or guts to do. In this manner of thinking (contemplative mode) what we are doing is creating alternatives for the intended acts or deeds that in reality we are incapable of doing or going through. Most of the contemplation happening in this manner falls under the category of fantasies or daydreams. And in this sense most of the contemplations are obsessive, which haunt us forever, unless we undertake self-analysis. Most of the times it is better to go ahead and do the act, which is one of the alternatives than endless contemplation. Mahaveer knows about these pitfalls in the proper practice of fasting, and is trying to make us aware of the dangers of blind following. Interest in any thing can be satisfied by relevant act and be done with it. On the contrary, contemplation about anything just goes on and on, but as contemplation is nothing substantial, then for the same reason satisfaction is not possible. But there is a possibility that just by the way of contemplation distortion of interest may happen very definitely. For this reason, any contemplation without reciprocating act is called as deviation and which is considered as a sin, only because we deviate from our basic nature. This is how Mahaveer looks at idle contemplation. Mahaveer is not bothered about outright act, but the thought behind the act, which cause the act to happen. Thought about murder, theft or adultery, to name the some are nothing but acts as far as Mahaveer is concerned. We also know that thoughts take forms, as thought is the primary motivational force without which act do not happen. As our mind is part of our body so thoughts in our mind are our responsibility. Furthermore, even though we are not aware of our minds way of working or about our thoughts, then our unawareness about the same is not reason enough to absolve us. In any court of law act becomes punishable only after its completion or happening, but in religious parlance thought before act, is treated as act itself.

So, any process that is going to develop our awareness and positive growth comes to fruition only when our mind as well as our body is in concert. Then we will understand the gap explained in the experiment of fasting.

Contemplation or deliberation should start and end on our say as the intelligent alternative under our direct command, but it should not be the idle occupation for the vagaries of our mind. So when the working of our mind happens as per our wisdom and awareness, is deemed, as a sign that true master i.e. our self, is present behind the process. But this very rarely happens, because mind as our servant has become master. If we have to validate this concept, lets do one thing; we will dictate our mind that we will not react by way of anger in any situation. Then look at the mind; it will create thousand alternatives as to how wrong we are, how to be angry is justifiable behavior on our part and so will resist to comply. In this regard, not only our mind, but all the organs in our body also behave in the same fashion and we as the master become pathetic. When we become habitual to go into every experience through the medium of our mind, then not only significant but also trivial habits become concrete, so to change or break these kind of habits become quite hard. And this happens only because we are not aware enough about our self.

Austerity is the way and process by which we regain the lost mastery of our self, where we should be. In this manner we come out of needless misery and suffering. Then no kind of troublesome attitudes or habits group around us because of which, we were used to waste our energy fruitlessly and were reaching nowhere.

We can go in to experiment of fasting only when we could dictate our mind. But since long we are conditioned to just think, to contemplate about everything, but were not taught about the mastery of our thoughts, what to think about or which thoughts are worth pursuing. In school, colleges, society and home, everywhere this is happening. So if our stomach says it is hungry, and then if we have to eat, then we will say OK we will eat. But if the hunger is of the routine nature then we will say that I am not going to eat, and the matter stands closed. But in most of the cases our mind, to defy us will start thinking about food. This kind of tug of war for assertion and mastery between our mind and our self is the reason we experience stress and tension. This happens everytime; the more we start to assert our self the more our mind starts to defy us. This happens only because no one wants to loose ownership of anything in simple manner. As our mind was used to be master of our self for quite long, then it will very definitely resist to part from the mastery. What we have to do is have patience and have to stand firm on our resolve to be master of our own, because our assertiveness will take some time to bare fruits, but here in this instance, our growing awareness and our resolve to assert will help us towards our mastery. This is how processes of austerity increase our awareness and make us assertive as well as master of our self.

When we say yes or no to any thing, how convincing are we? When we deny anything to the demand of our mind, then our first 'no' shows how resolute we are. And this phenomenon is well known to our mind. Then the mind resolutely goes on demanding and our successive 'no' becomes weaker, and ultimately we accede and say 'yes'. This shows lack of resolution on our part and how powerful our attitudes are under the dictates of our mind. More forceful 'no' show our weakness, as we know we have to use force only when we think or believe, that the other is more powerful than us. Understanding about self and self-analysis of the attitudes of our, makes us aware and more resolute. So when we have to say 'no', then our resolution should have to be so powerful that any further discussion and deliberation should not happen either knowingly or unknowingly. The way we resolve and commit our self to the resolution is major psychological step towards self-assertion.

Mahaveer is of the opinion that whenever we become resolute about anything, it is our duty to adhere to it with total conviction. Most of the times, we ourselves break the resolve or turn back from the commitment and blame outside circumstances, as the reason. But we know that this is fake excuse to camouflage the weak will power of ours and how powerful and insistent our mind is. When we go on repeatedly resolving and committing ourselves, but at the same time breaking or turning back from the same, then we are knowingly or unknowingly making our personality weak because of which we become more pathetic. It is to be understood that whenever we commit to change, we commit with our free will that the way in which we used to exist has caused endless miseries, stress, tension and disappointments, and to get out of this quagmire the choice to change is basically ours. What we have to realize is our self as well as our will is ours only, and so when anyone tries to stand or oppose his own self, then it becomes loosing battle, as we will never win. So when we have to resolve, then we have to stay resolved or do not resolve at all. When we do not resolve, then the choice remains open to us, that whenever we will resolve, then we will stay with it firmly. So, we have to start with everyday incidences and as our confidence grows along the way, then we will be in the position to set higher goals.

It is to be understood that our mind and its entire characteristic features, as well as all the attitudes and habits that are related to every sense organs and faculties is our creation. We create them for our use and convenience, at the same time all of them are not bad or troublesome, but they help to create our habit nature and we superimpose our habit nature on our basic nature. Due to our habit nature we behave in a set manner and this pattern of behavior is termed as conditioned behavior. In the existence and environment surrounding us, whatever is or exist, exists as per its basic nature, otherwise it will not exist. So when our imposed habit nature do not correspond with our basic nature as well as the other elements existing in the environment, we start to experience disappointment, dissatisfaction and emptiness. Fundamental importance of understanding and practice of religious doctrine makes us aware about this disparity and with this awareness we have to change our perceptions and beliefs, so that we exist in satisfactory manner and with joy. On the other hand, if we stick with our erroneously steadfast beliefs and misunderstanding, then we go on living in sorrowing and unhappy manner that ultimately causes psychological and behavioral abnormalities.

When we start to go into processes of austerity with the intention to understand and analyze our basic nature that will help us to regain our mastery over our being, then our mind and all the organs start to resist the change we anticipate making. This resistance happens because of deep-rooted habits ingrained in our total being as well as in all the organs. Secondly this resistance is direct confrontation between old master i.e. our mind on one hand and our awareness gaining self, on the other. It is to be understood that no one willingly part from the exalted position of authority and mastery so easily and without resistance. As we were not aware about the potentials of our self, and as we are conditioned since birth that our mind is the basic motivational and driving force to our being, knowingly or unknowingly we have made our mind so much powerful that any change we hope to make are resisted in tyrannical manner. Similarly we are not aware that every sense organ of ours is well capable to experience on its own, even if our mind is not involved as intermediary or medium. But even our organs, due to long association with our mind also start to resist. Resistance or fight over mastery happens in two ways; primarily our mind start to rationalize how intended change in the thinking process, altered perceptions and changes in habits are going to infuse our being with more hardships. On the other hand, when we start to ignore the demands made by our mind, then our mind becomes more insistent and goes on contemplating on the same subject. It is to be understood that there is fundamental difference between rationalization & reasoning. Rationalization happens when we are not ready to accept the reality, our basic perceptions and understanding is wrong but we like to believe otherwise, or we have become so set in our habit that we do not want to change. On the other hand, reason is fact as far as any incidence is concerned and is to be accepted when presented in logical manner and scrutinized under pure intelligence. Reasons may change in various circumstances but remain constant never the same. To rationalize is characteristic feature of pseudo-intelligence, which is nothing but an illusion of intelligence. Practice of religious doctrine helps us to increase our awareness in factual manner, and helps us to understand logical reasons behind our behavior, our beliefs, the surrounding and environment in which we are, as well as how to interact with other people who come into our contact.

Austerity is nothing but the process going through which, for the first time we start to become aware as to how our mind works. By way of this increased awareness, we can change and/or rectify our thoughts and the corresponding behavior, in positive and creative way by which all the ambiguity; erroneous notions and faulty beliefs of ours fall down. Similarly our personality becomes integrated i.e. our thought start to portray in our speech and our behavior corresponds to our speech.

Another characteristic feature of our mind is that it is very resilient. How we use this resiliency depends on us and for the same reason we have to understand our mind, and have to become adapt in harnessing its potentials. Witnessing the working of our mind, is one of the novel processes laid down by Mahaveer, and its application helps us to discipline or regiment our mind whereby we can use its potentials to the betterment of our being and existence. Why we have to discipline our mind, and why we have to keep it under control of our intelligence, has significance. Our mind accepts the concepts that are definite, finite and obvious, because at the end of these concepts it is going to become free again. And this freedom is considered as freedom to wander aimlessly. We have to understand that when wandering mind remain unchecked for any length of time we face mental disturbances and these disturbances may cause not only loss of energy but can create mental abnormalities also. So we have to start with manageable resolutions or goals, which in turn will be directed towards higher goals along the way. In this manner our mind remains firmly occupied as we are setting goal after goal to be achieved. And this is the manner in which our mind has to follow our dictates but aimless wandering stops.

The way in which we exist is the way of our habit nature. We think that there are so many things that are out of our reach, and this is a fact. Because when everything exists as per its original or basic nature and when we try to acquire them many times, we not only transgress but ignore our original nature also. So what we expect and what is not compatible to our nature will not fulfill our expectations and this non-fulfillment cause sorrow. Acceptance and understanding of this phenomenon is one of the basic aspects of austerity. As we are familiar with relationship of hunger and food as basic biological necessity to our being, concept of fasting is used as metaphor and this metaphor can be applied to all the organs and faculties, on which we superimpose our habit nature because of which many attitudes come into being.

CHAPTER 11

RESTORATION OF SENSES/FACULTIES

The meaning of the word 'Unodari' is 'not full'. The word Udar means stomach and Una means less; combination of these words means-'less than full', and the literal meaning is less than full stomach. But since start, it is to be understood that this meaning is applicable to all our faculties and its related attitudes, and not only with food and stomach. Synonymous word for day-to-day usage in English is 'moderate'. In reality very rarely we are aware of our biological hunger and food intake in relation to such hunger. At the same time we are not aware as to how our faculties function due to their association with our mind and our habit bound existence. Over-taxed faculties or misguided application of the same causes physiological, mental and behavioral abnormalities.

Most of the times the hunger pangs we experience are experienced because of our habit nature. In the same manner most of the organic demands we experience manifest due to habit nature only. In our body there is a biological clock, which is connected to every organ and its related faculty of our body. When energy reservoirs of any organ or faculty reaches minimum level then the said organ or faculty sends signals that its reservoir is empting and has to be filled. These signals are perceived as hunger for food, thirst for water or sleep for relaxation and rejuvenation. Once such demands are fulfilled then the organ or faculty again starts to work in its natural and intended manner. As mentioned in last chapter habit nature is human creation and the same habit nature imposes itself on our biological functioning. Working of biological clock happens in very subtle manner, and we very rarely discern its presence and functioning. Formation of any habit happens due to practice of the same act again and again, and the cause of repetition happens due to involvement of our mind.

Most of the eating habits are formed as per individual perception of hunger and the circumstances in which the individual exist. At the same time they are very rarely connected to biological reasons or natural hunger.

A Zen Buddhist monk was asked as to how he is living. His answer was so simple that people were not ready to accept or believe in it. He said that when he is hungry he eats, when he is sleepy he sleeps and when his sleep is complete then he awakes. People told him what is different in his way of life; we all do the same thing. Then the monk's answer was very mysterious- he told that if this really is the case, then it will be impossible to count the Buddhas in this world. What is the meaning of this reply? When we are not hungry, we eat, when we are really hungry then we may not eat. When we are not sleepy then we sleep and when it is really necessary to sleep, we do not sleep. When we wanted to be awake, we break our sleep. The Zen monk calls this behavior as perversion. And this perversion goes on and on. Similarly when this phenomenon becomes unbearable then either our body breaks down or our mind snaps. Mahaveer calls this perversion as habitual nature. When we superimpose this habit nature on our basic nature, we cause the naturally balanced existence to go haywire. What nature has awarded to each of us is very fine tuned and balanced as per our individuality. For this reason, every person is unique and so no one behaves in the same manner as the other behaves. To discover our unique behavioral pattern as meant by nature and existence, practice of religious doctrine is considered as scientific way of existence, and so religion is considered as super science.

The importance attached to any religion happens only because its understanding and practice according to existing environment make us aware as to what potentials we have, and how we are unique compared to others, as others are also unique in their own way. At the same time its practice shows us the way of living in joyous and sagacious manner along with those animate and inanimate elements and objects, that are also present around us. When any person understands and accepts the concept that religion is the science that is beneficial to our being and starts to behaves accordingly, then the said person is called as religious person. Most of the times we are not aware or do not understand that every time nature demands only that much which is necessary to our existence. But in habits, there is no end as we develop all the habits by constant repetition and regular practice. And as most of our habits are not according to our basic nature we experience dissatisfaction consistently even though we try to fulfill these demands regularly.

As mentioned above, stomach is denoted as metaphor or as an example. If we think that our stomach is an empty space, then the same empty space exist in our every organ or faculty, and this empty space is the stomach of the organ or faculty. We take food when we feel hunger and this food goes in to our stomach to appease the hunger. In the same manner, we put a kind of food in our sense organs that we consider as the food for the said faculty. The form of food for each sense organ depends on which sense it is intended for and representing. Sound is the food of ear, sight is the food of eye and touch is the food of skin. What generally happens is we fill up our stomach with too much food of various types, which is not needed or is not useful. The same happens with other sense organs also. We see, hear, touch, smell and taste more than necessary. In this manner we are not at all selective but on the contrary we overexpose or overindulge them. Overexposure or indulgence happens, or starts to happen at that time, when in spite of completion of intended function the said organ or faculty is kept operational. When any organ related to any faculty remains operational even after completion of its intended use, it starts to run down, looses its potentials and energy for further use. Then either the organ or faculty becomes weak or starts to malfunction. This phenomena compromise our sensitivity potentials of experiencing, and so this lack of sensitivity drives us towards repetition of the same act with the intention to experience anticipated satisfaction. On the contrary, if we do not experience desired satisfaction then there is a possibility of our loosing total interest in the act. When loosing total interest or not experiencing satisfaction even after repetitive act happens, then we start to experience emptiness. Manifestation of vicious circle happens when we keep trying to achieve anything in different circumstances without looking into our self as to determine whether we are at fault or wrong.

The observation that desires have no end is false; in the sense that natural and biological desires can be fulfilled but desires acquired by way of habit are hard to be satisfied. All the natural desires can be satisfied adequately, and at the same time they are felt only when they are spent in natural way. So until they are spent in natural way and manner, we do not perceive their existence and are not to be satisfied till the demand for fulfillment is made. We can experience emptiness or dissipation of the energy of any organ or faculty only at that time, when they are used or spent in intended and natural manner. So, if its fulfillment happens in the biological and natural form, then this phenomenon do happens in cycles only. Any animal, if it is sick will not eat anything or vomit the contents of its stomach, for the simple reason that most of the diseases happen due to food intake that do not agree with our basic and biological makeup. Secondly our stomach is power generation unit of our body. By way of not eating, the animals are lessening the burden on its stomach, and by way of vomiting they are throwing out that food that is not agreeable to their system. As animals exist naturally, all the above-mentioned incidences happen automatically. In reality we humans also have this capability, but due to our habit nature and lack of awareness, we have lost the capacity to experience these very subtle indications.

Fasting is the first experiment to experience and understand our natural hunger. So when we come to know our natural hunger, then madness behind food intake will cease to exist. Similarly at the same time no kind of food will remain, as cause of concern, to be weary of or no kind of food will be conceived as more interesting. In this manner food will be taken as a means to satisfy the hunger only. Habit formed hunger is psychological or mental hunger and it exists in mind only. We will go in to an experiment and know the difference. If we are habitual to have lunch at 1 in the afternoon, but if one of our friends reverses the clock by one hour without our knowledge, then what will happen is we will start feeling hunger at 2 in the afternoon as per the clock. Next important characteristic of natural hunger is; if more time lapses between true hunger and food intake then more hungry we become. But in routine or habit based hunger, the more time-lapse cause decrease in hunger pangs.

In this existence humans are the only species, which can function sexually round the year. All the animals and birds are season bound, so at the time of appropriate season they become aroused and act accordingly. On the other hand, humans are habit bound in the very basic faculty of sexuality also. We have imposed our will on this natural aspect of our being. And most of the time we do not know whether our arousal is biological or mental. Many people consulting psychologists are found to be concerned with sexual problems. Most of the times, the causation seems to be psychological i.e. preoccupation. The way in which we apply our superior intelligence in day dreaming, fantasies, ideal contemplation, curious ideas, suppression due to bizarre concepts, erroneous anticipation and expectations from the partner, cheap visual and written material etc. are all the stimulations and cues which goad us towards acts, and in turn cause sexual abnormalities. So when we treat our selves as superior in intelligence, then the proverb as 'Mighty falls heavily' is apt for us. As mentioned in previous discussions, and as the same is going to be elaborated in further chapters, faculty of sex is the only energy we have been given, manipulation of which will either make us superior or the lowest as inferior. Stereotype concept of more sexually active person is perceived as he-man or macho-man is sheer humbug. This is nothing but degradation of our own by our own deeds. In our current existence, kids of 13/14 years are becoming mature mentally. So till such children become mature physically and mentally, whatever baggage they are carrying since early age becomes condensed and habits are formed. On top of this all the cues are present in the surrounding like movies, print media, TV serials and behavior of the others. Unfortunately when this phenomenon happens, then these kids with fresh minds become adults with rotten mind. Most of the behavioral psychologists are facing this problem, as to how to educate these budding children about sexuality, its do's and don'ts, its significance and repercussions. No book about psychology is complete without a chapter on child sexuality, about how to manage the children who has experienced sexual harassment by the adults. It seems that in the first place somewhere to some extent we are responsible into causing these kinds of problems and when we are faced with bitter results, then we ourselves have to invent cures also. But the worst part is, due to all the exposure these children become wise in wrong ways, even before attaining proper mental and physical maturity. Then it becomes very hard to recognize or understand even the biological aspect of our sexuality or about its significance in nature, which they never know. Most of the times these unfortunate mishaps creates distortions for which we have labels as homosexuality, lesbianism, fetishes, transvestitism and gender identification, to name the few. Whenever transgression and encroachment happens on the natural, then we have to face devastating results.

So, in the practice of austerity, every pioneer of every discipline has stated that, the same faculty of our sexuality and its significance to our being is the only energy, which is the only vehicle we have and is capable of carrying us towards higher awareness and about our true nature. When we look in to eyes of all the animals and birds, we will see how innocent they are, even though they are also part and parcel of the same sexual union. Only thing is they exist naturally and behave in natural ways. Most importantly they are not stressed about their sexuality as humans are. On the contrary, sexual act is the boon for relaxation as well as release of this energy, which in turn also frees our mind and intelligence to pursue more creative and positive aspects of our being. No doubt the act itself will not elevate us towards higher goal, but at the same time it will not degrade us. Degradation happens only when we impose our bizarre ideas on natural.

So as happens about our food obsession, the same happens for our thirst too. Occasionally we do experience natural thirst. But most of the times cues as to we are thirsty come from outside. All the advertisements of all kinds of soft and hard drinks is nothing but psychologically induced thirst, which is as true as the drink depicted in the advert is. Adverts are creating demands for the products, which are not necessary for our day-to-day existence. But we fall for them only because our ego or our image is either challenged or reciprocated. These adverts are creating impression that if you do not have the object then you are loosing too much and your life is meaningless. Adverts are nothing but enforcers, to convince us that any product thus advertised is the only thing we must have, and absence of the same is the cause of hardships we are facing.

Let us imagine that we are wandering in the desert and naturally are very thirsty. Each and every atom of our body is crying for water, otherwise we will die. In this case a thimbleful of water will taste like nectar but any type of soft drink will not satisfy us. Only water has potential to quench real thirst.

After the experiment of fasting, Mahaveer leads us towards moderation. Intended message is, we do not have to go up to end or towards any extreme of any mental or organic hunger or experience, but have to stop before the conclusion or limit.

Let us look at an experiment that will help us to understand the concept. When we boil water upto the temperature of 100° the same water turns into vapor, but till reaching 99° it has potentials to remain as water. The same understanding and the related technique can be used in all the emotions, feelings and experiences we hope to experience. Similarly it can be applied to any fulfillment of demand our organ or attitude makes. When difference of 1° cause water to turn into vapor and we lose it forever, then with the same token we can save our energy by consciously stopping before arriving at the conclusive manifestation of our any action, that is going to happen in extreme manner. Our not consciously stopping before final conclusion or manifestation is the sign, that we are not learning from our past experiences and performance. At the same time, when any act gathers momentum but about which we do not become aware that even now we can stop, then we arrive at the point of no return where whatever is going to happen will happen.

Emotions, thoughts and feelings are generators of acts and behavior. Understanding the working of our mind in relation to our emotions, thoughts and feelings, and applying the same principle of moderation to them will save us from painful resultant behavior that happen due to such emotions, thoughts or feelings.

In the last chapter, we have discussed about two types of mechanisms. The same happens in the case of moderation also.

Till we stop well within the voluntary mechanism, then we can stop the act from happening. But if the same do not happen, then the momentum will continue unchecked and go into phase of non-voluntary mechanism after which, what has to happen will happen. This experiment can be applied to all the mental as well as all the faculty related attitudes, at any time and anywhere. This process is especially advantageous to shape our mind and its wayward workings.

In the context of topic under discussion, meaning of the word 'moderation' is taken as-to stop within voluntary mechanism, to stop before voluntary hands over the momentum to non-voluntary, to stop well within our power. According to Mahaveer, this stopping well within our power is to exist in the self, and going beyond is called as bondage, which is considered as sacrilegious, as any and all bondages cause sorrow. This is how we loose the mastery over our mind and attitudes, and this is the reason where subordinate i.e. our mind, dominate the master. Those people who know how the mind works, will agree that mind becomes satisfied only at the completion of any act, which is perceived by it as only when at any extreme or limit. But most of the times, all such acts and/or behavior that happen at any extremity, cause frustration and not satisfaction. Any desire that gathers momentum, which if not checked in time, starts to generate its own momentum, and the acceleration and pull experienced in this manner by our mind is the cause of emotional upheaval which ultimately make our mind weak.

Moderation is the process by which we can keep our mind well within its intended limit. It should be understood that, unchecked mind is wanderer by nature and at the same time idle speculation as well as needless contemplation dissipate our energy. Most of the people who just think but very rarely act, will accept this characteristic feature of mind as valid. Ask those people and they will tell that even a night's sleep do not seems invigorating to them, only because thoughts from conscious mind to unconscious goes on continuously. This phenomenon causes abrasion in their sleep pattern, which not only burden the mind but body also and this causes wariness.

Moderation helps to stop dissipation of the energy, which when stored, will make us feel charged. Thus charged mind can concentrate on any given function in its full capacity, because of which the work we do become qualitative. In the same manner all the faculties we have can be brought under the process of moderation, which will further stop the dissipation of energy.

Once we become adapt in this process of moderation, then refocusing of the faculties and its related attitudes becomes easy to handle. Refocusing becomes easy because, whenever we have to redirect or refocus, fresh energy output is required. So whatever energy we save and store by way of moderation becomes useful in refocusing.

In following of this concept by current Jaini's, the same concept is taken as shrinking of faculties and its related attitudes. But it should be understood that any shrinking is nothing but suppression. And a person like Mahaveer who is very positive in all the approaches, will never tell anything negative as process to enrich our being. As mentioned earlier, any following in blind manner cause distortion of the concept.

There is central core to every faculty where energy is stored that supply power to every act related to the concerned attitudes. But due to our habit nature and our belief, that every incidence should be experienced through the medium of our mind, all the centers of all the faculties are intermeshed, overlapped, and because of this happening, are confused. This confusion happens only because of the association of mind with the body with the core belief that our true existence is our physical form and we do not exist in any other form. Most of the times we expect and assign such a function to any faculty that is not capable to do the expected as well as have no potentials to fulfill the assignment.

So when something like this happens, then the same faculty has to interrupt its basic and designated function, and at the same time has to direct its energy towards expected or intended function, that do not fall under its natural potentials. In such a case two things happen; basic functional capacity of the faculty for its allotted function is interrupted, and as it has no potential and capacity to complete the expected assignment, the assignment remains incomplete. Then ultimately the said faculty becomes sick, atrophy or altogether cease to function. And the most important thing is, no kind of satisfaction can be experienced but only wastage of energy happens which in turn increase more frustration.

For example, the faculty of sexuality and its center is independent, as well as its function is very straightforward. Its biological arousal as urge to express, availability of consenting partner and ultimate act of intercourse between the both guarantees desired satisfaction. But when we involve our mind, then instead of direct and natural act, contemplation about the act starts. In this regard we are shifting the intended functioning of sexual center to our mind, which is not basically meant to be its function as regarding the actual act. Now what happens is, the satisfaction, which we will have experienced, will not happen to the same degree. At the same time, by involving the different faculty, energy generated at the proper faculty will not be released to the fullest, which will cause nudging to make us aware that residual energy is still in balance which is waiting to be released. On the other hand, our mind is intended to be functional for intellectual deliberation, but when it is burdened with the task that do not corresponds with its potentials, then this faculty of the mind will also be halted, where the intellectual capacity also gets hampered. Furthermore in all this shifting the proper satisfaction, which should happen at the end of the act do not manifest. So again we have to go into the act for desired satisfaction, but the same thing will happen again and again, only because unless we understand that only because of shifting we are experiencing non-satisfaction even after the act. And this is the reason because of which we have to repeat many acts again and again. Involvement of our mind where its involvement is not required, do nothing but contemplates, as contemplation is one of the thinking processes and not the instrument of direct action. Similarly this happening only creates illusions, and illusions are nothing but beings without substance. So the satisfaction derived by any illusion is nothing substantial, and for the same reason is not substantial means to any end. Illusions may just tantalize us, but we will reach nowhere as happens in the direct act.

So the moment we start to shift from the concerned faculty to any other, then the energy stored at the concerned faculty will remain dormant till such time when it is properly released. But when due to suppression or our shifting nature, the release do not happen, then the energy on its own breach the natural barrier and will flow unchecked in any direction. And when this phenomenon happens, we become surprised as to how this thing happened. But it is a law of nature, that whatever is stored will either wither away or if the inward flow of filling continues, then start to overflow or breach the boundary. To save ourselves from this type of overflowing or breaching and its consequent repercussions, the process of moderation helps us to release the stored energy in such a way, that optimum reserves are maintained. But as we humans are dynamic by nature, the flow of energy to fill continues. And in the case of humans, overflowing or breaching cause sickness of physiological and/or psychological nature, and can affect other systems also. Manifestation or happening of this nature is one of the causes of behavioral abnormalities.

Process of moderation is nothing exotic, but is the way of alienation of attitudes related to our faculties, with the intention of maintaining their inherent energy well within their natural limits. And in such a case they do not spill over or overflow if they are properly utilized. But unfortunately all of our faculties with their related attitudes are bunched around our mind and intelligence. So in this way only the faculty of our intelligence dissipates and we behave as idiots. Our mind as faculty of intelligence is for deliberation only, as to what course of action will be advantageous to do the intended job and once this is decided then the other faculties in the integrated and concerted manner are to reciprocate in completion of the assignment to the satisfactory conclusion. In this light our mind should be used as overseer, as the manager or administrator in any act we intend to do. But due to our conditioned habit nature and unawareness, we overload our intelligence, which not only function at below its capacity but no kind of satisfaction is experienced. Suppose we have to lift an object that weighs approximately 25kgs. Now our mind has to be involved upto such an extent as to how we will lift the weight so that no back sprain or other inconvenience is to be experienced. After this deliberation, it's our hands that are going to lift the load and not our mind.

We have taken birth with lots of potentials and are basically intelligent also, but the ways in which we are living and behaving do not show any application of intelligence or wisdom in our present existence. The states in which we exist portray chaotic living style. Similarly the way in which we expect and anticipate from others and environment shows that we grope like blind persons inspite of eyes. This trial and error method of our living happens only because of our not aware of or not understanding, our true nature and its potentials. Every process mentioned before and every process that is to be discussed is nothing but proper way towards just existence, i.e. to exist in creative manner with joy and happiness.

So if Mahaveer criticizes us in harsh manner, then the criticism should not be taken as bitter pill. All of us take birth with full potentials, except those unfortunates who are affected mentally since birth, but at the time of death most of us will die or dies as idiots. In reality this should not happen at all, but it happens. And all this happens only because of condescension of the habits we form, and go on repeating the same as real way of living. At the time of our old age or when we foresee that death is around the corner, then we start to realize that what we have imagined as the living was nothing but journey towards death. As mentioned before we do not learn from experience. Our past experiences are nothing but our reference library, and the faculty of our mind as intelligent contemplation is the means for this end only. But this powerful faculty bestowed to us is wasted in very trivial manner. Since long, it has glaringly become clear that the more we advance in age, then more set we become in our thinking, beliefs or assumptions. In reality, the more aged we are becoming then more mature we should have to be, as every experience gives us an opportunity to stop looking outside for each and every failure, and to start to look inside of us as to how are we wrong sometimes. When we criticize our younger generation, of which we have no right or authority, because they are not wrong as they are also following us and at the same time we are not capable to answer their doubts and questions. But as of now, since we have got this key to check by the way of going through the processes into our self, then we will come to know as to what reality is and change accordingly. So then when we become capable of changes in our self, and then at least we could help change others. This is how we as master come into being.

According to Mahaveer meditation is helpful in two ways. First is to integrate and concentrate the energy on individual faculty. This will make us realize the experience of each faculty to its fullest. Any experience, when we appreciate in its fullest, cause to stop us from senseless repetition. This helps us to conserve energy, which can be used towards self-realization or towards realization of the set goal. Repetition of any act, harmful or otherwise, happens only because full potentials of the related faculty are not properly engaged or when its core energy reservoir is depleted. Then whatever we experience become weak in expression, and to fulfill this weakness of experience we repeat the act again and again, with the hope that repetition may help us to realize full satisfaction. So when we understand this phenomenon with self-awareness, then harmful acts stop and creative acts develop in our personality. At the same time we come out of stagnation. Secondly needless contemplation of mind stops, which was happening due to continuous repetition of acts, which was happening only due to our unawareness. In this manner our mind's natural potential of intelligent deliberation becomes enhanced; as it is no more burdened to do other work, which was not it's allotted or intended function in the first place.

Any experience related to any faculty, when experienced and understood in totality leaves the full impression on our psyche, which make us free from the repetition, in the sense that the desired satisfaction from the act also happens in totality. And when we experience anything in this manner, then senseless repetition stops, but at the same time whenever necessary we can again go into experience on our say only.

Rise and fall of Hippy culture in America is the glaring example of the above-mentioned happening. Their way of life and experiences regarding expressions of human sexuality, without accepting any set rules of the so-called society give validity to above observation. All the males and females who were part of the Hippy culture were deemed as basic form of male and female as intended by nature. Everyone has freedom to choose anyone as partner. At the end, they come to know that not only any sexual act, but also the way in which they express the faculty of sex is very absurd. Most of the inmates from the group become celibate for their remaining life. This is in no way a suggestion that they lost the faculty completely, but any experience in totality looses its hold in this manner.

In total experience of any kind, senseless and obsessive repetitions of acts and the related behavior stops. When we cover anything, the covering cause curiosity as to what and why it is covered. Covering gives meaning to that, which is covered. Covering may happen with the intention of preservation, but at the same time it causes curiosity and gives meaning. In this regard, when we air the concept as to why anything is covered, then needless curiosity or assumptions about absurd meaning looses the hold from the observers' mind. The same happens in the case of any experience experienced in totality.

Use or abuse of all types of drugs happens in any civilization where materialistic objective are easily accessible and available. At the same time if taboos of any kind or nature are not observed, then the same thing happen as in the case of covering. The reason is when every kind of demand is met easily, and when any type of behavior is accepted under the freedom of personal rights then very few challenges remain for the general people to achieve. When it is understood that nothing remains to be achieved and when no thrill is perceived concerning the efforts to be taken to achieve something, then the void and vacuum perceived due to seeming non-activity cause us to behave in the manner that may be considered as bizarre. In such a case the usage of drugs comes in to vogue to experience the same thrill and to fillup the resultant vacuum. So if such kind of people get attracted towards religious following, then this kind of following do not happen due to sudden quest for enlightenment but because of the rituals related to the religious concepts that fascinates people, which in turn help them to come out of everyday boredom. In the same manner meaning to marriage as sacred institution is to be reinstated to give meaning to the sexual relations as something to be cherished about, and not mere act to be gone through or just to empty the body of excess energy. Psychiatrists practicing in western societies are of the same opinion, and are trying to restore faith in marriage, as fulfilling institution is one of the pointers that validate above-mentioned thought. In all the Indian cultures and societies we face relatively few incidences of above-mentioned nature only because hold of religious doctrine is still quite strong. But very few people are following the same with the proper and scientific understanding.

We have to keep in mind that each and every faculty, and its related attitudes are for our betterment only. All the religions are trying to do the same thing, as the doctrine under discussion here is trying to do. Each and every faculty, along with its proper experiences are meant to be gone through with understanding, and with concerted efforts towards realization of self-only. All along, this has to be our aim, as we are destined to be like that. Nothing is against us or nothing is causing us to deviate. Only our conditioned thinking process and the behavior as per our assumptions is the cause of sorrow and unhappiness. Not only Mahaveer but also all the persons like him are of the opinion, that humans are to live and to exist in fulfilling and creative manner, as only humans have the potentials to be like that.

Our mind is the most powerful faculty in all the known existence, which is given only to human race. And at the same time the intended function of our mind, as pure intelligence is meditation. By way of meditation our intelligence is experienced in its purest form. So when it is experienced at its purest, then we become wise in true sense. Then such a wise person understands as to what life is about, and why we are as we are and what is intended from us. Enlightenment is nothing exotic, but the state of our mind at its purest crystallized form that makes us totally aware about our self and about total existence.

If we look at our body and all the faculties we have; then it can be compared with any town council, where every branch of administration and management is present, which functions individually as well as in concert with each other for the betterment of its inhabitants. The same branches are present and working in our body also, which are our faculties. Our mind should work as main branch of intelligence, as the chief executive officer works as coordinator and overseer over all the subordinate branches of the council. When our mind starts to work in this fashion then all the faculties fall in line.

When moderation of the faculties is restored and when each faculty starts to function in its allotted field, then needless dissipation of precious energy stops. We start feeling at ease with the self for the first time, as no reason for stress or tension remains. Our resolution to start to understand our being, and its practice to follow as we resolve, starts to make the desired changes in us. Then whatever energy remains, and the energy very definitely remains as surplus, because now there is no chance of its spending on trivial; then it is to be directed or can be directed towards the realization of the self. This procedure is called as refocusing of the energy. Outside of us there is nothing, which should cause sadness or unhappiness in us. Including us, every thing is present as they are bound to be. When nothing in this existence is against us, and when everything exists in joyous and contented manner except us, then we have to recheck our self. So now let us decide, that hereinafter we are not going to look outside for anything as cause or reason of our sorrow as well as for our happiness, but we are going to analyze our self for all the reasons or causes.

CHAPTER 12

ABOUT INTEREST AND OUR BODY

What do we mean by interest, and what causes anything as, or why anything becomes as interesting? Experience in relation to any object or any act, when corresponds with any faculty that is associated with our mind with the preconceived notion, that the relation with the object or the act is going to be pleasurable or desirable, causes development of interest. With the same token the object thus used or the act happening in the above manner, is called as interesting act.

When we eat any food as tasty, then what we experience is assumed or pre-expected taste i.e. interest, in the said food. Biological reason behind any taste happens due to taste buds in our tongue. Suppose a person is sentenced to death then he will start to loose the interest and taste in the food in which he was very much interested as well as according to his liking. But as the time of execution nears, he will loose total interest and taste in all the food. In such a case, even though his tongue is still intact with its potential to taste the food, but his mind that was the driving force behind all the interests, likes or dislikes, will not be interested in any food, because of the certainty of death. In such a case his force of life as Prana will recede to its core, as parting from the physical body is perceived as glaring reality. The purpose of this explanation is to clarify that the real we, as the force of life/Prana as our true nature of being when associates itself with our mind is the reason we experience the phenomena of taste and interest.

As mentioned repeatedly, all the processes we are discussing here are to break those core beliefs that are based on erroneous or mistaken thoughts. These processes are to be used as a tool to break our old mold, which will help us to understand our true nature. In psychiatry, ECT as a way of therapy is suggested in major mental disturbances whereby best results are sought. Application of ECT causes momentary severance between association of affected mind and force of life; whereby the link of altered psyche with our force of life is broken. Then the gap between the links is used to recondition the affected person towards normalcy with the help of medicine and psychotherapy. Purpose of this doctrine and its various processes is applicable in the same manner as ECT.

Concept of re-shuffling and refocusing of any interest, is the process by which every faculty and its related attitude is brought under the magnification of our intelligent self that helps us to understand them better and in their true form for the first time. Once we become aware of it's true nature and significance, then it becomes easy to refocus them in creative manner or in right direction.

No object has taste of its own, but they have individual and inherent potentials of taste. In this manner, at the most they can be termed as cause of the taste. And the same happens about colors. When we look at any object and when we perceive the color of the object, then we say that the object is of any specific color. But what we see as the color of the object is not its real color. It would be more proper to say that objects do not have colors of their own, till we, as observers are not present. This fact is very disturbing, but it is scientifically proven. Light itself is the source of all the colors. When light falls on any object then the object absorbs all the colors present in the light, except any color not absorbed or less absorbed is reflected back. And this reflected color is experienced as the color of the object. And this phenomenon happens only when an observer i.e. we, are present. Then does it mean that unless there is no observer, the colors do not materialize? The answer is, yes. They do not materialize. When we want to see something, we focus our eyes on the desired object. In this focusing the same kind of light is projected on the desired object, the properties of which are the same as natural or man made light. When someone becomes blind, then people says that such person has lost the light of eye is a factual statement. Chemical function of the brain generate the same light which is similar to the light we are getting from the Sun as natural light. So if there is no observer to look at the objects, then the objects do not project any color. And as we know that every person is unique, then the energy he has and can generate, is also unique compared to any other. This is the reason, that the same object is not perceived in the same intensity in regards of dimension and color in the same manner from person to person. Some difference is bound to happen in their experience and perception. So the potential of the object to reflect any color do become the color of the object.

The same phenomenon happens in the case of taste of food also. Sugar is not sweet, but it has the potentials of sweetness, which can be experienced and understood only when sugar is kept on the tongue. Then taste buds situated in our tongue and potential of the sugar grains collectively give us the experience of sweetness. Similarly the same potential is present in all the animate as well as inanimate objects, and these potentialities are to be considered, as distinctive nature of the objects. To help us understand about these potentialities is the unique importance of religious practice. Manifestation or happening of anything is the result of fusion or merger of two potentialities, and this phenomenon happens when some percentage of both the potentialities are compatible to each other. When any person evolves and develops in positive and creative manner, irrespective of circumstantial hardships, the happening is treated in psychological parlance as model personality, and the same person is considered as a person who has realized his potentials. The same happening in religious parlance is considered as realization of self.

So once it becomes clear to us, that all the objects of food that are interesting or tasty, happens due to relationship between taste buds situated in our tongue and the potentials in the object, on the level of our mind only when our force of life is in concert with our mind. So when this scientific fact is understood and accepted by us, then the methods of all and any process of austerity will become easy to understand.

So once we come to understand this scientific relationship between interest and objects, and how we experience the end result, then whatever we do as acts turns into creative living. At the same time any act as blind following is only surface act without understanding the principle behind the process. But the so-called austerite is trying to make his tongue insensitive by unnatural means so that clinging to interest in any taste will be nullified, or do becomes fearful and wary of all the food, with the erroneous perception that it is food itself that is cause of interest. But we have to remember that any willful distortion of the related organ or suppressive attitude about food only make us more pathological, as without any of them our natural existence do not remain integrated and we become sick. Majority of eating disorders comes into being due to many reasons, and some of them are caused due to personal perceptions, erroneous understanding of religious concepts, social acceptance or rejections, notions or assumptions ingrained in the psyche of the person or family. More eating, eating of any one-item to the exclusion to other, less eating than natural and biological requirement of the body or casting away of certain type of food as the way of following of doctrine, is nothing but disorders related to food in general. And to punish our tongue as demanding organ of food is nothing but paranoid behavior. Mahaveer has not presented the process due to any of the above-mentioned aspects. But when we go on contemplating about eating or not eating, make us so preoccupied that there does not remain any other existence to our being. And to bring us out of this trivial attitude the process is presented. What we are meant to understand and appreciate is, why we are behaving in the way we are behaving, and how we have created the attitude which is not only pointless but will cause sickness in our body also. We still do not know that how healthy the proper austerite is physically, because he knows the importance of proper food at the time of real hunger which is a boon and not a curse. When we have to go in to process of proper austerity our physical body is the only vehicle we have which will help us in our endeavor, so it has to be healthy.

To deny anything is nothing but subtle kind of suppression. Denial happens due to phobic fear of loosing control on the situation. And due to any phobia when we start to avoid any thought, act or attitude, then avoidant behavior starts. But if we try to go into depth as to why we are avoiding any thing, then most of the time we will come to know that, our behavior was happening due to our unawareness, so once we come to know the nature of the phobic fear then such fear ceases to exist or we become aware about the ways in which the said fear can be overcome. So the same thing happens about food and eating disorder. Whatever is suppressed remains dormant and in such a case, chances of the suppressed to fester in more pathological form are more imminent. Any process of austerity is nothing but way of self-analysis. And in this exercise we come to know the cause of our behavior. Once this is understood then we do not have to avoid anything, but we come to know that what we were avoiding is, if inferior can be cast away or if it is necessary, then we have to accept it with understanding. The same thing happens in self-inflicted damage on our sense organ like our tongue. Merely damaging our tongue does not free us from the taste and interest in food. Because to develop any habit our mind is much more powerful rein- forcer than all of our sense organs, so if at all we have to change the habit or to be free from the same, then we have to change our mind and not the sensory organ. Because all the sensory organs have their inherent potentials of expressions of related experiences, which till we are not fully aware about our self, accept the commands of our mind. So it is safe to state that austerity is nothing but to understand the workings of our mind, and is the way to alter or change the mind in such a manner that it will stop working in conditioned and assumed way as per our beliefs, but should be in correspondence with our basic nature and temperament.

To exist in stress-free manner our mind is to be in concert with our self. All the branches of psychologies are working in response to the disorders of mind, which happens due to discord between our self and our mind. So the more we try to suppress our mind, then more resistance it creates. This happens only because till now we have never tried to understand our mind and it's working. Furthermore the same happen in case of reasoning with our mind also. It should be understood that by nature our mind is unruly, and the reason of this phenomenon is our unconsciousness and unawareness. We have never tried to regiment our mind in any way. What should happen is that the mind should involve on our say only and this will happen only when we are more aware; as masters of our mind and not vice versa. To cast away or to give up any thing, happens only when our force of life and mind in concert comes to understand, that what we used to do is inferior to our being, then we do not have to abandon or leave aside anything but whatever is inferior automatically falls down or we elevate ourselves above the situation. On the contrary if anything remain as it is even after this acid test, then it has to be accepted with the understanding that what we were intending to cast away is necessary to our being.

Mind on its own do not accept or reject anything. But when

we apply our intelligence in conscious manner to our force of life or Prana, then our mind and force of life in association creates that which is creative and necessary, and all the other that is not necessary drops down without our doing anything. The same happens in case of any taste and interest about food or our eating habits. Potentials and capabilities of our mind are infinite, so neither its bottom nor its peak can be discerned or experienced in any ordinary way. But austerity is the only way by which we can understand the working of our mind as well as our true being.

Process of witnessing is the exercise to understand our mind, but more than that the process will make us aware for the first time, that is it necessary to involve our mind every time, are we out of habit involving our mind where the natural involvement of any of the sense faculty is more than sufficient. In a nutshell, witnessing is the weeding process whereby involvement of our mind, voluntarily or automatically, tapers off and we start to become an integrated personality. Mahaveer is not against food, but what he is asking us to do is very simple experiment. Let us have our food and let our tongue experience the taste of the same, let our mind experience the interest in food, look at the stomach as how its hunger pang is appeasing, and in all this exercise we do not have to do anything but have to remain as witness of each morsel as we keep it in our mouth. Now we have to truthfully analyze as to where the satisfaction of the eating is experienced and who is benefiting by way of eating. This will, for the first time make us aware that what we are doing is satisfying the very biological need of our body, to recharge its depleted energy by giving it the food which is nothing but fuel to regenerate further energy. And this awareness will free us from mad filling of our stomach every time, as this habit is harmful to our physical and mental health.

The moment we become witness and this concept becomes condensed, then we do not have to avoid any thing. Then no kind of food will make us fearful and we do not have to punish our tongue or suppress its demand for taste. Unnecessary repetition stops, and what requires to be repeated is looked at as the way of life. Any vicious circle happens due to our subconscious habits. Meaning of vicious circle is the behavior pattern that is harmful to our mental as well as our physical health. Best example of vicious circle is repeated use of alcohol or smoking, which happens due to our subconscious mind.

Consumption of alcohol or smoking starts by way of initiation from the other person who is habitual of either. When he says that alcohol or smoking helps to release stress and tension immediately because he has experienced the same thing, then this belief of his, re-enforce or assures us to act at least once in the same manner. Now nicotine in the cigarette directly stimulates our nerve centers as well as stimulates our heart function that in turn boosts our blood pressure. Circulation of the blood at higher rate carries more oxygen to all the parts of our body, which is experienced as surge of energy, and this surge causes mental bonding or association between smoking and its usage as tension relaxant. So in this manner whenever we experience tension and when we intend to experience the release, then we continue to smoke. The same happens in the case of drinking of alcohol, which again directly affect our nervous system and blood pressure. But in the case of alcohol, when control over our brain function is affected, then association of worrisome thoughts from the conscious mind are blocked, which again cause release from tension. Then in all the similar incidences and in all the other situations, where we cant cope or do not have the necessary coping skills, the act of alcohol consumption continues. So unless and until the person is taught as to how stress and tension can be released naturally or in regimented manner, this kind of behavior goes on like an addicted person. Both of these substances and various other type of drugs are addictive, which is a fact, but our habit to assume or believe in them or to associate their use as tension releasing agents, is much more powerful that makes them more addictive, and this behavior is known as substance dependence.

There is a very interesting hypothesis that a child deprived of maternal love and attention because of which if feels insecure and abandoned, as well as if it experiences hunger, the child starts to suck its thumb, which is perceived and substituted as nipple of mothers' breast. The same feeling of insecurity leaves its impression on child's psyche and may remain dormant in the subconscious mind forever. So when the same child become adult, and when its near and dear deserts him again or the child -turned-adult perceives that he will be abandoned again, then instead of sucking his thumb he will start to smoke, as shape and size of cigarette symbolizes the thumb. Another hypothesis is similarities of experience between alcohol and meditation. Under the influence of alcohol the person not only forgets about reality and surrounding, but becomes cut off from the others also. This detachment from the others also happens in meditation, but where the feeling of calmness and tranquility is experienced. But the major difference happens where all the feelings of calmness and tranquility disappears when the influence of the alcohol wares off and the entire primary worries and tensions are felt with re-doubled force, which do not happen at the end of meditation.

Whenever we identify our self as mind then this type of behavior happens. Faculty of our mind is mercurial by nature. So the more we try to hold it; more slippery it becomes, more we try to shape it; it changes the shape. We have seen vast amount of emptiness or void, like open sky or endless expanse of desert, which is beyond our capacity to shape, change or fill up. The same void is our mind. One of the five elements of which our body is the configuration, our mind is the same void that is the sky. It will be more proper to say that as we see clouds on the background of the sky, in the same manner we can experience our thoughts on the background of our mind. While meditating or at the end of meditation we experience calm and tranquility for the reason that in this experiment we remain as witness to all the traffic of thoughts. To benefit from meditation, it is to be understood that to think on the thoughts materializing in our mind is not going to help us towards calmness or tranquility until we remain as witness. In witnessing our conscious being should exist like a tolerant guardian in charge of many playful children's. So whenever we remain in the capacity of witness, then gradually thoughts stop materializing and our mind without any thought cause tranquility. Most of the restlessness, stress or tension we experience, happens due to continuous flow of contradictory thoughts and our willful conscious involvement in or about such thoughts.

We have to understand that all the emotions we feel or experience, happen due to our mind. So when we say that I am angry, we have to look at our mind and then we will understand that emotion of anger is experienced at the level of our mind only. But when we start to look at all the thoughts and emotions as the witness, then the attitude of or habit to, portray anger on any occasion starts to ware off. Similarly when we start to apply the same technique to all the attitudes of ours, then those that are not positive and creative, loose their hold from our mind. Any obsessions about anything, thoughts or acts, are nothing but our erroneous association with our mind, which is deemed as our true self or our basic form.

Attitudes are visible forms of expressions of our faculties. Up to certain extent they are natural, in the sense that to see, hear, feel and taste as sensory inputs are necessary to our survival. But when all these sensory inputs are believed to be expressions of our mind and not of the faculties, then perceptual association starts to manifest. At the same time when all the experiences of the attitudes are perceived at the level of mind, then the desired satisfaction of the act do not become fulfilling, only because to experience any thing on the level of mind do not end anywhere.

In this manner the capacity of the mind is boundless. On the contrary any desire to be experienced as fulfilling should happen on the level of related faculty only. In this manner mind should be useful as the medium of experience. When we go to any musical concert and when we listen to the entire program with concentration and do not concentrate on the conversation of the other people, then the experience become fulfilling. But if we are not capable to concentrate on program only, then we remember snatches of the concert as well as the conversation of the other people also, and then we do not experience the anticipatory satisfaction of the concert. Here our basic aim was to listen to the concert and not the conversation of the other people, but due to wandering nature of our mind we loose the intensity of the experiencing and the faculty of our ear becomes frustrated. So whenever any act related to any faculty is not experienced because of the intervention of our mind, then we do not experience full satisfaction. Anticipatory energy stored or generated at the intended faculty is not fully released, and then what energy remain in balance cause us the feeling of dissatisfaction about the act and again we have to repeat the same act again and again.

Any faculty, to be fully realized and experienced happens when we are present as witness in the whole act. In this process our mind is also remains involved, but only as medium of experience. This is the proper way to use our mind. When we as master are present then there do not remain anything to choose because whatever we experience, the experience takes the form of total experience. Anything experienced in totality make us aware as to what is worth perusing and what is worthless. Then that which is positive and creative start to manifest, and we as creative personality gather momentum.

After the process of witnessing comes the process to understand the frailty of human body. Vedic and Jaini doctrine takes the meaning of this concept as physical discomforts.

According to Mahaveer the term is Kaya Clesh. Meaning of the word Kaya is body and Clesh means pain or sorrow. As we know that our body is the configuration of five elements present in this existence, and as everything in this existence is ever changing, our body also changes in the form of aging, sickness and diseases. It looses the pliancy experienced at young age and become more firm and powerful at the middle age. Then at the time of advanced age it becomes infirm and all the faculties start to loose their respective powers, which most of the time cause various illnesses. These organic illnesses make some faculties useless or they start to function below par, and ultimately death happens. All of these changes are experienced by all of us and still more changes we have to experience. At the same time we can see this happening in the elders of our own family as well as in our surrounding.

The reality, that every thing or every form-animate or inanimate do not remain as constant or consistent, but have changed, are changing and will change, is used to break our false belief that are we really body or something else. We have seen various dead bodies of other people, so what difference do we see? The body remains same as it was in the animated as well as in lifeless form. But in the death, the element that animates the body departs. The element that animates our body is accepted as force of life/Prana. So in reality this force of life/Prana is real 'I' of us.

Basic meaning of austerity or Tapa is to create or generate heat. But the traditional meaning is taken up in the literary sense that is out of context. So when we look at the so-called monks who are going through the so-called austerity, we see gaunt and cadaverous people. They appear to be listless, bowed down, without spring in their steps or smile on their lips. They perceive the human body as bondage that holds their soul prisoner because of which they are feeling sorrow and unhappiness, and so consider the body as enemy. Then the meaning of austerity is taken as to break the body in any manner possible. Then they start to fast so that the body can be starved, which will make all the faculties weak and will stop demanding various things. Stand naked and expose the body to the elements, which will again make it weak. Stand on any one place for extended period to tire it or stand on one leg to break its resistance. All this behavior happens to make the body our slave. Similarly they will light the fire all around the body and sit in the middle, so the fire will hot up the body from the out side. No doubt, in austerity our body becomes much more hot, but the reason is when all the faculties start to function in the intended manner, the excess energy generated is directed towards our core. And this excess energy is experienced as more hot than our previous experience, which was lukewarm in comparison.

According to Mahaveer behavior of the so-called austerite is not the behavior of true austerite but of a masochist personality, who is still violent. And the person who is violent towards self, then the chances are that he will be violent towards others in future. To Mahaveer our body is our vehicle, with the help of which we are going to reach ultimate flowering. We do not discard any vehicle because of any mechanical malfunction or punish the same due to same reason. We mend it and start the journey again. In fact looking at the body of Mahaveer, we see a very healthy, brimming with vitality and proportionate body and nowhere it seems, that he has abused the same in any way. *But people who are masochist by nature got religious sanction under this doctrine and the irony is all the other people who have no guts to follow and understand the significance of the process on their own, are bowing down in front of these masochists whose ego is ascending in direct proportion to these masses of ignorant followers.*

How we are conditioned and behave accordingly, and how this phenomenon is erroneous is proved by a French Gynecologist. He used to suggest to all the expectant mothers that at the time of delivery, these women are not going to experience any pain or discomfort. At the same time he told them that they would not be anesthetized in any way at the time of delivery. They are going to deliver naturally, as all the females of all the species deliver without any assistance or from any outside help. According to him the moment a woman starts to experience labor pains; they believe that now they have to go through an ordeal. Then the moment the child is on its way, the mother in anticipation of the intended pain starts to contract the pelvic region, which does not help the inner push to deliver the child. Natural contraction happens to expel the baby, but when the woman due to anticipatory pain start to contract on her own, then both the contractions cause resistance, which cause pain. This conditioned behavior happens due to description heard by the other women, who has gone through the process of delivery, which was very painful to them, only because they were not given suggestion in the above manner. At the same time scene's of the same process shown on the TV and in any film are shown in such a way that, knowingly or unknowingly the spectacle gets etched on our memory, which associate pain and child birth as inevitable experience. Then what happens at the time of actual delivery is conditioned behavior, as a painful experience. His suggestion has benefited upto five thousand women till now, and those women has accepted and validated his concept as a very natural phenomenon that happens without any pain.

All of us at various times have experienced pain, either real or imaginary. In any pain the muscles at the affected area are contracted to dull the experience as well as to restrict further movement that may cause more damage. This contraction happens very naturally as non-voluntary defense mechanism of our body. Even in any impended accidental impact, our body tends to become tense and contract and this happens only to stop us from experiencing pain that we anticipate in advance. It is nature's way to save us from traumatic experiences. We can see the behavior of any person who is unknowingly going to fall down. The manner in which his arms spread and the neck bows to arrest the fall, the way his hands shield the back of his head; all these actions and related behavior is way of nature to save the vital systems from injury or trauma, and to save the life. All these actions are natural reflex actions.

But all these actions can be done with awareness, which will also save us from the pain. Specifically sporting events like boxing, football etc. where contact injuries and injuries due to falling down are very common occurrences. At the same time the participant also anticipates the same beforehand and is prepared also. In such a case he will experience the pain but the same will not be disabling, so he can continue with his activity. The same happens in the life of soldier, while he is fighting in the battle. All the pains of the injuries he experience at the end of the battle but not while his actions to defend or to attack are going on. This type of behavior happens only because of his heightened state of awareness to save the self at any cost.

In all the above explanation the intention is to show that the pain depends on our perception. More aware the person is and when the same awareness is focused on the pain, then preoccupation in focused manner enhances the feeling of pain, but if we have to feel less pain then we can shift the awareness from the affected area that helps to lessen the pain. We know that growth of hair on our head, growth of nails on our fingers and toes, is growth of dead cells. So when we shave our head to the scalp, and when we cut nails of our fingers or toes, we do not experience any pain. Intention behind Kaya Clesh as the process of awareness is to make us aware of the conceptual reality, that attachment and association with our physical body where our mind is deemed as central to our being, causes pain and discomfort in this existence.

When people start to meditate, initially they experience unrest and mental turmoil. The reason being till we start to meditate we were used to be extrovert. And in this manner whatever impression we have collected, were collected without any thought as to their inferiority or superiority. All these thoughts remain in our conscious, subconscious and unconscious mind as they are. But when we start to meditate, then what we face initially are the same stored thoughts. As mentioned above we collect everything without any awareness. Then the same stored thoughts are perceived as very bizarre and against the assumed concept of our ideal personality, which we are projecting. And this phenomenon creates the unrest and confusion that as we are not at all like this, then why we are experiencing these types of thoughts? But prior to meditation we were used to think about anything and everything, without conscious choice and this type of indiscriminate thinking leaves its impressions of their own on our mind and the same impressions are retained as they were. So when we start to meditate we encounter the same junk initially. But we are not going to despair, because in the start meditation is going to be a cleansing process of all the stored memories in our mind. Similarly all this stored memory is kept in the form of beliefs, assumptions, perceptions or interpretations. But as we go along meditating, then after some time as we go on discarding what is trivial and retain that which is useful and creative to us. This is the process to clean our mind and at the same time to make room for positive growth. But we have to be very steadfast in this process. Because once we start to meditate then the process should not be stopped in the mid-stream, otherwise the sediment of old thoughts we have churned by way of meditation will keep us pre-occupied and restless. So now let us decide that we are going all the way and will try to understand what is inside of us, then analyze the same, and keep only that which is necessary and at the same time are going to download the baggage that is not worth keeping. Then what calm we experience will be a very novel experience.

So when we start to become more aware of the way our

mind works, then the same is reflected on our body also. In this way, for the first time we become aware of limitations of the physical body, its pains and discomforts. In our heightened awareness we experience everything in its true form. There is pain in our leg, but in our sleep we do not experience the pain, but as we awake we start to experience the pain. Our awakening does not cause pain, which was present even before that, but awakening makes us aware of the pain by way of experience. Intention of this process is to make us aware that physical body in itself is source of pain and discomfort, various illnesses as well as ageing. Whatever we are going to experience from birth to death is to be accepted as part and parcel of our being in physical body. We have to accept this fact with equanimity and without sorrow, with the understanding that it is the basic characteristic nature of our physical body. And in a nutshell, this is Kaya Clesh.

Mahaveer do not ask or suggest us to cause pain or further discomfort to our body, as he knows that our body in itself is more than sufficient source of the same. But he tells us that the acceptance of all the limitations of our body is an austerity in itself, we have to just understand and accept the same with awareness. He is against the so-called austerite, who is inventing new ways to punish the fallible, which is bound to perish as its basic nature. Do not torture our body by way of false austerity, because to be in this body is torture in itself.

Why we invent various means of comfort and happiness, because by this way we camouflage the existing being of pain and discomfort. We have to arrange for joy and happiness. Then we start to believe that the same joy will be experienced, if not today, then tomorrow or in future. What we are doing is we are denying living today and postponing the living on tomorrow, but each tomorrow does not remain tomorrow, it become today till we are ready to face it. And this is how illusions come into being. We do not analyze our being, as to why we are not happy and joyous. And in this regard Mahaveer calls us as future oriented people. Once we analyze our self then what we understand frees us from illusions, otherwise when we are rudely disillusioned, then we become frustrated.

The way of austerity is to exist in present. Then anything we experience becomes experience in its totality. In this manner we do not remain insistent to repeat any act, as in this process whatever we experience makes us aware that to act in the same manner is very futile, and then the habit to act in the same manner is cast away as unnecessary or trivial. But at the same time those acts, which are positive and creative to our being are kept as necessary and productive, which in turn helps us to make our being as an integrated personality. False anchors, which we have created with the hope of realizing in future also, become futile and we save our self from future related stress and tension. At the same time the true nature of our body and our faculties as to what they are in relation to our being, is understood and with this understanding we accept the same in its true nature. But at this stage it should be understood that as our body is our vehicle, so whenever it becomes as necessary, then its ailments or sickness has to be treated at proper time, so that our journey towards self-realization is not interrupted. This does not come under the heading of pampering of our body, as it is the only instrument we have which is very useful.

In this existence everything is present due to its own nature and including us, everything is part and parcel of the same existence. Our not understanding this phenomenon is of no importance. So to avoid or ignore the fact that we are also a part of this existence or to attach excessive attachment to the same existence is the cause of all the sorrow and pain. At the most, we have to use the resources available to us that are also part of this existence as per our need, and leave them aside once the end is achieved is the best philosophy. The same is applicable to our body also, as our body is the combination of the five basic elements of the same nature, then its deterioration and ageing happens as per its nature. When we understand this fact, then the unnecessary attachment and clinging stops, and we go on the search as to what we are, and what will be eternal and nonperishable. According to Mahaveer, this is existential phenomenon and acceptance of this fact causes a big transformation in us. Facts make us uneasy and seem to be troublesome, only till they are tested and understood as they are. Realization of this fact keeps us out of conflicts, and our being out of any conflict becomes cause of tranquility and peacefulness.

CHAPTER 13

ENERGY CONSERVATION

The word Sallinata used by Mahaveer is synonymous to energy conservation, but at the same time the word denotes tranquil mind and also includes functioning of all the faculties in the intended manner and well within their intended limits. So the overall meaning is to be understood as, total tranquility in our being. And this process is the last of the six processes laid down as outer procedures of austerity.

Traditional and cultural following takes the meaning as; there should not be any physical movement more than necessary. Primary meaning by Mahaveer is when our Prana/force of life remains tranquil then it does not cause any ripples or tremors, which can be discerned or experienced on the surface of our body. Even if our fingers twitch, then the cause of the twitching happens due to tremors in our force of life.

We know how earthquakes manifest and have experienced its effects. There are plates under the surface of earth, which are not always connected with each other, and generally remain where they are in dormant manner. Till the plates under the surface of the earth are dormant, the surface of the earth is experienced as solid. But because of various reasons when any one plate comes into contact with the other plate, then the friction caused because of their meeting is experienced as tremors on the surface of the earth. This tremor is called as earthquake. Contact of the plates happens without our knowledge and beyond our sight, but its friction as well as its effects we experience as tremors. The same happens in case of our body also. Our body reflects the same inner turmoil at the time when our force of life and mind are associated, and when our mind becomes influenced due to thoughts or emotions, then the influence causes movement in our mind that reflects on our force of life. Then the same movements in turn cause subtle tremors and these tremors are experienced on our body. To go into practice of Sallinata, first we have to observe and understand as to how our mind, all of our faculties and its related attitudes function, and why they function in the said manner.

When we are angry, have we seen the expressions on our face, how we talk, how our fingers twitch, the way we clench our jaw. Have we observed when we are depressed as to how we walk in bowed down gait like there is heavy load on our shoulders? In this emotion our eyes are down cast. In the moments of joy, there is spring in our steps, our eyes are shining, and we hold our head high. Now we have to do one thing, whenever we are in one of the above mentioned states of mind or in any other state, we have to go in front of the mirror and look at our reflection. In this manner we will experience something new every time and will find that we are different than our perceived or anticipated self-image, which we try to project.

In every one of above-mentioned emotions, we unknowingly project those expressions that are clear-cut indicators of the thoughts going on in our mind. Very subtle changes in our thoughts generate corresponding emotions, and then the said emotions reflect not only on our face but in our gait as well as in our expressions and behavior also.

Our bowed down position shows that we do not think there is any future for us and so we think that we are hopelessly lost, as happens in most of the cases of severe depression or when we are sick with worry. In our elated mood or emotion, we express so much exuberance that in this heightened state nothing seems to be impossible to us. In our old age, not only our backbone deforms or changes shape, but in most of the cases the proximity of the impending death and introspection about our past life shows to us that we are very much empty and have not achieved anything of substance as yet. This feeling of wasted life and hopelessness that we have lost countless opportunities, make people bent and bowed down. But all the people like Mahaveer or their pictures do not show them as bent people. What we have to understand is this phenomenon do not happen due to vanity, but such people has experienced true life, it's meaning and so are not worried about death, which is very common but inevitable occurrence in our existence. They have experienced eternal bliss, what life and living is about, due to which they are joyous.

In psychiatry observation of the body language is considered as important as verbal explanation. The reason being most of the inner feelings are conveyed in such a manner that the affected person feels either inability to express the same verbally or due to power of internal conflicts because of which the persons ability and judgment also becomes affected or impaired, because of which his narration becomes garbled. In such a case the therapist remains in the dark as to determine the causation. Similarly most of the times the affected person do not convey about his suppressed thoughts, emotions or feelings, with the notion that those are not significant enough. Any trained psychotherapist or palmist, read up to 75% of our body language, which helps them to arrive at proper conclusion most of the times. Even we are of the same mindset generally, that when some one is talking about something, and if the subject is not to our interest, then we sit in relaxed manner and let the other person completes his talk. But if the subject is of our interest, then we sit in straight posture where our back does not touch the back of the chair. Furthermore, if the part of the talk is of sensational nature then we bow in front with baited breath. In this manner our mind influences our force of life and these influences manifest on our body, which are experienced or expressed in the form of facial expressions, gait, postures, twitches and ticks etc.

All these changes as our demeanors can be used as study of our self in front of the mirror and in this regards we become witness instead of subject. We do not know our facial expression in anger, but others have seen it. But when we see our self in this emotion then very amazing thing happens, our emotion of anger starts to dissolve. When we become witness, our association with the emotion breaks. So if the emotion is concerned with anger, hate, greed or of the nature causing stress and tension then its dissolution reinstates peace. And if the emotion is concerned with love, sympathy or compassion then by way of witnessing we experience joy and happiness. In this manner our faculties remain as they are, but inferior attitudes are cast away with total understanding.

In the above-mentioned process, Mahaveer presents the view that humans are not monopsychic but are polypsychic i.e. we have more than one mind or simply put there are more tracks in our mind. Because if we were monopsychic, then we would have behaved in consistent manner and presentation of our emotions will also remain consistent. We have to validate this view only because if we really are monopsychic then it is not possible to deviate from the norm i.e. either we will adhere to our basic natural nature of behavior and expressions or due to learning potentials of our mind, we will stick to the pattern of learning we have had. But it is our experience that at various times we experience multiple emotions at the same time, which are diverse from each other. Our thoughts and emotions are ever changing, and according to these changes our behavior also changes. What we are in the morning, the same does not remain at the afternoon and in the evening we are totally different person. Looking at all these changes; leave aside others, but we our self does not know what we really are. And this continual change in emotions and related behavior happens due to outside stimulations and cues. In this manner we are like automatons, any thing and everything can move us to act.

When we are calm in mind we sit in relaxed manner, our breathing remain deep, and regular, and similarly our heart also beats in regular manner. But if we are emotionally disturbed then our breathing becomes shallow and our heart beats starts to accelerate. In agitated situation if we are sitting down, then our legs start to move like we are trying to walk sitting down or we start to walk in circles in the room. These kinds of acts happen to release the paint-up mental energy generated due to our disturbed state of mind. A brisk walk or any type of sport or exercise for physical fitness at evening is suggested only because, when we follow any of the above regimen, it causes vigorous movements of the body which helps to release all the paint-up mental energy stored in our body throughout the day and our mind becomes calm.

Sallinata in itself is the way in which we can conserve the energy, which we are indiscriminately spending or flushing continuously all day long. When we become capable to observe our self, then all the emotions, which cause drainage of energy stops and thus the conservation of energy happens. This conserved energy can be directed towards meditation, which again helps us to delve deep in our mind.

Anger is the everyday experienced emotion in every person's life. So when we are going to be angry, then we are going to stand in front of the mirror and while looking at our face, we will try to superimpose features of calmness and peacefulness on our face. In this case two things will happen, anger will seethe in the mind and peaceful expression on the face will be seen, which are contradictory emotions to each other, so both will evaporate at the same time. Then what we will experience is pure tranquility, neither anger nor peace. This is the technique of active witnessing, and in this way also tranquility can be experienced. This is how consummate actors act. Their personal problems are very much apparent to them, but when they face camera or spectators, then all of their problems are kept on back burner and the emotions demanded by their role are presented to onlookers. Any association with any emotion can be broken down only if we become capable to create contradictory emotion at the same time. Association happens only because we concentrate on any one emotion, which is easy for our mind. But when we create contradiction, then mind cannot concentrate on the both at the same time. In this regard our mind is of singular track only. To change or drop any attitude uses more energy and we have to concentrate fully in this way. But in creation of opposite emotion, both emotions try to dominate each other, so in this conflict of supremacy both become weak and ultimately dissolve. As we are acting as only witness, dissipation of energy stops. In this manner we have to behave as politicians do - divide & rule.

First we have to become aware or to understand and accept, that the way in which we behave happens in conditioned or in very routine manner, like robots. Any driver becomes expert driver only when he talks with others, listen to the tape but at the same time braking and acceleration of the vehicle happens automatically. It seems that vehicle is running on autopilot. But when anything unforeseen is going to happen which may disturb the smooth ride or will cause accident, then the driver consciously concentrates and avoids the calamity. Due to his continual practice of driving his subconscious mind takes over the task of driving. The same happens in most of our general behavior. Minor stimuli's and cues from the surrounding cause us to act in preplanned ways and this happens due to our subconscious mind. But when something unforeseen or not previously experienced happens, then we feel inadequate and has to think as to how to react. Sallinata is the way of understanding our unconscious mind, and to know why we behave in the way we behave in our day-to-day life. People who are staying in foreign countries since long; talk the local language very fluently, which is convenient for local interaction. But rouse them from the deep sleep and ask any question in their mother tongue, then they will reply in the same language. Any language heard, learned and talked since birth becomes the first and original language. Any other language learned afterwards always remains as second language, in spite of its fluency. The same happens in our every day acts and behavior. Most of the times we are not aware, but behaving in conditioned manner causes dissipation of energy. Sallinata is the process to stop this kind of repetitive behavior and to act only when necessary.

It is proved that what we accumulate and learn up to the age of 7 years by way of language, attitudes, habits, mannerism, as core beliefs and assumptions; 75% of the same molds our personality or is retained in our psyche as primary conditioning. All this learning makes the first layer in our psych. Then whenever we learn anything new by way of necessity or as hobby, connects to our basic layer, which at the most can be called as habit nature. So whenever an old person of the 70 becomes really angry, his presentation seems very childish, which corresponds to his basic learning upto the age of 7 years. It happens in love also. The very first experience of the emotion of love happens in our young age. Then we just go on repeating the same theme again and again. In adulthood we behave with restrain, because other will ridicule our constant regression to our basic and formative conditioning. But if we look at our inner emotions then we will find that the thoughts and emotions are very much childish. In behavioral psychology, it is accepted as a proven fact, that our mind has compartments where all the memories are kept stored and the same are presented, displayed, expressed or are consulted as and when the necessity arises or the situation warrants. Roughly the behavior happening in any situation can be analyzed in reference to these memories, and they are labeled as child like behavior, parental behavior or adult behavior. Any act or behavior happening by any person whose presentation shows that the age of the person and his deemed intelligence quotient, is not happening as per the accepted norms, is behaving in the childish manner. Similarly when any person is sticking to his parental suggestions given at his adolescent period or is following the mannerism of the same, is behaving as per his parental upbringing pattern. In such a case the person can be analyzed as well behaved person, but at the same time his independent maturity as an adult seems to be wanting. We have came across some people, who most of the times act and behave, in the manner which even though seems to be corresponding to all the accepted norms but their age do not warrant such behavior. In such a case the person is deemed as wise person beyond his age or a person of mature outlook or a person who has developed as an adult person. Doctrine laid down by Mahaveer has potentials to negate all the classifications accepted by behavioral psychology, as going through the process in the right way with understanding and awareness, any person can achieve sound wisdom and maturity irrespective of his age, upbringing, accepted caste or creed. Most of the time it seems that we are not ready to accept our self as we are. If we are in privacy of our home and no other member is present; then either we will watch TV, listen to the radio, read the same newspaper again which we have seen in the morning only. But we never face our inner thoughts or emotions, which is called introspection. There is a proverb in Marathi language that- what we think about our self, our enemy will not think about us. It is very unfortunate that we have lost the ability to honestly appreciate and understand our own nature, which is most of the times, is alien to us. We contemplate, but about other matters which are not so important than our self. Our self-image is based on the expectations and anticipations of the others, which we very much like to be. We set goals which were achieved by others, but do not check in our self, as to are they well within our capacity. This whole process of contemplation is nothing but tantalization and daydreaming. And in this manner we set a goal, but when the same is not achieved then we either strive hard or become depressed. We do not understand or do not accept that if we have no potentials to realize the same, then this phenomenon of continual disappointment or failure happens again and again. Most of the psychological problems stem from this kind of behavior, without honestly understanding our potentials, drive, willingness to change, commitment etc. Comparison with anyone is harmful in this regard. Then we unnecessarily become cross with others but never try to be even. This kind of behavior happens only because we are not ready to accept as we are. Comparison with others and to become like our idol causes untold miseries and frustrations because we have our own potentials due to which we can be unique in our achievements. But when we try to be other than ourselves, then neither we realize our potentials nor we can mold ourselves as per our idol as we have no potentials to be like our idol. Process of Sallinata is the process to understand our potentials and act accordingly. Then and only then our being will be creative and fulfilling in the true sense.

Process of sallinata is to understand and apply the faculty of any kind in its intended form, with our presence and awareness. At first we have to let the eye, the tongue, the nose do their work and remain as witness. If our mind wants to wander, let it wander but only in our presence. In this manner we can understand why our mind wants to wander and when we come to know that this wandering is senseless or fruitless, then we have to pull back. When we actively pull back in this manner then the mind looses the drive and starts to behave as per our dictates. Till now our mind was wandering without our awareness, but when the master is present then this aimless wandering stops. But our mind could not remain idle for any time, so we have to give it a direction towards which it can move. And in this manner we start the process of meditation.

Meditation is not only useful in self-awareness, but is useful to ascertain if we have any difficulty and how to overcome the same. If we have any goal, then how to achieve the goal falls under the domain of meditation. In this manner we can understand if we have the potential to realize the goal, if we have to change where this change has to be made, are we committed enough to go through the efforts and are we willing to accept success or failure at the end of the process. This is the true work of our mind. Then once we decide the course of action, then mind hands over the task to other related faculties and remain in the capacity of overseer only. This deliberation of any intended action on the part of mind saves lots of energy and the rate of success automatically increases. All that is worthless do not happen as act, only because it is screened and dropped down at the plane of our mind. Most of the time either we do not want to confront our mind because of all the chaos we feel in it, or our not understanding the true function of mind. This happen due to our conditioning, as we do not know that all of our faculties are capable enough to experience the outcome or the results of acts related to them. We try to experience anything and everything through our mind. And as mentioned before; that unless the energy generated at the center of any faculty for its related act is not used at its fullest, then the residual energy cause dissatisfaction. So whenever we experience the same dissatisfaction in our mind, which in reality is happening in the concerned faculty, then we have to repeat the same act again to achieve the desired satisfaction. By nature our mind is nothing but a screen on which we experience all the thoughts and emotions, which are nothing but the projections of the experiences of the faculties. Sallinata is a means by which we identify the means for which any faculty is useful and its applicable limits. We have to use our mind as overseer only but not as a substitute for any faculty. In reality our mind is the bridge between our self and all of our faculties.

We feel full in the emotions of love, compassion and sympathy. Similarly this fullness makes us calm and peaceful. But on the contrary in anger, hate or disgust we have to step down from the mental equanimity, which ultimately causes unrest. If any common hoodlum bullies us, to reply him we have to be on his level. And this stepping down is called as deviation. We have to deviate from the peaceful state of mind to reciprocate his action of bullying us, because this is the only language he understands. We do not have to go into details if we have to remain tranquil as to why others react to any real or imaginary stimuli and in which manner, because generally, to understand as to what others are thinking or the causation of their behavior is beyond us. So the same is applicable to someone bullying us. At the most, we have to accept that to bully any one is his nature, and as we are only the cause that induced him to behave in the above manner due to our presence at the precise time. So rather than react, if we pass away, then we save our self from deviation. Not to react to a seemingly unwarranted action from the other may be perceived as avoidant behavior, but sometimes this kind of behavior is necessary to adopt to maintain our peace of mind, for which there is a good proverb; to kill the bastered, is to ignore him.

Sallinata is the last of six outer processes, and is the gateway of inner austerity. But we can start on the inner only when we have understood and have applied all the six in proper manner. Then our personality starts to emerge as integrated person, and the gateway becomes real gateway. Till the completion of all the processes, our awareness also increases, so we come to know more about our selves. All of these processes are related to the twelve organic aspects of our being. They are very much related to each other, and when we understand this relationship, then only integration starts to happen. At the same time all the five processes are also inter-related as conservation of energy. This conserved energy is our fuel to go into inner six processes, which we are going to discuss afterwards. Partial understanding or halfhearted practice of any process will hamper our integration of personality. What we are trying to conserve is like a bank balance. If we spend all the energy on the outside, then in a sense we will be bankrupt, as there will not be sufficient reserves available to us to go into inner sanctum.

If due to carelessness we leave our bathroom tap on while coming out, then all the water will go down the drain. This is what happens in our general behavior also. All of our energies are flowing outside, without gaining anything. So in advanced age what remains is so puny that the same is wasted on needless worries and repentance, which is not going to help us at all. These processes are important and substantial only when we have sufficient energy; any change is possible only when we have energy to change our selves. This energy helps us to change, and at the same time make us capable to sustain the pressure we have to bare while we are changing. Possibility of this type of happening is easy in younger age or at the middle age, only because we have vast reservoirs of all the types of energies at our disposal. Every kind of energy makes us elastic and pliant, which helps us to change. We have to be elastic like wet clay, and then we can mold ourselves in creative and desired manner. We have to understand that water in the clay is also a form of energy because of which the clay can be shaped in any desired manner.

According to Mahaveer practice of religion is nothing but day-to-day code of conduct for the human being. Only because of our superior intelligence, this type of model conduct has to be applied. But due to blind following as well as lack of awareness, practice of religion is done at the start of late middle age or at the time of more advanced age. But till such time all of our energies and drives are on decline or at the lowest ebb, next we become so set in our ways that any type of change becomes impossible, as any change requires energy to change. If we look at the history of all the religions and its pioneers, then it becomes apparent that all the pioneers have started at an early age and are known as pioneers only because of this early start.

It is the general attitude of the human race, that we go on making hey while the Sun shines. But this kind of Sun shines for very short duration, and in most of the cases the same shining become pale than a candle. Religious practice of any doctrine is not applicable to the masses as the only salvation, because every individual is unique. But on the contrary adoption of any one from various doctrines according to individual potential can create a religious society where every one will be creative and joyous. Potential to realize our self or ultimate flowering as a human being, is inherent in each and every male or female in this existence. What is required is, free choice to every one to follow and practice the doctrine of his or her choice. Every doctrine is nothing but a formula of self-realization, and is tailor made as per our capability. It is told at countless times that religion is eternal and remains alive, and blossoms again and again in new forms. This is the true meaning that all and every religion is eternal but ever changing.

To sum up all the chapters we have discussed till now; we have to observe our organic functions, has to understand as to how our organs and mind function individually as well as in association, then we have to go beyond all the functions and its association by way of meditation to ascertain as to what is real "I" of ours is, because of which all this exercise has to be gone through. In this manner we come to understand our true self.

Initial feeling on start of meditation is of suffocation and more of a mental unrest. But these are only passing phases, as to meditate in proper form is new art to us and as the way is not charted as yet; suffocation & unrest are initial by-products. No one dies while meditating but the feeling of imminent death is experienced only because all of our energies rush back to our core, which is what happens in real death. At the same time this experience of death like feelings will show us as to how our notions and beliefs about death were erroneous, and at the same time we will come to know consciously what remains after the death. This type of awareness will make our being more fulfilling and creative.

CHAPTER 14

WHY PENANCE AND NOT REPENTANCE

In various stages of austerity, Mahaveer laid down the first inner process of or about Penance and this happens with reason. Popular mix-up of repentance and penance is so fine to be separated, that both are merged and only repentance has remained in practice.

In this regard, Mahaveer seems to be very hard taskmaster and knows the basic habit nature of the human being; i.e. to extricate the self from any situation with his ego unscathed. Dictionary meaning of the word "penance" and literary meaning taken up by the followers of the doctrine is altogether different but in actual practice the same is taken as repentance. Repentance means guilt or remorse felt after the act. But when we accept this definition, then the possibility of any change do not remain.

Repentance felt after any act is the indication that the said act is not according to accepted social norms or our beliefs, and so we feel guilty or remorseful about the act or conduct. In this case repentance concerns only about act but do not concern to the person by whom the said act is happened. Basically we are very decent people, but due to surrounding and the circumstances we act or react. In our subconscious mind we think and believe that we could have restrained ourselves from instigating the act, but still what happened happens besides our self or in spite of our self, and for this reason we experience the emotion of guilt, and we repent only because we experience the feeling of guilt. So whether we accept it or not, but generally repenting happens as an excuse to negate the act done or happened by us.

Feeling of repentance is experienced because of our altar ego, which is nothing but sentinel to safeguard our basic ego. If we do not repent, then the continual feeling of guilt clashes with our basic ego, which causes unrest, and in our own eye we become pathetic. In this regard repentance is used as a direct means by which we pardon ourselves and again start to live with a clean slate. But have we ever thought that repentance reinstates us at the same position where we were before the act? In this process what happens is we do not change at all, but by way of repentance we free ourselves from the feeling of the guilt. Repenting does not change or alter our way of behavior or change us in any significant way. Repentance is like dry cleaning of our soiled image from the stains of guilt and we start from square one again, like superficial dressing on a festering wound but nothing else.

There are number of incidences in our life and in various past experiences we have come to know that in emotions like anger, greed, hate we have suffered mentally. So every time we have decided that hereinafter we will not succumb to the same and suffer again. But still every time we have repented and started again. Most of the times we blame outside stimuli's or cues or some one other than self. But in all this exercise we do not count a common factor that is always remains present i.e. we, our selves. As mentioned earlier we do not learn from the past experiences and we think and believe that we are not fallible. Basic condition applicable in psychology, as far as any change is concerned, is to start from the self. We know that surroundings very rarely change or if they change at all, then the change may not be to our liking. Similarly how others behave is beyond our control and may not happen as we anticipate. So in all these circumstances to change the self is the easy way out, but in this regard also, either we are not aware about this fact or so we blame the others for our emotions. At the same time we forget that any other person, due to which we feel anger or hate, is very much the same human being like us and with the same emotions like us. So repenting in this manner does not change us at all, but only reinforces our ego that we are ever ready to accept the blame for our acts.

Whenever any person went to Mahaveer with the desire to be ordained, then Mahaveer asked him to go through the process of Jati Smaran, which is nothing but the contemplative meditation in which the person was asked to go through his past wherever and whenever he has repented. The importance of this process was to make the person aware that repentance has not changed him an iota and is not going to change at all. When this phenomenon is accepted and understood in its entirety, then Mahaveer used to ordain him.

Repentance is related to the wrong act happened by us, and penance is related to the fact as to how wrong I am. Meaning, application and the final outcome is diametrically different in both the cases. In the former there is no hope of improvement and the later is to accept the blame with the intention of making changes in the self. The basic question has to be, not because I have erred so I should repent, but as I am not aware which or what is causing all the erring, then I must change.

In our existence there are so many things that are present only because of their own nature and maybe without them this existence may not have been complete. Once we understand this phenomenon then practice of penance becomes easy. In a nutshell, penance is nothing but transformation of the self as per our own standards or as per the present existence. If we have to live as per our own standards, then we have to leave aside the existence and live as per our standards irrespective of all the consequences we have to face. But if we have to live in this existence with joy and tranquility, then we have to accept the laws and ways of the existence.

As per Mahaveer, penance is death of the person who was erring till yesterday. And repentance is the resurrection of the same person again and again, who erred then repented, then will err again and will repent again. This is called as to stuck in a vicious circle, but penance is the way out of this circle. According to Mahaveer, penance is like breaking off of the old mold and try to be alive for the first time. But to repent again and again is like a step ahead and to step back again. And the irony of this later exercise is, it just creates the illusion of movement in which we reach nowhere. To repent is to live in an extremity where we act in any extreme manner, but when due to the act we experience guilt and remorse, and then we go to the other extreme and repent. This is nothing but the game of unconscious mind.

Let us think about an emotion of love in which when we love someone then we select some qualities of the others that appeal to us or reciprocate our anticipations. We call this choosing and selecting of certain aspects or characteristics of the other, as love. In reality pure love happens in a manner where there is no question of choosing or selecting, as true and pure love happens only when we accept the other in totality. But in our type of love what we have basically accepted starts to bore us, as by the way of acceptance we take every other aspects or characteristics for granted with the belief that nothing contrary to our expectation will ever manifest or happen. But when the initial novelty starts to ware off and what we have primarily assumed or believed that will never happen, starts to happen or manifest. Then the love about the person or the object turns into hate and rejection. In this manner we start to experience all the negative emotions instead of love and then again repenting starts.

What we have to understand is, that it is the law of nature and existence that all that exists exist because of the opposite. Flowing of river happens because of both the banks, night happens because of day. Our not knowing or nonacceptance of opposite in any thing is our fault or shortcoming. And here is where awareness becomes important, and with awareness comes understanding and realization. But till we come to this understanding and about the pitfalls of selection and choice, we have to experience depression, heartbreak, disappointment etc. Association with any facet of emotion or non-acceptance of anyone or anything in totality definitely causes mental anguish.

In this regard the basic characteristic of our mind as a pendulum has to be understood. Our mind due to our selecting and choosing perceives, assumes and exist in duality. Then today's love will turn to hate tomorrow, today's God will be devil tomorrow, and today's friend is going to be an enemy tomorrow. So if we have to get out of this duality, then either we have to accept totally or reject totally. Penance as a practice is to be out of choice or selection of any thing or any one aspect of anything or anyone, but to understand that whatever we are facing or experiencing is as it is. But if we cling or behave in adamant fashion to any one aspect, then our act will cause us to repent again and again.

Common experience and expression of the emotion of anger on our part always deemed as justifiable presentation. Either we express anger to justify our behavior or to rectify the behavior of the persons that are very much near to us. Furthermore we explain this emotion of anger as just cause for the betterment of our son, wife, friends etc. But have we ever seen any one developed in positive way because of our anger? Our father was trying to mend our erring ways by being angry with us, but have we changed? It seems that most of the times anger is used as disguise to mask our shortcomings and our frustrations. Whenever someone criticizes us as totally wrong, this criticism haunts us. Criticism of one act and criticism of our being as an erring person, are two different things. Act under criticism can be counteracted upon and we may get out of sticky situation, but criticism of our being as erring personality pricks like thorn in the side. In this regard anger expressed by us takes the form of rationalization or berserker fury. Whenever our ego gets bruised because of criticism of our personality, then our self-confidence also shatters. Penance is the process, which can be activated on our own or as a direct result of our being criticized by others. It is hard to accept the opinions of the others about us, but at the same time it is the easiest route towards change in our self. Penance is the process of changes to be made in us, in positive and creative manner. But this miracle starts to happen only at that time when we criticize our self with honesty and in all the nakedness. Then penance starts from within and visibly starts to manifests on the outside.

The reason behind keeping this process as first among the total of six inner processes is of paramount importance. Unless and until we are ready to change wherever we are deviating, it is not possible to go into austerity. Focus of the penance is not on the act but on us, as perpetrators of the act. When we come to understand that because of our habit nature and conditioning we are going to be acting or behaving in the old and set manner, then whatever we will do will be erroneous. This differentiating factor will make us aware as to the difference between repentance and penance.

According to Mahaveer there are three categories of people and they behave accordingly. First category is of those people who are on the lookout as to how the other is wrong. Second category consists of those who accuse the acts of the self as well as others as wrong and still repent, but there are very few of the third categories, who after due deliberation find themselves as wrong. In the first category there do not arise any question of repentance, as to them all the others will always be wrong. In the second category there are still hopes that due to continual repentance, there are chances of experiencing frustration because of which they will stop blaming the act and start blaming the self, in which case they will change. But the third category is the best, because the moment they find themselves wrong, they immediately change, which is nothing but instant penance as well as transformation. This is how Mahaveer looks at the process of penance. According to him penance is not a life long process, but once we with total awareness breach any one barrier, then the breaching of all the other barriers and similar transformations starts to happen simultaneously.

Penance shows us that the other is never wrong. And this statement is not mere hypothesis but is fact. When we accept our self as thinking, feeling and expressing human being, then how we can reject the same fact about other human being as something different than us? What we have to remember, accept or understand is that the other is also feeling the same thing as we feel. At the most the intensity of the feelings may be different in degrees, and priorities may be different, otherwise all of us are the same. So when what we feel about other, with the same token the other will be feeling the same about us. When we are disappointed due to other, then the other is also disappointed due to us. And when this mutual disappointment is felt all around, then every one is unhappy due to the other. In this regard we do not have any right to declare the other is wrong. And this understanding and awareness is called as penance. Once this phenomenon becomes clear to us then we stop blaming others and start to change our self.

Most of the acts happening by us are provocative by nature and most of the times the provocation is very subtle but nonetheless intentional. Our intention being we are expecting some kind of reaction from the other. So when the other reacts in the anticipatory manner we become satisfied. But it should be borne in the mind that anticipatory reactions do not happen every time. And this is the gist of whole of Bahgawad Gita. Every action cause reaction, but each and every reaction is not according to our anticipation. At the same time reaction may happen immediately or in near future, but it very definitely happens. When reaction is immediate but not according to our anticipation then we feel sorrow and frustration. This frustration turns to anger when we have to act again and again with the expectations of anticipatory reaction. Now when no reaction happens immediately, then as our attention span is limited, we forget about the act happened by us, but still when the reaction happens in future, then we become bewildered as to why this is happening to me? Then we start to curse all and sundry, curse our destiny, curse the God in which we believe, which again cause anger. Reaction to any action never happens to be in direct proportion to each other, and as far as human emotions is concerned, this is the fact. As mentioned above each and every human being is unique in itself so how everyone reacts to any act of similar nature is hard to tell. But when any two persons act and react that is complimentary to each other, then this happening causes birth of relationship. Then this exercise is applied in every situation and to all the other persons. And this is how conditioned behavior manifests.

When we come to understand this maxim of the penance that other is never wrong, then we start to change. Any fact-finding excursion on our part at the outside happens due to our ego and due to our image about our self. But those who have gone through the penance; people like Mahaveer, Jesus, Buddha etc., are very compassionate and so they dare to point us towards the kingdom of God, which is never on the outside but is within us only. They are compassionate because they know that we are unconscious people. Have we ever blamed a person under the influence of alcohol as wrong person? We think we are normal person only till we visit a mental asylum. But when we experience the abnormalities of the inmates, then what we come to know by way of first hand experience is beyond our imagination. But if we try to explain our experience to the other people who have no knowledge of such a place, then no one will believe in us. The same happens to all those pioneers who look at us as people with mental problems, then they do not talk or write about what they have experienced.

What is applicable to human relationship is also applicable to all the objects, which are even though inanimate but are still coveted and are necessary in our day-to-day existence. Again it has to be understood that even though they are inanimate, they have their own nature, and are useful and advantageous to us in their very limited capacity. What is called as materialistic achievement is nothing but acquisition of the same objects, which make our every day life easy and pleasant. In this regard materialistic achievement or any other achievement is not bad or sacrilegious in itself. But the ways of acquisition are most of the times questionable and violent. Mario Puzo author of the book "The Godfather" wrote before preface of the book that," Behind every prosperity there is sin". This statement seems to be truth, if we look at today's environment of mad rush behind acquisition of anything and everything. People are no more wary as to how they are going to acquire what they wanted. Any means is acceptable. And when comparison is made between everyone, then this disease takes very dire form. Mostly our attitude of comparison with others is causing much more mental anguish and depression nowadays. It will not be much off the mark to note that comparison with anyone or everyone is the root cause of most of the mental disorders, which today's therapist has to face most of the time. There is no need of any exhaustive research or study in this regard. We all are comparing our family with other family, our child with other's child; husband is making the same thing with the other's wife and so on and so forth. As we very well know that every individual has different potentials but very rarely they are equal to the other person. But we knowingly or unknowingly disregard any person's individuality and potentials and expect the same level of achievements or results from everyone. Even though the surrounding is same for every one of us but still success or failure ratio remains different. So when any person is criticized in harsh manner, then either he tries harder to fulfill the expectation imposed on him by others or become depressed for the whole life. When he tries to achieve in insistent manner, then to prove himself he starts to cut corners as to achieve the goal at any cost or by any ways become justifiable. But in this way, if not immediately then in future, his inner voice in the form of divided psyche always torments him, which may culminate in fragmented personality as happens in schizophrenia. Depressed people commit suicide for the simple reason that their efforts do not bare fruits as they anticipate and at the same time constant criticism and comparison with others makes them more pathetic in their own eyes. The same happens in case of students who appear for the exams of SSC & HSC or any other competitive exams, passing of which in flying colors is must. Those who fail or those who do not get the class corresponding to their future goals, become depressed and to save themselves from further criticism commit suicide. Now the question is, was Mahaveer so far seeing that he has anticipated these kinds of problems and has given us some solutions? The answer is 'no', but he was very much aware of human nature and acquired attitudes. So it is our responsibility to apply old maxims to new problems, as in reality we have never changed to such an extent. No doubt environment at the time of Mahaveer is no more, but the human element is more or less remained as it was. Socio-economic gaps felt by people in general, happen due to hoarding of materialistic objects. Then various groups of downtrodden are formed to balance the inequality and to resist them the achievers has to form their groups to safeguard their own interest. Then for the sake of identity groups of caste and creeds are formed, with the intention of special privileges. Then even though you have merit, the minority will be awarded your intended place, only because he is from minority class. To take advantage of these situations politicians are ever ready. Then lobbying starts. This is how we exist.

Social workers as well as thinkers from various walk of the life are of the opinion that affiliation between religious following of any group of people and politics has to be separated. Every person should have the right to choose his education and career as per his potentials irrespective of his caste and socio-economic standing. Whenever this thought will be applied in practice, then most of the unrest felt by the masses will decrease, and related mental suffocation will gradually subside. In psychology we are taught that when a person becomes mentally disturbed, there are numerous causes which cause the disturbance, like genetic, upbringing, family atmosphere, society, environment, religious following, peer group, sex differentiation and nationality. The list may go on forever, but if this is the case, then humans are very tenacious species. Because the burden we are carrying is so huge and suffocating that we have to be declared as endangered species. But really are we so weak, pathetic and shackled down that we are not at liberty to make, remake or change our being. What we have to understand is religion and its practice is basically intended to be used by every human being as a means to become master of our being whereby we will appreciate the inherent potentials of ours and make our being more fulfilling and creative.

Penance is the process of rude awakening, as to what is the meaning of our existence, why we are behaving in the manner we are living, what is the purpose of my being in this existence and am I reaching anywhere? Coming back to the point, we think so highly of our self, that after us there is going to be a void so big, that the world will stand still and to fill the void after us will be impossible. If this is going to be our attitude or notion, then we are very naïve or our ego is very inflated. Let us leave aside the mortals like our self and look at the powerful figures like Emperor Ashoka, Alexander the Grate, Napoleon, Jesus, Mahaveer, Buddha and countless others of the same caliber. All have came and went. Some are still remembered but very few were mourned for any length of time. In spite of this nothing has stopped and nothing of any substance has changed to any perceptible degree. All the cemeteries and funeral houses are full of them. But still what these people has left behind is the formula, a blue print, a way by which they have reached, with the hope that somewhere someone will be tough and pliant enough to practice the same means by which he will also reach the same destination where they reached.

Penance is the process by which our true self can be realized for the first time. But to repent and repent again and again means, pardoning of the unconscious by unconscious being. As our being and everything in this existence is ever changing due to the dynamic force of the existence, then penance is the resolution that our unaware being until yesterday has turned back, and now it is infused with awareness as we have resolved to change. So if all of you are gracious enough to pardon me then it is perfectly all right, but if no pardon is forthcoming, then as I have changed by way of penance, my old self is no more because now I am very much conscious and changed. Whatever I have done till now was because of my unconsciousness, but now I am changed not because of my acts but in my being as an erring entity. This is how creative and positive penance happens.

There is logic behind the unconscious or mentally disturbed persons. These people are very convincing because there logic is absolute, in the sense that what they experience in hallucinations or illusions takes form of reality for them. Then if we try to show them reasonably how wrong they are, then they start to rationalize their experience in vivid details, which is not known to us. Now what we have to do is place our self in religious context and ask the person who is enlightened being as to how he perceives us. Then he will perceive us like mentally disturbed person. The way in which we are shackled by traditional religious beliefs is nothing short of illusions. And this is the reason why most of the times we have to rationalize our acts and general behavior.

According to Mahaveer meaning of the religious practice do not mean rituals or to follow all the tenets from letter to letter, because this type of practice is nothing but bondage as well as unnecessary burden. What we have to do is understand our nature and inclination as to which doctrine appeals to us. Then we have to understand the meaning of the doctrine, make necessary changes in the applications, which are in correspondence with present environment. Then we have to try to integrate them in our every day existence and then by doing so we will experience the pleasure of achievement and fulfillment. And this is the manner in which any religion can be practiced. Then the statement that every religion is alive, eternal and ever changing becomes fact.

A theory presented by Darwin that we are in the process of evolution is correct, this is true in the sense that as humans we have higher intelligence, and this higher intelligence is not accidental. Potentials inherent in every human being are so vast that we have the capacity to reach higher peaks of awareness because of which we can realize the causation of our being in relation to the surrounding. In this light we have to appreciate that each and every religious doctrine is nothing but a formula guiding us towards total awareness. So after we reach the said awareness stage then our evolution becomes complete.

Most of the behavioral patterns of the humans are very much predictable. Transformation from the normal to abnormal seems to be happening all of a sudden. But this is not the case. Sudden presentation of any emotion happens due to suppression of the same emotion. Most of the times this presentation do not happen because generally the circumstances are not right or the wrong person happens to be present at right time in front of whom we do not like to express our emotions. A younger member of the family who habitually arrives late is accepted as the norm or routine, but once in a while the same member is severely punished or criticized because of his lateness by the elder of the family. This punishment happens only because of suppressed emotions, which were seething to come out on various occasions and which happens at the lateness of arrival under the guise of discipline. This type of behavior is nothing but an excuse to give our pent-up emotions an outlet. Even in psychology about discipline of children, it is stated that any punishment should be just and rewarding. When any child comes to know that sticking to routine accrues brawny points, but to deviate is the cause of punishment or criticism, then he behaves consistently.

As parents it is our responsibility to behave consistently towards our children and only then expect consistent behavior from the children. If we have double standards, then they will tolerate us till their coming to age and then they will retaliate. In this instance our chances of beaten in our own game are very high, as now they are major legally and at the same time physically they are more powerful than us, as they are much younger than us. This is how child delinquency happens and antisocial behavior starts. In such a case these children not only defy their parents but will also defy all those persons who are of the same class as father figures or persons with authority. In such situations no kind of therapy or drugs for mental disturbances will work, because both have passed the point of no return. At the most the child will remain subdued under the influence of drugs, but the stigma of his supposed ailment will be with him forever. Since last forty years America is trying to help those soldiers who have fought in Vietnam. All types of drugs and every branch of psychiatry and psychotherapy is constantly failing to make any positive change. It seems that all the help they are trying to give is not reaching where it should reach. Psyche of these soldiers is so damaged that fear of unknown is constantly haunting them and most of them are written-off as lost forever. Basically all the related problems started due to egomania of political figures that intervened in the problem that basically was not their problem at all. And all those political persons were perceived as father figures.

In our general behavior we have to act with caution and this is every day occurrence. The reason being the way we act is not in accordance with our thoughts; so a step out of line and we may inadvertently spill that which we are trying to hide. But once we become aware then we know what we can expect, but at the same time we remain ready to face the consequences if our act is not reciprocated as per our expectations. Similarly if the consequences are not worth experiencing then we can altogether avoid the act. So in this regard if intended reaction happens then we are satisfied, but if it does not happen, then as we are prepared beforehand the outcome do not bother us and we do save ourselves from avoidant or compromising behavior.

In penance we have to accept our self as it is. Then according us, if we are dishonest, sinful, lecherous or whatever, or if our behavior is subject to criticism by others then we have to accept it. We know what we are and because of which we have resolved to change. Hereinafter we are not going to blame anyone or anything or circumstances, but we are going to change towards that which is positive and creative to our being. This resolution is to be made in front of our self but we are not going to declare it to any one else. Whenever we declare that I am not honest in front of the others, then others get much attracted to us for wrong reasons and their belief in us is reinforced. According to Mahaveer this is bound to happen, and for the same reason he has restrained us from public declaration. Because if such is the case, then our ego gets more inflated and we tend to exaggerate our wrong doings in manifold manner for wrong reasons.

Repentance has to happen in front of the other, because our act may have harmed the other. But penance has to happen in front of our self, as we have to accept and change our self. There is a possibility that in front of the others we very rarely disclose everything, the reason seems to be our ego, which never allows us to be truthful in front of the third person. At the same time when we start to talk in front of the other we go on improvising which may be different than our original thoughts. Again the reason being our image, which is nothing but the form of our ego, restrains us due to fear of staining the same. And this is one of the reasons why Mahaveer rejected the existence of God. People are very clever; they behave and act as per their wish irrespective of outcome or repercussions with the notion that God being almighty and forgiving of any or everything, the believer will be pardoned and absolved of every thing. With this kind of assumption and belief the believer or the devotee confess in front of the God by way of repentance and frees himself of all the responsibilities arising due to his acts and behavior. So this is also one the reason for which Mahaveer is of the opinion to remove the prop of the God, so that people will realize that no one is going to pardon them but they have to redeem themselves.

Any person who is ready and willing to go into process of penance will experience much unrest initially, because due to his increased awareness he will come to know what type of hell he has created. Then in such a case he has to change as his growing awareness and understanding will haunt him forever. If the house is on fire, then we do not have any choice whether to remain in the house and burn with it or to get out of it and save ourselves. In practice of penance realization about creation of self-made hell causes us to transform. Mahaveer says that hell is nowhere else, but to remain in our unconscious being is hell itself.

CHAPTER 15

HOW TO BE HUMBLE AND WHY?

Our being humble either happen naturally or we have to achieve this virtue by practice. But we know that by way of practice when we acquire any virtue, it is superimposition on our basic nature. And anything superimposed in this manner is nothing but whitewash or camouflage, which do not take roots in the bedrock of our original nature. Traditional following takes the meaning as meekness, like follow all the dictates of the doctrine to the letter with total belief, where to debate the concepts for verification or doubt about the same is frowned upon and so are not entertained or tolerated.

But to Mahaveer this meaning is not acceptable as well as practical. According to him humbleness is the end product, which happens only after successful conclusion of penance. Unless and until we are aware that due to our expectations and anticipations we are dependent on the others, then there is no possibility of penance. We have to understand at least once, that no one is responsible for our sorrow and unhappiness, but due to our misguided beliefs and assumptions we expect everything from the others. Humbleness as a virtue is acclaimed by all the known religions in the world for the simple reason, that to be humble is the basic key that makes our mind mellow and receptive where by expected changes to be made in our psyche becomes possible.

To Mahaveer virtue of humbleness is comparable only with prominence of ego and in inverse proportions. So if a person is very egoistic, then his chances to become a humble person are less. Very subtle food of ego is our basic belief, that other is always more wrong compared to me. Basically why we are so much interested in accusing others as wrong happens because in this type of comparison we seem to be less wrong. And this comparison happens only due to our image or our altar ego. In reality to prove anyone as wrong is very futile effort. So let us leave aside the others, but is it possible for us to prove our innocence? Because the moment we have to prove our innocence, we come under the shadow of doubt as innocence is a being or state and to prove the same is very tough matter.

If someone tells us that a person has reached prominence in the society by honest means then it becomes hard on the part of the listener to accept. But if someone tells us that a person is not honest and will go to any length to achieve his aim, then we accept the statement at its face value. In both of the above instances how subtly our ego works becomes clear. In the first instance we feel inferior to the other so we do not accept his honesty as it will show that we are less honest than the other, and in the second instance we believe that the other is very inferior, is to show that we are more superior than the other so the statement is easily acceptable. This is the manner in which the conditioned human mind and ego works. So if we have gone through the process of penance, then let us wait for sometime and check whether we are humble enough to accept how we are and at the same time accept the others in the same manner as we are. Because if really this phenomenon is happening, then we are becoming humble. After this we have to see that whatever ego we have then where it is anchored and in what manner it inflates. Whenever we have to praise someone then we are very reluctant. But whenever we have to criticize someone then we do so mercilessly. On our subconscious level what we are doing is just balancing the demands of our ego.

Humbleness is the flowering of the human psyche, which

happens after application of penance as an initiator that weeds out our mind of its false notions. After penance our attention is refocused on the self, which shows us what we are. This focus makes us humble and at the same time we become considerate towards others who really are not so radically different than us. Mahaveer do not ask for egolessness. If we have to eradicate our ego totally then the process may take our full lifetime and still the task is not possible. Mahaveer leaves the concept of ego completely aside. According to him to reject the ego is acceptance of the same. In this manner our ego will draw a camouflage net and will present itself as egolessness. But this camouflaged ego is much more troublesome than original ego as it will torment us forever. What he suggests is, leave aside the ego altogether but asks us to elevate ourselves above the ego so then we can arrive at humbleness.

Any person who does not perceive any fault in the self is more critical about the faults of the others. On the contrary when he comes to know about his own faults and accepts that due to these faults I am fallible, then his thoughts about others become much more considerate and sympathetic.

Person who is caught as lawbreaker and prosecuted may become hardened criminal, as this happens because of our judiciary system. The judge who is presiding on the proceedings is generally a straightforward person and his concept about right and wrong are very well defined. But as he has not gone through the privations felt by the accused, his judgment is going to be harsh. Passing of harsh or strict judgments is the pivotal factor that may turn the occasional offender into a hardened criminal, because most of the times the circumstances and to cope with the same in not possible for the offender. So when the same is not considered with sympathy and understanding by the judiciary then to retaliate or avenge the system the casual offender turns towards further crimes. Humbleness as the virtue works in this manner. Most of the people, who are by nature sinful of conduct, are more considerate about others than the people who are very principled about clear-cut concepts of right and wrong.

By the way of tradition, the followers of the doctrine take the meaning of the concept of humbleness to show respect or revere the superiors from all the walks of life. This superiority is attached to advanced age, achievement and designation, as well as to all the people who are connected with religion. The thought behind this respect is all those who are above our station are to be respected. But to Mahaveer this is not happening due to humbleness, but due to our own shortcomings and our belief, that as we are less superior than such people then we have to respect them. But what we do not understand is, if we respect any one as superior to us then our respecting in this manner does not mean anything on our part, as it do not make any change in us. Similarly our respecting the other is not our virtue, but is a declaration of our belief that the other is so above us that we can never reach the same state as the other has. Furthermore our respecting or neglecting the other is not going to make any difference to the others being. Basically our respect to any one or anything is acceptance of our shortcoming, and at the same time whenever we respect any one in this manner then, this happens very grudgingly. At the same time whenever we accept anyone or anything as superior, then by the same token we have to reject ourselves as inferior to make the balance. What we forget is in this manner we are again going on the same path of choice and selection, and so knowingly or unknowingly we are again going to experience stress and tension.

When we start to select in above-mentioned manner then we loose much more and gain very little. When we accept any religion by birth, then we have to accept the pioneer of the religion as the master and final authority beyond which we could not reach. So in future even if we think that any other doctrine is much more adaptable to our nature, even then we could not fallow that practice due to fear of criticism by others.

All the religious doctrines and all the pioneers of the religions have shown the same path towards higher awareness. At the most the way in which they reached is somewhat different than the other. But in this manner we are so unfortunate that to us our religion by birth becomes more important and all the others become pale in comparison. Then various people of various religious following reject other pioneers as well as their doctrine, except their own. But again in their own practice they feel suffocated as they are just following without understanding its true significance in every day life.

Kohinoor is the gem of gems. Its preciousness happens to be its basic nature and its own virtue. Our acceptance or criticism as to its rarity is not going to affect its value. Our appreciation is not going to enhance its value or our criticism is not going to devaluate it. But when we become capable to discern the same value in every stone and pebble, then our capacity to see beauty everywhere becomes our virtue. This is how humbleness comes into being. When we appreciate everyone and everything as praiseworthy in this existence without selection and comparison, with the understanding that everything and everyone is like us, then what transpires is humbleness.

Everyone and everything, animate or inanimate, in this existence exist with reason. Our not understanding the reason behind their existence does not make them inferior or superior. If they are useful to our being then well and good, but if we could not use the other in the same fashion, then it does not make them inferior. It is only our association with such persons or objects that make our life joyous. But if we anticipate what is not inherent in the nature of objects or humans, then the fault lies with us. If we expect cooling from fire then fire is not at fault, but our expectations and understanding is faulty. When we are ready to accept all as per their nature and form, as they are, is called on our part as virtue of humbleness. In this regards nothing is superior or inferior, but everything is part and parcel of this existence. There is a saying that; it takes every kind to make this world.

Quality of superiority attached to anything or anyone is conditioned behavior on our part. What history teaches us about towering personalities is written at much later date. But when the same people were very much alive and had the capacity to change values and thinking of the society and whose effects were felt at every level at that time, were treated as troublemakers. In such a case whom we are going to accept as superior or inferior? In the same manner when we accept the religious practice in inherited manner, without any conscious efforts on our part and without any efforts to understand its significance then what right we have to look at other religions as inferior to ours? Most of our impressions are formed on surface appearances. A person donning saffron robe is automatically taken as a monk and a person flamboyantly attired will be taken as a worldly person. But we have come to know by various experiences that appearances are most of the time deceptive. Now, to whom we are going to perceive as superior in above two examples. But again, as we are conditioned since our birth we become surprised and disillusioned most of the times due to our beliefs and superficial notions.

To Mahaveer humbleness is inner virtue, and precondition of its development is penance and understanding, that whatever exist, exists because of reason. But in our needless comparison nothing is going to be more superior than before or more inferior than before. Secondly we are not going to gain anything in this fashion of any significance. Humbleness is the virtue of understanding that whatever is, is. If all of the existence is not grumbling about its being as it is, then who am I to criticize their nature and existence. And if all the others are to think the same about me in the same fashion, then am I going to accept the criticism about me in the same fashion and with equanimity?

Respect or reverence without any reservation, reason or comparison is humbleness.

I will accept you when you behave in manner desired by me, is not respecting the person but to respect our precondition. In child psychology when parents behave in this fashion with their children, then such children develop clinging personalities. Every time they behave according to dictates of the others, they expect to be rewarded. But in later life these children become incapable of developing any lasting relationship on their own, only because of their expectant nature.

Process of humbleness is kept after penance because while going through the process of penance is like looking in the mirror every time in all our nakedness. This process make us realize what we are, the reasoning behind our behavior. Then when we realize our self inside out, there are chances that we become aware that we are not so much different than the other. And this realization is the cause of birth of humbleness.

In a nutshell humbleness is reverence for life. Any person who is happy and joyous to be alive, and is in concert with his surrounding, is the person of highest order. And such person will never criticize any one about anything, only because he knows that every one exists according to his nature. And when I am living as per my nature and all are accepting me as I am, then I have no right to criticize others as to how they exist or why they are present.

There are various religions in our world, but all the religious practices under Hindu banner are steadfast about bindings of acts or Karma. Whatever we do, are doing and will do, is predominantly happening as per our basic nature or due to our habits and conditioning. And the same happens in the case of others also. Emergence of relationship or bond between others and us happens when the acts are either reciprocal to or opposite of each other. Friendship, love and trust are some of the relationships where acts are deemed as reciprocal to each other. In the same manner enmity, hatred or indifference are some of the emotions that are experienced because they are perceived as against to our nature or the expectations from each other are not reciprocated. The person who understands this concept very well will not repeat the same act again with the notion that he is going to reap the same results again. Understanding and awareness of this fact enable us to save ourselves from continual frustrations. But if we continue to behave in the same manner with various persons or objects, then we will be unhappy. Causes or reasons of various types also work in the same manner in other's as well as in our case. Till we are looking for the causes of our unrest on the outside, we are going to experience misery and unhappiness. As mentioned above, outside causes are like stimulants and cues, so before responding to them if we go into the reason as to why they are stimulating us, then our chances of unhappiness will remain low. Proper changes in our self will manifest at that time, when we will understand as to what ticks us. The same applies to the criticism made about us, by others. If the criticism is valid, then we should be thankful for making us aware, but if the others are just blowing hot air, then the act by the other is to be taken as his nature to criticize all and sundry. But all the pioneers have praised the critics, as means to our positive development and growth. Reason behind this observation is critics are like bucket that dips in our mental well and draw such material from inside of us about which we were not aware. Whenever their criticism nettles us or disturbs us then we start to look at our self in critical manner and this manner is the key that induces us to analyze our self for the first time. Doctrine of every religion is of the same nature as critics are, and its application should happen in the manner whereby our habits, assumptions, notions or beliefs can be tested, verified and if necessary can be changed.

To sum up as per Mahaveer, humbleness happens at the time of dissolution of our ego or existence without ego. In this manner whatever happens to us by others is causal. What we are doing is due to our basic nature. Good or bad, hell or heaven, whatever we create is our responsibility.

CHAPTER 16

STUDY OF THE SELF

In all the known religious practices and in the entire civilized world, only Christianity accepted the concept of Service as the central theme of religion. Similarly Christianity and most of the Hindu religions believe in prayer as part of the austerity as well as devotional and practical aspect of the religious practice. But to Mahaveer Service/Seva has different meaning. But after Mahaveer, his follower's accepted the meaning of Seva as parallel to Christianity. In this regard, what Mahaveer intends to convey and what present followers has accepted, do not correspond with either Christianity or Mahaveer. To render service or Seva to anyone is believed to bring back rewards in the form of materialistic gains of each and every kind. Similarly the belief or notion that Seva accorded in this manner assures the placement in the heaven after our death. We may accept it or not, but the same is happening since inclusion of service or Seva was incorporated in every religious practice as one of its tenets.

In all, meaning inferred and intention behind rendering of service/Seva seems to be future oriented. Like we are going to gain something in return for the services rendered. It is something like provision for rainy season, which can be useful in our old age or on the Day of Judgment. Intention behind this kind of service is to secure our future. And in this regard service is considered as some kind of investment, which will help us in future. Service rendered in this fashion happens with purpose and the intended purpose may be towards further riches or more achievement.

To Mahaveer service should have to be spontaneous and without any thought of gain and is past oriented. This means that whatever Seva we render is to cast away that which we have colleted in our past by way of knowing or unknowing acts and behavior. As per Mahaveer when we are intending to go on to journey of self-realization then whatever we have collected in the past has to cast away or left behind to make us shed unnecessary load because of which our journey becomes light. In this regard this type of service can be called as active penance for the past sacrilegious acts and behavior. To undo what has been done. And the most important thing is our ego does not have any chance to remain intact.

Our rendering of any service to anyone is nothing but completion of the original act, which we have started in the past. At the most service is to be considered as the other half of the previous act. And in this fashion we are nullifying what we have done in the past. This concept of Mahaveer is very novel in the sense that whatever we have accumulated is castaway or left behind.

To our way of thinking any act is deemed to be complete when reaction to action happens. When we act on our own initiative or act as reaction to the act of others, then either we repent due to guilt or go into penance and try to change our self. In our day-to-day interaction or behavior something always remain as incomplete. Seva/service is the manner or means by which we can complete that which is remained as incomplete. Service rendered in this regard can take form of financial, physical or mental assistance. This concept requires further explanation to understand its significance. If someone has to bear financial loss due to our act or behavior, then obviously that other is going to suffer in various ways, so services rendered by us to such person by way of monetary assistance or by other means is deemed as adequate recompense for his prior losses and our rendering the service as counter act, will make us free from the responsibility. Most of our acts happen in careless manner or with malice, and when we come to know about the repercussions borne by the other, then either we repent or go into penance. But our repenting or penance is not going to help the other in any substantial way. Generally we do not know that our act has caused misery to other when the other is unknown to us. Service/Seva is the means to balance the books. Whatever is the cause because of which the other is suffering, then if we are present and have the capacity to lessen his suffering, then with spontaneity we have to render the service and pass away. But the condition that Mahaveer has attached to this kind of act or behavior is, we are not to believe or assume that we are going to gain anything in return but on the contrary are going to unload our past acts in this manner. Furthermore we are not going to think afterwards that we have behaved in noble manner. Even our thoughts in this manner are enough to sway us forever and inflate our ego.

Consciously or unconsciously we very well know the reasoning behind our every act or behavior before its execution. We may act due to malice, carelessness and greed, to cross the other or to get even with the other. Mostly we act and behave out of turn, which may be harmful to others. In this regard our memory span is very short. We just do not forget about our acts or behavior but we even forget about those people against whom we have acted. So Seva is to be treated as the only means by which we are trying to set right or compensate our basic intention or motive behind the act or behavior that was our original act. This concept of the Seva is nothing but our repayment against our wrongdoing. In light of this explanation we have to understand that there is nothing honorary in rendering of any service.

In the process of service it becomes immaterial to attach any value to our self as a person of big heart or of helping nature. At the same time, if we intend to take credit as superior human being who is ever ready to serve anyone then this belief will negate the basic principle of the concept. And for this reason only Mahaveer is stressing the point of spontaneity. In any act, which happen to be spontaneous, we do not have chance to be prepared beforehand. Someone is in difficulty, we are present and can help, then Mahaveer says give the assistance and go away. This is Seva/service.

On road junctions there are traffic wardens, whose primary duty is to keep the traffic flowing. Some children or aged persons feel difficulty while crossing the road. In such instance the same traffic warden helps them cross the road and afterwards stands on his point to direct the traffic again. Do we think that he will think about how he has helped those children to cross the road? What he has done is rendered the spontaneous service and forgotten about it. It is applicable to us also. On our way if we can help someone, then do the helping and go on to our intended job. But after completion of the helpful act if we are going to think about it, then we are again associating our self where no association is necessary.

If we are under the pretension that as the other is unhappy so I must serve him, or the other is helpless so I should serve him; then our this kind of thoughts are going to create much inflated ego. But we must not forget that if we are going to realize our true self, then any type of ego is going to be hindrance. According to Mahaveer service with any intention or emotion cause resurrection of ego.

This concept of the Mahaveer about service was very rarely appreciated and practiced. Basically general people as well as followers do not accept the concept as given by Mahaveer. The reason behind this reluctance seems that people like to invest not only their money and expect returns on the same, but they expect returns from their acts also. In this light what Mahaveer intends, seems to be bizarre. But as mentioned in earlier discussions about Mahaveer being psychologist par excellence and as even modern day psychology accepts, that to develop in creative manner we have to shed previous load from our mind which causes blockages in our psyche. In psychology the therapist asks the counselee to focus his mind on new concepts and in religious doctrine Mahaveer has given a way out to the practitioner by the conceptual way of service.

Why Mahaveer stresses the importance of spontaneity has various reasons; people serve to take credit, which either inflate the ego or is future oriented with the anticipation that at my lean period others will help me in the same manner, which cause attachment. Similarly serving without spontaneity may develop into bizarre interest in the hardships of the others, due to which the person intending to serve become passionate and starts to live on other's miseries like a parasite. We have to remember that our ego can take any form and to serve anyone at any time become obsessive behavior. Any and every obsession has capacity to sway us from awareness of our self. Further, if due to our association anyone is suffering then to get away from the situation is also considered as a form of service. In our relationship with others, we generally attach our self to such an extent that the other feels suffocated. In such a case, to extricate our self from the relationship is also treated as service. In everything, habitually we are very much passionate, so when we serve with the same passion then the act becomes binding as well as painful to all concerned.

Due to our habit nature we become so passionate that even in religious practice we show passions as if we are fanatic. Our insistence, our stubbornness is nothing but forms of our passionate nature. Even to acquire any merit we have to be passionate; meaning of the word merit is used as Punya in religious parlance. Passion about anything makes us unconscious, at the same time to fulfill the passion we have to be aggressive, which again is the form of violence. By our conditioned nature, we bargain for every thing and anything.

And in this regard we are so driven that if we are going to cast away any attitude that is cause of our degradation, then in return we expect to gain something in its place. This is how Mahaveer says that any person who is passionate by his habit nature is unconscious or a dense person.

To make any change in us as a basic pre-requisite is, we should not expect or anticipate anything in return. We are willing to change, means we are not happy prior to the intended change. But when we feel sure that after the change we are going to experience peace and joy, then this happening is sufficient reward in itself. The same rewards showers on us in religious practice and austerity.

To Mahaveer's experience Seva/service is like medicine. Its spontaneous practice will help to regain our mental health. And we know that peaceful mind is basic prerequisite of good physical health. Mahaveer believes in the concept of traveling with light baggage. In this manner we do not have to concentrate on the upkeep and safety of the baggage, but should be open to experience new sights and beauty of the surrounding. The same concept is applicable to the journey between birth and death. We collect all kinds of baggage on the way, but Seva is the process by which we can discard that which is not necessary as well which is useless for the ultimate destination. As happens in the long drawn illness, when we start to regain health we feel that something is missing. In reality nothing is missing but what we are missing is the discomfort we have experienced in the illness, which we have associated with our being. As we go into spontaneous service mode, the same emptiness is felt at the level of mind, but this type of emptiness is rejuvenating. Not only conscious thoughts, but thoughts, which are dormant in our subconscious mind also affect us. These thoughts make us preoccupied and at the same time we loose the ability of our mind to concentrate on the tasks in hand. Unknown to us, each and every action and reaction of ours along with relevant thoughts, remain stored in our mind. If such thoughts are not purged from our mind from time to time, then our mind become like overflowing reservoir, where input continues but no output happens. Seva/service is one of the process by which we load shed of our mind from excess thoughts, and can experience peace and tranquility.

Our definition of truth and its application is very functional. At the same time some truths keep us changing frequently. Let us go through an experiment that for 24 hours we will behave truthfully and see what happens. Most of the people form our immediate surrounding will find us hard to tolerate and will complain that we are behaving in bizarre manner. To us and to all persons around us truth, as we define, understand and appreciate, is nothing but functional edition, which will help us to go on behaving as per the social norm. And this edited version is called as common sense. But at a very subtle level this is nothing but mutual playacting. Our truthfulness change from person to person. One version is for spouse, another is for children; still another for partner and the next will be for all the others. All the enlightened person tells us that truth is ever changing, and its realization happens to various people in various forms but each form is novel and different from each other. But we are much more enlightened than all the pioneers, as our version of truth changes many times in just 24 hours. This phenomenon happens only because of our habit to exist with double standards.

Next process of inner austerity is study of self. This concept is to be understood as study of self, but for this study no outside study material is available. Tradition takes the meaning as study of books concerning religion and its doctrine. The brake-up of the word and what Mahaveer intends by the way of meaning are totally different. The word used is Swadhaya- Swa Adhaya; study of self. Whenever we study or read any book concerning religion, the book is presentation of the concept or contains experiences of the author, as to how he has arrived at the conclusion. At the most, such books will be called as book of instructions. But again the experiences mentioned in the book will be of someone else's and not ours. To verify these experiences we our self has to go through the process and experiments. In this regard such a book will help us. But if we are going to declare that just by reading we have become religious, then this thought is nothing but illusion. Even in experiments of general scientific natures, we have to verify the information in laboratory and then we can say that whatever information is given in the book is correct. The same principle applies to the religious books also.

Religious doctrines are nothing but the formulas for practice to be gone through in every day life. But as the subject i.e. we, are animate, then the results varies from person to person. And this novelty of the different results for every person makes religion alive and the truth arrived at is experienced as ever changing.

To Mahaveer every person is ultimate scripture. That what is known, was known and will be known is present in every human being. Every human is nothing but the scaled down version of total existence. In a nut shell study of the self is but study of the existence. Learning about human emotions in the book of psychology is instructive, but learning about our thoughts, emotions, feelings and attitudes is study of the self.

Mahaveer defines human potentials in very radical manner. To him human knows whatever is known and furthermore whatever will become known is going to be known by the human only. But if the knowledgeable is known or encountered i.e. the element that is our basic being, then everything is known. One who has known all the existence and when the knower is known or acquainted with, then there do not remain anything to know. This realization is called as enlightenment.

Knowledge about anything happens in two steps; first, the one who knows about anything or everything i.e. subjective, the second is to know about the knower i.e. objective. Religion is related to the knower who knows.

Knowledge about objects is every day occurrence, but knowledge about the seeker is mystery. In this context the more we know about objects, the more we forget about the one who perceives and experience the knowledge. Religion is the ultimate science, which helps us to know and understand about the knower, which in religious parlance is known as self-realization.

Heaps of knowledge does not help us to identify the ultimate seeker of the knowledge. To Mahaveer's way of thinking, the person who has knowledge of everything except the seeker is pseudo-intellectual. But once the seeker is identified and experienced, then the austerite is very near to ultimate explosion i.e. enlightenment. This stage of transcended enlightenment is termed as re-birth. The term Dwija (Twice Born) used in Vedic doctrine is the same as re-birth. After this stage true revolution happens in the life and being of the person.

Religious books and its doctrines are important and instructive to only those who are intelligent enough and who understand the meaning and go through the experience on their own. Most of the times the so-called ignorant jumps heedlessly and reach, but the so-called learned remains under the illusion that by just reading the books, he has arrived. Even in Upanishada the same is stated that; 'ignorant wanders in the darkness but so-called learned wanders in pitch darkness'.

We can really listen or really see only when our mind is not involved. The statement seems to be so superficial that this phenomenon has any validity is very rarely perceived or experienced. But once we become adapt in using this technique its validity will be experienced as fact. Further, in such a case the true identity of who is listening to or looking at, can be also be experienced. Such is the nature of our conditioned and habit-bound mind that it starts to interpret the meaning of what we are listening to or looking at, before the completion of the act of hearing or seeing. In this regard our mind starts to refer to our past experiences of the same nature as reference library. But by experience we have come to know that whatever we are going to listen is something different than before; the speaker is new, even though the subject seems to be the same the presentation is going to be different. But when instead of us, our mind start to meddle, then we do not get the satisfaction of true listening. What we have to do is make our attention as dual directional; we will concentrate on the orator and at the same time we will concentrate on our self as the true listener. In this fashion what we listen will be understood in its entirety and at the same time the emotions of the orator will be received by us in its true form, which will change us. This is how awareness helps to change us. The main advantage of the dual attention process is we could verify the experience of the orator with the knowledge of the self.

Study of the self is nothing but going into each and every act of ours, and experience with total awareness of our self, without letting our mind meddle every time. The best example of mob psychology happens at the time of political rallies. 10/15 supporters of the speaker in the rally are placed at various places in the mob, these supporters have knowledge of the speech beforehand, at the same time they are told to clap at the utterance of certain statements. When during the speech these people start to clap then all the other people also clap. The reason behind this type of behavior is people are not sure about self, but clap none the same with the belief that they will look foolish or ignorant if they do not clap. And this mutual nonsense of the masses is termed as the success of the rally.

It is said that humans are social animals, but when humans remain in herds then our personalities become absent. We start to behave in collective fashion. According to Mahaveer we are not only absent personality, but we become absent from our self also and this being is called as extrovert personality. Study of self or self-awareness is to remain present in all the acts, situations and experiences i.e. nothing should happen without our knowledge. In such awareness even alcohol will not intoxicate us but in unconscious state even water will intoxicate us with strong suggestion. When we are thirsty water is available and thirst is experienced but the element of self, which is going to experience the quenching, remains absent. Logically the self should be initially present, then thirst should be experienced and lastly water should be sought. This is the way in which study of self or remembering of self should happen.

Inferior or superior is different from person to person; mostly this distinction depends on the individual's nature. If we start to differentiate these qualities from person to person, then the task will be daunting. But in study of self, the process even though common to everyone, gives results to every individual as per his nature and this is the novelty of the process. Study of self is nothing but analysis of the attitudes of the person who is going through the exercise, as well as a step towards awareness. So if any attitude of ours is not according to our nature or if we are interpreting any faculty of ours beyond its intended purpose, then this wayward behavior tapers off and stops happening. As discussed before, repetition happens because of our unconscious being which is cause of loss of energy as well as frustrating.

Awareness gained by way of study of self shows us that either our expectations are erroneous or we are placing expectations against such an object or individual where the fulfillment is not possible. In this regard awareness is nothing exotic or special, but is the way to change our thoughts as to what to expect from other. This key in the guise of awareness is the master key that helps us to be free from all the sorrows and frustrations.

So when Mahaveer says that live and exist in totally aware state, live in wide-awake manner so that no sin will happen. Meaning of the concept of sin as we know or understand and the meaning of the same concept intended by Mahaveer is radically different. As per the pioneer, any act happening by us is called as sin only if we are not aware as to why and what we are doing. Do we think, that if we remain aware at all the times or most of the times, then will we go through any act indiscriminately or in repetitive manner? Any act happening with awareness is not perceived as sin but at the most it can be said to be happening as per our nature. In this context and for this reason, any act is called as honorary act of one person but is considered as sacrilegious act by the other. This distinction happens only because we compare acts and not the nature of each individual. This understanding and to understand that each and every person is unique, to understand that all the objects present in this existence do have their own distinct nature is called as awareness. This awareness frees us from all the bondages, all the anchors, from the stigma of right or wrong. Awareness is like burning torch because of which we do not have to grope in the darkness or bump every time but now we can see the way out.

Study of self is to shift the focus from objective to subjective. Till we are focused on objective we are bound to bump, even if we change the object every time. The person who used to walk to work will consider purchasing the cycle when his income increases. In the same manner his focus of attention will go on changing as his income goes on increasing. This nature of our attention to change from object to object is called as extrovert nature. Study of self shows that this change do not happen due to our self but due to needless intervention of our mind for acquisition of the various objects for the same purpose. According to Mahaveer when all the acts and behavior of any person is influenced or dominated by his mind alone, then such a person is to be considered as unconscious person. Similarly a popular misunderstanding that we concentrate due to our mind do not happen till our self is presiding over our mind.

Various external stimulants and cues either disturb or provoke us. Again this emotional oscillation happens due to focus of our mind and due to our conditioned behavior pattern. What we have to do is focus on the external and at the same time be aware about disturbance or provocation experienced at the level of our mind. This exercise will help us to understand, as to how our mind works and its causation or reasoning. This understanding will very definitely change us towards creative and more fulfilling way of life.

As study of self is new process we are going to adopt in our otherwise routine existence, initially we have to face and experience very disturbing thoughts and beliefs about which we were not aware. This happens because till now we have collected various beliefs, ideas, and concepts, and go on hypothesizing with the intention that some of this collection may help us towards betterment of our future. But once we start to study our self then we start to realize that most of the collection seems to be inferior. We are not going to despair because of this inferior collection, because now we are getting acquainted with the potentials of our mind that can store anything or everything. In this light, what we have to understand is whatever we have collected, is collected due to our unconscious nature. So when we encounter this inferior collection then it is a indication that the cleansing process of our mind has started, and we have to go through this experiences with equanimity, after which we will understand for the first time as to what our core is like and where we have to alter or change. So as we continue with the study of self and due to which as our awareness about our self increases, then that which is inferior or not necessary to our being starts to fall down or cast away, and in its place we can install positive and creative concepts that will better our being. Similarly for the first time we are going to be face to face with our original self. It is basic rule of existence, that whenever we are going to get something of true substance then we have to let go or to loose something less substantial in return. Most of the times traditions are inferred or understood without proper understanding because of which we cast away inferior as well as necessary but do not replace or install creative concepts in its place. Then the resultant void or emptiness causes preoccupation, depression or disturbed mental state. It is the law of nature that either we reinstall or replace self generated void or nature on its own will fill the gap. The novelty of this process is we are going to cast away those aspects of our being because of which we have experienced sorrows and frustrations.

This process makes us capable to live as per our nature then automatically we start to live with our self. Similarly our being in heaven happens nowhere else but when we remain in our nature then we are in heaven. We create hell due to imposition of our habits and attitudes on our basic nature and start to behave in conditioned manner, without verifying whether they are compatible to our nature or not. Study of self does not demolish anything, but make us more aware as to what we are at our core and helps us to change accordingly.

CHAPTER 17

MEDITATION: HOW AND WHY?

Mere instructions about any concept may increase our instructive knowledge but till the knowledge is not applied to gain the experience, our understanding remains as theoretical. Meditation is the next process to increase our awareness and its application in practical manner is going to be beneficial to us.

Experience of meditation and swimming are very much alike. Sitting on the bank of a tank or river, we may imagine what the swimmer is experiencing. In the same manner, when anyone practicing meditation will tell us about his experiences then again we may just imagine as to what he is experiencing. But as to imagine is mental exercise, we will not experience as to what feelings we will really experience till we physically participate in the experiment. To meditate is an existential experience, so mere knowledge about its theory is not going to make much of a difference in our being or life.

Mahaveer defines meditation as two-way path; one is objective, which is called as obsession or false meditation, and the other is subjective, which concerns self of the practitioner. Latter meditation is considered as true meditation. Any thought or emotion, because of which our focus of attention consolidates on the object or person other than the self, is false meditation. Intense anger, hatred, greed, attachment, attraction, revulsion are some of the emotions which cause us to focus our attention on the other. Increase in intensity of any one of these emotions become so all consuming that our self as separate identity is totally forgotten. This forgetting of the self is deemed as false meditation. But most of these emotions are never felt to the exclusion of all the surrounding as well as our self, like berserker fury, which when experienced fully will show pyromaniac display of destruction a human is capable of causing. Even this kind of intensity will give us a glimpse as to how meditation is experienced. In proper meditation we shift the same focus from objective to subjective i.e. towards self.

Not only in presentation of anger but also in most of the emotions we are very lukewarm people. We become fearful that if we do not restrain our emotions, then the emotion will get out of our control. Even in joy, happiness, love we restrain our self from full expression, with the same trepidation that if our emotion is given free rein then we will make fool of our self. This restraining causes unease in our mind and body with the nagging feeling that what we have experienced is not to the desired limits of expected satisfaction and intensity, with the persistent feeling of dissatisfaction, that something is still missing. This reasoning is not to be taken in literal sense or as sanction to give free rein to all the emotions, but any one of these will have shown us as to what potentials we have. In subjective meditation we are not going to restrain our self, but are going to be witness to the happening at the plain of our mind, and this is the proper manner by which we are going to experience our being at deep meditation.

Why Mahaveer has termed objective meditation as false and secondary, because in this meditation we will be spending our energy on fruitless endeavor, only because any other or object, is going to remain separate from us, no matter how intense our meditation is. At the same time in this kind of meditation we forget about our self, as the processes we are going through and discussing are concerned only about self, as the main aim of every religious doctrine. Dynamic force of our self is given free rein in meditation for the reason, that then we will come to know what we are, what is our nature and then this understanding will elevate us, which is termed as realization of self or enlightenment. All the elements of the doctrine discussed till now are but preliminaries and by going through them we become capable to go into meditation as the ultimate means of introduction to our self. In fact, to meditate is the basic art as well as science, of productive and creative living. But we are unfortunate in the sense that we have lost this faculty of our being due to our extrovert nature and superimposition of learned habit nature on our basic nature.

People become interested in meditation as last resort to experience peace of mind and tranquility. Restlessness, stress and tension not only affect our mind but also affect us physically, which in the long run is the basic cause of various ailments and diseases. As we are conditioned since birth and as we start to take interest in any religious practice by the time we reach middle age, natural aging of the body as well as chaotic mindset takes its toll. We lose much of the energy and drive till we go for meditation, which again become a chore to be followed as prescribed but not as a pleasant exercise to be cherished. This predicament of human psyche is very much understood by Mahaveer as well as the entire pioneer's of every religion. This is the reason we have to follow and understand more processes of the doctrine before we reach the process of meditation. Then we come to know that the manner in which we existed till now, and whatever we have created is nothing but junk, the way we are creating relationship is nothing but a method of trial and error method where we very rarely experience fulfillment and joy of being together. This understanding takes us towards study of self in which we become aware as to where we are deviating, where we are expecting something that is not going to manifest. Then we have to plug all the leakages, clean the store and only then we can start to meditate.

Meditation is the process where we have to be witness with

the precondition that we are not going to think either for or against anything i.e. thoughts, emotions, feelings etc. but we are just going to witness the same as they occur or felt. People take meditation as a form of contemplation or introspection, which is not meditation. Contemplation is the faculty of our mind where we weigh pros and cons of the action and its effects in relation to us before it is taken. In retrospection we think on our past experiences and acts happened by us or about the acts we were part of. Similarly it helps us to decide whether we want to go through the same act again or not.

We do not know that to experience peace and tranquility, nothing is necessary or anything special has to be done. What we have to do is extricate our self from the chaos we have created and then what we will experience is peace. Peacefulness is not an achievement but it is our basic being, and so we are not going to invent anything but are going to discover our basic state. It is really unfortunate that even though we human's are the most intelligent in the known existence and have invented so much for our comfort but we are loosing the main ingredient of our basic being i.e. mental equilibrium and are becoming pathetic, only because we have lost the touch with ourselves. As mentioned before and as going to be repeated in further discussions also, in our headlong quest for materialistic advancement very few people has touched the base of realization and understood as to what makes us tick and how we can be contented in our life. We do not know that only because of our superior intelligence, there has to be a frame of religion around us so that we can experience joy and tranquility. If religion seems to be very heavy word with the ring of mystery or orthodoxy around it, then we can make it light, as code of conduct for humans, which will help us to exist in peaceful and contented manner.

Let us use meditation as an instrument to check the validity of above statement. All the sense organs of ours are basically meant for our safety and continual survival till our natural end.

Similarly they are meant to be data collection apertures also. Are we really using all the faculties or any one of it in intended manner? The answer is very definite 'no'. We taste and use such substances which are not meant for humans, we see so much of what we want to see at and why we are looking at looses its true meaning, we eat when we are not hungry and do not eat when we are really hungry, we crave to touch and feel anything and everything with preconceived notions but in doing so do not feel desired satisfaction because in our craving we loose sight of the basic reason as to why we are doing what we are doing in the first place. All this madness is happening because we have never studied or understood as to why we are given these faculties and in what manner to use them. Momentary thrill experienced through the medium of mind in association with faculty drives us towards repeat performance with the expectation that the same thrill will be experienced again and again. This repetition of the acts of the same nature is the reason of development of habitual nature, which is imposed on our basic nature and the related faculty. This kind of behavior is termed as conditioned behavior.

Any obsession is termed as false meditation only because it is other oriented i.e. separate and independent from the self. This is one of the reasons why Mahaveer even denied existence of the God, as God is also other than us. According to Mahaveer and Buddha realization of the self is termed as godliness in the form of human. In all the other Hindu religious practices, merger of the self of the devotee with the God is termed as the state of Adwaita (Existence of only one). But in Jainism, Mahaveer says that the realization of the self in its pure form is also state of Adwaita. To merge with the God we have to prey and to submit ourselves to the God, whereas to realize our self, we have to meditate.

The way of prayer is always an application for help and guidance from higher and superior being than us. In meditation we are going to be ultimate authority and so are going to realize our self on our own. Given or granted to us by anyone or even by the God as ultimate authority, can also be taken back, recalled or foreclosed in future because anything given can be revoked and this phenomenon depends on the whim of the giver. So, if such is the case, then are we bold enough or have guts enough to challenge the superior authority? Whenever anything is granted or given in this manner then there are chances that the same can be taken back, and in such a case we are again going to experience sorrow and heartbreak.

To Mahaveer, every individual irrespective of any gender has potential of self-realization. And to arrive at this state initially we have to cast away all that is collected and acquired, to make our slate clean and then start again in the prescribed manner and then our existence will be model existence. The meaning of the word relation means association with other. The other may be animate or inanimate. In such a relationship even if we are happy or contented to continue the relations, but if the other is not ready and willing to continue as he has the same right to discontinue, then the relationship stops being valid. Association by way of relation has a hidden proviso of disassociation. It is a partnership of will.

So when each and every relationship, however close or intimate, has the inherent quality to be discontinued from us or the other, then Mahaveer points to the one and only relationship we can have and will be maintained forever i.e. be acquainted with our self or with our basic nature, which was, is and will be forever ours as eternal. A word used by Mahaveer for meditation is Samayik, which is combination of two words. Samay means time, the ninth dimension and momentum of our being as human being and it means; to be in self, to be in or dwell in our pure conscious, is called as Samayik.

Since long scientists are working and studying about our existence in relation to our surrounding. They agree that our existence is three-dimensional i.e. it consists of length, width and breadth. We perceive and experience all the objects, animate or inanimate, only because of these three dimensions as well as we have potentials to perceive them in this manner. But as all the things are ever changing and to understand as to when and why this change is happening takes some period. The intervening period that has to be passed away so we can register the changes that happens in relation to the objects or animates, is termed as time. So to establish the relationship between existence and time, a term is coined by eminent scientists that is Spaciotime or space-time. By the application of this concept the changes happening in relation to human elements, natural elements, as well as natural or manmade objects can be determined and the results are stated in the units of time. As per Einstein, time is the fourth dimension and a bridge between space and objects. It is further accepted that time also is an energy force. And 2500 years back Mahaveer termed human soul as time.

Now it becomes clear to understand, that without time existence of objects is possible, but life force without time is not conceivable. Dynamics of life force happen in time only. We leave our home for office by way of car, bus or train i.e. physically we are in any one of them. But our mind would have reached our destination long before we physically reach and this dynamic force of our mind happens only because of time.

Happening and existence of our force of life in this dynamically flowing condition happens due to time, and our being in this manner is called as Samayik or meditation. When our life force remains dynamic but at a neutral state or keeps running as an idling engine, then ultimate Samayik or meditation happens. This state of being is known as -Just is.

If we look into an enclosed room with but a chink in the ceiling through which a ray of sun is coming, then in this sunbeam we can see dust moths floating and can also see that they are coming and going continuously. This traffic starts from the darkness and ends also into darkness. This is how our mind works. Our thoughts are like dust moths and our focus of attention is like sunbeam. We appreciate and experience only those thoughts that come under our attention. But this phenomenon does not mean that the thoughts we experience are the only thoughts in our mind. Our mind is also like an enclosed room where various thoughts are floating everywhere like dust moths but to experience or encounter them we have to shift our attention.

Psychology divides human mind in two broad sections and this happens due to our focus of attention. Section of mind under our focus of attention is termed as conscious mind and the other section is termed as unconscious mind. Those people who are very much habit bound or behaves in limited routine become restless when unknowingly thoughts from unconscious mind come under the focus of attention. As such thoughts were never experienced before in daily routine, they become baffled as to how and from where these thoughts are coming? As mentioned before, we see indiscriminately and think about anything and everything in the same manner because of which everything remains stored in our mind. Then the same thoughts we have collected in this unconscious manner start to haunt us when they come under our focus of attention.

Our mind is full of thoughts as atmosphere is full of air. When air in the form of breeze or wind touches us we experience its presence and the same happens when our thoughts come under our focus of attention then only we perceive them. In this regards our mind is like atmosphere, in the sense till thoughts are perceived we do not experience our mind. Again there are two ways in which we can save our self from experiencing the existence of our thoughts; one is to totally switch-off our focus of attention, which is not possible, or to focus our total attention on our mind whereby no nook or cranny of our mind will escape from our attention. And this is where study of self and meditation is useful. Our mind is like screen in the theatre where beam of our attention helps to project and identify our thoughts so that we can see and experience them.

In our sleep we do not experience thoughts only because our conscious attention is switched-off to let our body and mind have much needed rest. Use of alcohol and all the psychotic substances cause the same effect; they sever the relationship between our mind and thoughts and so any person under the influence of any of the above substance is called as unconscious person.

Similarly, recital or chanting of any specific prayer or mantra helps up to a certain extent, only if the practitioner knows the proper posture of sitting and is capable of proper pronunciation of the words of the prayer or mantra. Regularized breathing, proper posture and proper pronunciation create such waves in our being that our mind start to become occupied with the recital and focus of attention shifts from thoughts to prayer or mantra. But in the longer run this recital become as self-hypnotism. When we recite anything then focus of conscious mind shifts towards reciting and thoughts present in our mind recede towards our subconscious, but do not totally dissolve. After recital we experience calm and tranquility because thoughts from unconscious take some time to emerge in our conscious mind and the gap between the two is felt as calm. Further, any recital practiced for extended period of time causes boredom and this boredom lulls us to sleep. Practice of recital is good for disturbed sleep pattern or in insomnia, but in self-realization it is of very limited use.

In general there are two techniques adopted while meditating; the first is to firmly imagine an idol of chosen deity or a sign considered to be of value in religious parlance. The said image is to be visualized in the mind as if we are sitting in front of the deity or sign. At the same time the practitioner has to relax in body and has to fully concentrate on the mental image. In this manner we do not have to think over the thoughts coming under our focus of attention, but look at them in detached manner. What Mahaveer suggested as witnessing is applied here as detached observation. But most of the times the practitioner due to relaxation as well as total concentration goes into deep trance, which in turn become sleep.

Way of Mahaveer is the way of effort, for which he has coined a word Shraman. The meaning of the word Shram, which is of Sanskrit origin, is to do efforts. In this technique maximum pull is applied to the body and Zen Buddhists and Sufi fakirs apply this technique most of the times. What is suggested is that we have to pull all our muscles to the utmost like crazy. At some point we feel that if we continue to pull then something will tear apart or we will breakdown. While we are pulling in this manner a curious thing starts to happen; that our mind starts to relax in direct proportion to the pull. After this continuous pull we are advised to let go all the efforts behind the pulling, which in turn relaxes us to the utmost not only in body but in our mind also. At the same time this kind of relaxation after profound exhaustion does not take us into sleep, but we remain fully awake in detached kind of mental frame. Then this relaxation of mind and body is used to go into meditation. Here I will like to mention a warning before going into meditation prescribed by Mahaveer about which we are going to discus and are to be considered as preliminaries. We are not going to by-pass any of these preliminaries otherwise we will not only experience disturbance in our physical functioning but disturbance in and damage to our mind also.

Preliminaries or three steps are remembering, returning and re-living. Completion of these steps will help us to go into active meditation. Most of the time at the end of the day we feel that some actions or reaction of ours keep us on the tenterhooks, in the sense that the way in which we have behaved lack something which we should have done at that time or should have done in somewhat other way. This unease in our mind makes us restless and we remain in contemplative mode as to in future we will act or react in different way. But next time either circumstances change or we forget about our resolve and do the same thing again. Repetition of the same kind of acts, because of which again our mind becomes disturbed, makes us a brooding person. Similarly we also know that the acts happened by us in any circumstances is water under the bridge and in whatever fashion we may act in future in the same circumstance is not going to negate the previous act. Time is the reality in the sense that what we have done cannot be undone by further act or counteract. Above-mentioned steps are processes to ease our mind as well as an antidote to change our being towards better person.

Remembering is concerned with recalling of our past memories. Mahaveer states that our past memories are to be used as references. By returning he asks us to start from square one; from the point from where we have started. And reliving is concerned with to exist again in the same incidence in the same manner that has happened. It is to be understood that all these steps are mental exercise only and we are not going to change anything by way of imagination or according to our deep-rooted concepts about anything. In a nutshell, this process is nothing but a concentrated version of witnessing. In this process our adaptability to the role of just a witness or as an observer becomes enhanced and at the same time we will come to know at what time we were not present as self or as a person of awareness, because of which we have slipped. Process of reliving is like recorded cassette; any segment which is important, can be heard again and again with total concentration.

Any person who is desirous to go into active meditation must go through this process at any time. The time suggested as ideal time is when we go to bed, for the excellent reason that in this manner we will become easy in mind that will help us to sleep peacefully. We have to start with all the activities we have gone through since waking up to the time we are ready to go to sleep. Most of the times whatever we are doing, we are not aware about our surrounding where some thing is always happening. For example, at the time of our breakfast sunlight was streaming through the window, radio was on, wife was working in the kitchen, children were talking or arguing with each other, our neighbor was going out and the noise of his door opening and closing can be heard, there were vehicles running on the road and their horn's were blaring. About how much we were aware of all these activities? In remembering the only thing we recall is we were having breakfast and thinking about the appointments we have to attend. But our mind is so sensitive that even though we are not actively aware, it records all the activities happening around us and all this information is stored in our subconscious mind. So we have to start with remembering and then an amazing thing happens that upto 80% of the stored information will be remembered once we focus our attention in this manner. The moment we start to remember what has happened since we woke in the morning then we have to return to that point and to recall each and every act through which we have gone, and look at them in witnessing manner. One more thing to remember is, as soon as we start to remember the acts then we have to recall the pertinent details of the specific acts also and to again relive them in the same manner as we have gone through or experienced.

In this process some basics are to be always adhered to; we are not going to change the sequence of the actions or reaction, we are not going to change our emotions or thoughts behind any of the acts, we are not going to contemplate any ifs and buts about the causation of the acts, we are not going to think about the manner in which the other has reacted to our act or whether the other was right or wrong; in the sense we have to firmly accept that whatever actions or reactions has to be happened has happened.

There are various advantages to this process; to start with we become more aware about our self, we come to know about our attitudes whether they are creative or troublesome, our faculty to recall become enhanced, conscious and unconscious mind are de-cluttered so that tension and stress decreases, as every thought and act is recalled and relived then preoccupation of the mind also decreases. Major advantage of this process happens to increase in our understanding and it becomes clear to us as to what assumptions, beliefs, perceptions and thinking pattern of ours needs changing, upgrading or discarding. At the same time repetition of the acts, which were of no value tapers off and stop. We experience dreams only because in our hurry to act and to go through the routine, our thinking process behind any act remains incomplete. Incomplete thoughts and its relevant acts remain dormant in our subconscious mind, which are given free rein in our sleep as our conscious mind looses its hold on the total mind when we are sleeping. But as we are going through the remembering, recalling and reliving process, all that is happened is again experienced by our mind and there do not remain anything residual to bother us. In this manner our dreaming also stops. Then the sleep that we start to experience becomes total and rejuvenating sleep, which is the basic important function of sleeping. Then our days become new and fresh and our concentration become total. Aimless wandering of our mind stops. Continuous thinking is an obsession, which happen due to non-attention of our intelligence as conscious mind on our thinking process, which in turn causes suppression of thoughts. But when we start to relive all the thoughts and its relevant acts in the manner mentioned above then they are again felt consciously, which weaken their hold on our conscious as well as unconscious mind.

In all, this process which we have discussed above takes 3 to 4 months to master. Then whatever thinking and act happen happens for the present only. Then each and every act becomes a complete act. When every act becomes as complete then unnecessary acts or repetitive acts stop altogether.

As we relive and experience our past constantly we become free from our past that may be perceived as troublesome. Burden on the mind lessens and in the same proportion our mind becomes uncluttered because of which we start to experience peace that was illusive to us till now. We knowingly or unknowingly create our future, good or bad, only because our present happens in unawareness. Our habit to postpone any change in our self happens due to our perception of improper circumstances, which is also our erroneous belief. Most of the times circumstances are out of our reach of change, but in any circumstance we can mold our self. In the above process as we become more aware, we stop from blaming circumstances and start to change our self. When any act happens due to total awareness, then it becomes a complete act and we do not feel any trepidation about future. Now as we have got the formula where whenever we have to act or react then the happening is going to be total.

Any ailment of mind happens only because we are not aware as to how our mind works. In the above process we learn to look at our mind in detached manner and in this manner only it become possible to look at our mind as to how it works and why it works. Again this process helps us to purge our mind from overload of various thoughts, which time and again creates confusion. Each and every person who is following any religious doctrine can adapt this process and will understand the nature of his mind and can save the self from its pitfalls, which if not checked at the initial stage may turn into any psychological problems. Every psychiatrist and psychotherapist plays the same role with the counselee i.e. try to pinpoint the thoughts, beliefs or assumptions that causes the problem and how to alter or overcome them. The process mentioned above is nothing but the process of self-evaluation and the same directs us towards changes that will help us grow in positive and creative manner.

In a sense, we all are somewhat eccentric but the more eccentric is to be treated and less eccentric remains in the gray area. We the general people are deemed as somewhat eccentric but are still accepted as sane people only because our behavior pattern somehow coincides and seems to be adhering with the accepted norms of the society and culture to which we belong. And by the same token when anyone from us either goes beyond the same norms or completely breaks away from them is termed as abnormal. The statement that we are somehow eccentric is to be accepted by all of us, only due to the fact that even though we stay in the society of somewhat likeminded people but still our capacity to understand and perceive as well as our potentials to express are unique than any other. And this is the beauty of to be a human being that each and every one of us can reach different heights of achievements with the help of the same concepts. This fact bares fruit in reality, when one child out of a whole class tops in the exams even when all are taught by the same teachers, one athlete wins the race against his opponents as well as against his contemporaries also, even though the contemporaries have got the same training as the winner has. The same happens in master-acolyte relationship. Most of the times the acolyte surpasses the master, the son surpasses the father and then we say that the achiever is chip of the same block. What we have to understand is that whatever is manifesting on the out side is the projection of our inner perceptions and if the meaning of the same perceptions are not analyzed from time to time and if the erroneous assumptions or beliefs are not purged from within us then the same may become cause of concern in future. So meditation is as much necessary to our being as the food we take every day.

We accept the habit of daydreaming as common mental pastime. Daydreaming is a way out to the actual behavior or act, which we do not dare go through because of its nature. Most of the times we daydream only because we do not have the capacity to pursue them in reality or it take the form of an alternative to the actual experience gained, which is not as per our expectations. As many of our activities are of routine nature, this chain of thoughts considered as daydreaming does not disturb us. But once in a while we have to halt the routine and have to think why this break has happened, why we have to stop the routine, which has become as our second nature. The reason being, the continuously flowing train of thoughts nudges our surface concentration and we have to look at the disturbing thoughts. This distraction of our mind as well as flimsy concentration can be overcome by way of remembering, recalling and reliving.

Most of the children of 12 to 16 years of age go into daydreaming because various hormonal changes are taking place in various parts of their body. These changes are not affecting only their body but are affecting their mind also, which in turn alter their way of thinking. Most of the children become brooding, cantankerous, surly, sullen or outright insolent only because they are not made aware beforehand as to what is taking place and how it is affecting them physically and mentally. But this is the proper time to let them know the importance of changes happening and its effects in their body and mind, as at this stage their personality starts to take irrevocable shape that will remain with them till the end of life. So if some misguided concepts or core beliefs become firm in this age, then the child will face trouble and may be cause of trouble to all the others around him.

What is the meaning of gestalt? To change our perceptual outlook or try to change our basic perception by pursuing different aspects of any thought, emotion, concept or hypothesis in conscious manner. How our perception can change is verified using various pictures. There are two scenes in a picture, but we cannot see both of them at the same time and the other is perceived only when we look at the same picture after we consciously alter our way of perception. Mahaveer suggested an experiment; the moment we wake up in the morning we will concentrate fully as to which thought materializes first in our mind. In this manner an amazing thing happens, that till we are concentrating on manifestation of the first thought, it's happening will take inordinately long time say up to 5 minutes. Then after 5 minutes the first thought will materialize, but in this intervening period what we were looking at was our mind, and after the manifestation of the thought what we are looking at is our thought but not our mind. This is how with our conscious shift in attention we either see the thought or our mind because presence of one is the cause of the absence of the other. We experience our mind only when there are thoughts in our mind, but at the same time when there are no thoughts we experience only peace. Period of thoughtlessness or of no thoughts at all is the cause of peacefulness. As mentioned before thoughts are always in our mind but in meditation what we do is look at all the thoughts as witness only, which after sometime help us to experience the same peace which we have experienced when we were attending our mind. This is how concept of gestalt can be understood.

One experience of our mind with total consciousness and the experience of peace as its result change our total gestalt to look at our thoughts show how the coveted peace can be experienced again and again. This is the way in which we can come out of the jumbled state of mind. The phenomenon of our witnessing every thought, act and emotion is termed by Mahaveer as Science of Division. We are having lunch; then there is food, consumer of food i.e. our body and our self. We have to witness the process of eating in this manner. Food would be hot, fresh, tasty and mouthwatering smells are emanating. Our tongue will taste the food and will find it delicious, our stomach will appreciate the appeasement of hunger. In all this procedure our self will be present as witness only. In this exercise we will come to know that our self is not having the food, but the body in which we are dwelling is eating the food, as hunger is the basic feeling of the emptiness of the body but not of our self. This separate existence of our self from our physical body is the intention of this exercise and witnessing is the process, which is condensing this understanding that we are not body, but are life force or Prana or our consciousness.

CHAPTER 18

PREPARATION TO PART FROM THE BODY

What happens in death is our force of life (Prana) separates from our body. Various reasons and explanations are presented by various religious doctrines. Most of the doctrines states that allotted time given to live like human come to an end, some believe that as our apparels (body) become old and threadbare so we discard them for new one so death happens. Or our force of life discards the body that ages and become infirm, so leaves the old one behind and takes birth in new one. According to Mahaveer, the dwelling becomes so infirm that to remain in the same becomes impossible, so death occurs. But about inevitability of death all the theosophies and all the religions are of the opinion, that death is part of our existence.

But for most of the people we have seen and in general the description about the dying is explained as painful and wrenching experience. No doubt death due to violent means is and will be painful i.e. accidental death or murder. In such cases the reason can be understood as suddenness of the happening. In spite of this most of the natural deaths are not only perceived as painful but even to think about death causes restlessness, anxiety, stress and trepidation. Most of the times the reason behind this inevitable impending experience seem to be purely psychological.

Human mind is a powerful faculty and it expresses itself through the medium of physical body only. So unless and until our awareness or understanding is not clear enough that we are not really physical body but something else, then our mind does not believe in our separate existence from our body. This association of our mind with our body as our true form of existence causes all the pain and misery about death. To Mahaveer, this kind of death is the cause we take rebirth; powerful association of mind with the body as our true form is given as a cause of going into the cycle of birth and death again and again.

Any firm belief of our mind can be altered or changed with the help of proper suggestions and monitoring, but death has become so significant to humans that any change in such deep-rooted belief is not going to be easy to change if association between our mind and body is firmly entrenched in our psyche. And in this regard Mahaveer prescribes meditation as ultimate conclusive alternative whereby our real being and its form can be experienced. We have to remember that in-depth meditation does not change our belief but it helps us to face the ultimate reality of our true being. So once this phenomenon is experienced with total awareness then reality about death becomes clear where our mind do not have to meddle and cause pain, fear, tension or frustration.

What happens in death happens in meditation. And meditation comes to fruition only when all the eleven processes mentioned before are understood and gone through as firsthand experience. At the peak of meditation the practitioner experiences that his total force of life is receding towards his core and the powerful feeling of partition from the physical body becomes very much condensed. All the extremities become laden; heartbeats come down to such an extent that every beat can be differentiated and distinctly experienced. Mahaveer cautions the practitioner that he should not become fearful or restrain himself from the experience, because this is what happens at the time of death. And once any one goes through this experience with awareness, then for that person death losses all the meaning so for the first time and in true sense he becomes fearless.

This is the twelfth and last process in the chain of austerity. In any humans life various anticipated desires may be fulfilled or not, various achievements may happen or not, humans by their habit nature may anticipate happening of various incidences of which some can be fulfilled or all may result into futile endeavors; but one phenomenon is going to happen ultimately and that is death. No animate is going to live forever; it may change, grow, age but dies none the same and the same happen in case of inanimate also, as they too change in appearance over the period of time. If we think hard and honestly, then the entire struggle we undergo is directly related to evade or postpone our death.

According to Mahaveer the cycle of birth and death happens only due to our unconscious being. We may have gone through the same cycle of birth & death in the past and so maybe today we are again a living being. But we have forgotten about our past only because at the time of our previous death we were associated with our body through our mind, because of which at the time of death we have become unconscious due to pain of parting. And this unconsciousness has caused our rebirth. Whenever we die in unconscious manner due to fear of death then our memory of past life's experiences are shrouded and this is the reason that every time we are born, we think that we are making a fresh start. As mentioned before all animates die; but death in relation to human and other animates have diverse significance. All the animals, insects or plants accept death as integral part of living; primarily because they exist as per their basic nature and, secondly their intelligence and awareness is not as developed as of human. Superior intelligence awarded to human is for the purpose of self-realization only. And this is the reason that religious practice and meditation is deemed necessary to human race. Religion and its doctrine is the intended code of conduct for human to reach self-realization. A very thought provoking statement is given in the Bible that –"Man that is born of woman hath but a little time to live – In the certain knowledge of the Resurrection and the life thereafter". If the meaning of this statement is loosely understood then it become clear that any person who understand and practice any religion of his choosing will come to know the meaning of his existence, otherwise he will have to go through the cycle of birth and death again and again. As we have seen in all this discussion till now, hell or pain, sorrow, disappointments along with all the miseries we experience do happens only because of our unconsciousness about our true nature or being.

What happens in meditation is our mind is by-passed as meddling faculty between our force of life and physical body. As we are conditioned to live through the interpretations of our mind that has vast reservoir of past memories and experiences, whatever experiences we go through become etched in our mind along with its interpretations. People erroneously take this bypassing of mind as end to its existence or destruction. But nothing of this kind happens, on the contrary when we willingly experience our pure being by way of meditation, our mind in the form of pure intelligence experience our natural state of existence for the first time and this experience alone changes the gestalt of our mind forever. Now it will become clear that we do not have to sacrifice anything in any way or destroy any of our faculty to save our self from any habit or attitude. Once the futility is understood by our pure intelligence or once the focus of our intelligence is properly directed, then any attitude, habit, preconception or misconception about other persons or materialistic things does not cause us sorrow and disappointment. And this is the reason why we are evolved into more intelligent species in this existence and to practice religion remains as the only way by which we can arrive at this conclusion.

There is one more popular misunderstanding that at the peak of meditation possibility of death increases. But we must understand the fundamental difference between natural death and death like feelings we experience at the end of meditation. In meditation we are willingly going into process and our self remains as witness, where we can come out of the meditation whenever we will like to stop, whereas in natural death even though we would like to stop the death from happening, the parting of the force of life as self from body happens, on which we do not have any control. In a nutshell meditation is mock death, at the most a trial run of the actual event, which make us aware beforehand about death and about what perishes and what remains.

Meditation is the process by which we experience that even though our mind exists but it remains at neutral state. And this existence can happen without the shell of the body to which our mind is attached. Meditation is the ultimate verification of our existence or being, irrespective of destruction of mind and body. This phenomenon of being without the covering of physical body is also known as Atman or pure consciousness. And this is the importance of the doctrine of each and every religion that make us aware that whatever happens our self remains forever. What perishes is not self but our body. The same is mentioned in Bhagwat Gita as; that no fire can burn, no water can drown and no weapon can cut is what we are. Arrival at this stage of being is called as realization of self or self-enlightenment.

For this process Mahaveer used the term as Kayotsarga – the words are from Sanskrit language and meaning is; Kaya for physical body and Utsarga means to part from or partition, partition from physical body. At the time of our natural death we have to remain present as witness only, to be witness to the ceasatition of the association of our self from the physical body.

As a part of indoctrination, Buddha used to ask his trainee monks to live in the crematorium for some time and to look at the bodies that are burned on the pyre. Those monks used to ask Buddha why you are sending us to these rituals, as we are still young and healthy. Buddha used to answer that; I would like to make you aware that what is burning is not you and it will help to break your association between your self and your body once forever. Similarly you are going to experience the same phenomenon at the time of meditation and will realize that you are not body but are something else.

Why death like experience is important by way of meditation is that the experience once gone through makes us totally aware and this experience makes us fearless about death. This kind of willful encounter with death with total awareness is also termed as rebirth or twice born. So, do we think that any person who has gone through this experience will again behave in childish manner or in the conditioned manner in which he used to behave?

There is a term as fallen monk or about monk fallen from grace. The meaning is, a person who at the peak of meditation turned back from going into death like experience. Water was boiling and was at such a state that within a degree would have been turned into vapor and evaporated, but at the last moment heat was turned off.

In our case where we are and the state we are in, we identify our self with our body. As we have no experience of our real being, all the pain, sorrow and illness happens to us. We experience hunger, thirst and exhaustion. Anger, greed, love, hate are treated as our emotions. Old age makes us old and then death also happens to us. As per Mahaveer this kind of thinking is nothing but pure illusion and the cause is our mental association with our physical body.

Mahaveer has to lay down six primary processes of austerity only because of our unconsciousness due to which we are extrovert. As we are very much acquainted with the outside, first six processes are about outside influences. But we have to understand that what is outside of us is also connected to our insides. Our understanding about our inner can be understood only when relationship between outside and inside is explained to us. This is the reason why all the pioneers have to start with outside as primary processes of austerity. But the followers only practice all the rituals which can be seen by others, with the erroneous notion that what they are doing is as per religion without being aware of its inner relationship. In such a case we will never reach anywhere only because even outside remain incomplete without understanding its relationship with the inner working. Even death is considered as surface happening; a living being till yesterday is no more today, but this happening does not make any difference in religious context. In religious parlance death like experience by way of meditation is considered as towering achievement and after this happening the occurrence of natural death is considered as just a formality to be gone through. To general people like us religion is of no value except mundane rituals, meetings, processions and festivals. We have to remember that even Vardhaman has to go through all the processes to become Mahaveer- the ultimate brave, Jesus become Christ and Gautama become Buddha, all these and other pioneers like these personalities died as we are going to die or all the ordinary people has died. Even though happening of death seems to be in the same manner in case of all the pioneers and us, the radical difference happens in its perception.

About religion, there is a general belief that it is to be practiced by aged people who have gone through all the facets of living and for whom nothing of any significance remained to be done, or for those who have lost every thing in spite of their efforts and gained nothing of significance. But what we have to understand is mighty and rich and the poor also dies in the same way and this is the reason that death is considered as a great leveler. In a sense, religion can be looked upon as art of living or science of how to encounter death.

Capacity to part form the body at the time of the death is nothing but acquired equanimity on our part to let go willingly, and at the same time understand with awareness as to what perishes and what remains as eternal. In a nutshell, the basic intention behind every religious doctrine and meditation as its integral part is to understand death in its proper perspective so that we can resolve all the dilemmas regarding ideal living before natural death occurs. And so going through this experience and after understanding what death is, the secret of the real and fulfilling living start to happen.

Mahaveer also considers one more mode of death that is suicide. According to him suicides happens due to extreme obsessions. Any person who is thinking to commit suicide is ready to live only if his conditions are met otherwise he is ready to end his life or die. A martyr is nothing but a person who has the same mindset as any other have, but only differentiating factor is his ideology or cause in which he totally believes and the same goads him towards the extreme and the same is greatly applauded by the masses that believe in the same ideas or cause.

Nowhere Mahaveer has made such a statement or behaved in such a manner that shows that he is against life or living in fulfilling and creative way. On the contrary all of his processes are tools of self-analysis to verify on our own and to check the authenticity of the statements made by him, after which we can also start to live in joyous and contented manner.

Those people who believe in God say that we are made in the image of God. Whatever I have is of God, my body is of God and still further states that God is mine. But in this circuitous route they arrive at the self at last. Is there existence of God or not is a mystery to us, but a person like Mahaveer better knows this phenomenon. Even his denial of God as Supreme Being is not of importance, only because he knows how in conditioned manner human behaves and how we are looking for scapegoats for our failures, in which we even curse God if our expectations are not fulfilled. And this is the reason Mahaveer denied God. For the first time in the history of human existence and the advent of religious movements, Mahaveer is the only pioneer who has removed the crutches even of God on whom we people may bank. This revolution has its own reasons; first to jolt the people out of their lethargy to be always dependent on others for fulfillment of every anticipations and expectations. Secondly even psychology accepts the vast potentials inherent in every human being, which Mahaveer expects should bloom to its full glory. For this reason he says that you are your self and your body is configuration of basic natural elements. Every thing is as it is. Every thing has its own nature and it always exists as its nature is. Associations happens but still they maintain their own nature and identity, similarly because of their specific nature they are useful and do remain in association till they are useful. The moment the intended use or reason of association is complete, they separate and become independent again.

The airs we inhale become ours but before that it was in other body and after exhalation it may enter into other body. Now if we could ask the air about its ownership, then the air will tell us that I am mine. In Christine burial the Father intones that dust to dust- ashes to ashes. What is the meaning of this statement? Air is associated with our body only at the time of breathing as all the elements of the body disintegrate at the time of cremation or burial, and merge and become one with the original elements from which they have come together to form the body. This is how associations happen and after completion of the purpose merges with the original. Then Mahaveer asks how our body becomes ours and how we become owners of the elements that are of different nature than ours. After partition from the physical body what remains is our pure self.

Appreciation of our pure self happens only after going through the experience by way of meditation. Theoretical understanding will remain just that, just understanding but not experience. So when ownership about basic elements becomes clear, then all the madness about owning the other stops. Then what remains is pure self, pure knowledge, just knowing. This state of being is called as self-realization, enlightenment, Adwaita – only one.

Scientific and materialistic developments are meant to be for the betterment of human existence and to maintain natural equilibrium, but now it seems that we are becoming more subjective and in the same proportions deviating from our self. Increase in difficulties, tensions, stress, mental disorders, general physical debilities, sorrow, unhappiness and hatred are on the upward move. The more we are accumulating materialistically the more we have to be on guard to save them. And the more ownership on the objects is to be exercised, the more we are going away from the self. If this is the price we have to pay for development, then somewhere something is very wrong, because hereinafter no one will dare to step out of his lair for the fear, that on the outside there is more danger lurking. In a sense, it seems that the more we are advancing in all types of technologies for the betterment of mankind then more fearful we are becoming.

Every kind of ownership starts with I and mine, and even our body that is going to be separated from us at the time of death is also treated as I am the body and body is mine. Basically it is the intention of every religion, that we are to be warned and checked in time so that if we are facing continual hardships and failures, then our ways of living are erroneous, but if we take pains to understand the doctrine laid down then there are chances that we can still mend our ways that will guarantee contented and joyous existence. So if this observation is to be accepted as truth then we have to also accept that we are not religious in proper sense. Then whatever we have achieved by our old ways is the cause of hell and it is of our own making. So it is to be understood at least once in a lifetime, that every religion is the scientific method, which will guide us to the destination that is intended to be ours from the start.

According to all the pioneers and Mahaveer, the joy of being happens only when we owe to no one or own nothing. Mahaveer's criteria about materialistic development and achievement are very simple and straightforward; things that increase our joy and happiness, creativity and awareness are good. But if this achievement is causing subjective retrogression then it is of no use to anyone. If we could get scientific and authentic reports of proportionate increase or decrease of mental and behavioral disorders after Mahaveer, then the ratio of sane versus insane will be staggering. Then either we have to change ourselves or change the definition of insanity.

On every step of life we have to choose from alternatives as to which course is proper or right and we decide about this alternative at the very last moment. It is not something like we have not faced similar circumstances before, but as most of the times we are unaware and as most of the actions happen due to our habit nature, we loose the opportunities of learning from our past experiences. This happens either due to our so-called image, which becomes barrier or our ego about self becomes barrier. Now if we accept the average life span of 70 years for any person, then he faces so many alternatives because of acquisition of his habits, assumptions and beliefs, that if he tries to take advantage of everyone of them then he has to live for 210 years to act upon the same. Do we think that this is normal way to exist? Because even inmates sentenced for life imprisonment are released after 14 years for good conduct, but we will not be released as the sentence is self created and imposed. Again the point to be stressed is very few people learn from their past mistakes. And all this happens because of our attitudes, desires, greed, anger, lust and what not which we have superimposed on our basic nature.

What we have to do is just turn the focus from outside to the inside. If at all something from the outside remains as pending or undone then we are going to leave it aside, as on its own it will pass away. For improvement in the self there is never late, we have to start as of now. Only thing we have to decide is whether our body is important or our self. We have to go into experiments without let or hindrance from others. If our experiments make us aware about the experiences pertaining to our body are pleasant and are worth pursuing, then we have to let go about our self and will fulfill all the demands of our body. Then we have to make it our sole aim. As this will be our conscious choice, then we are not going to be afraid of criticism done by others as no matter what, people criticize anyone in any situation or condition. To become decisive or to be assertive do not require guts but firm resolution is must. And this happens only when we believe in ourselves and in the cause in which we have unshakable faith. To be assured about our self and to have faith in our own capabilities and potentials, are the maintaining factors and driving force that makes positive and creative changes in our personality. We have become so lethargic and exist in so lukewarm conditions that we achieve very little worth mentioning. Because of our habit bound nature and conditioned behavior, we create so many alternatives that to choose from them any one of value or of true substance becomes impossible. This statement is not mere hypothesis but is consistently proven and tested fact, that the more choices people have then more confused they become, and as confusion causes increase in stress and anxiety, people generally stick to the old. To decide on our own and to go on the chosen way builds confidence in us and in such a case even if death ensues, then we are prepared with the understanding that this is part of the game. Living without any choice will make us free from all the tension and stress, and then we will say that now I am contented and happy and it is pleasure to be alive. This phenomenon of decision-making and to stick to it means to get out of any bondage and the same becomes purpose of our living and being. In austerity this state of being is called as standing on the threshold of getting out of quagmire of indecision. We exist in ambiguity when we think over any thought in half hearted manner then such thoughts start to weigh heavily on our mind, which in turn cause tug-of-war between conflicting emotions and causes mental turmoil. When positive thoughts surface then at the same time negative also make their presence felt and then we become mere helpless spectators. There are too many people who live aimlessly as drifters, the reason being they are living in the limbo of conflicting and opposite thoughts and emotions about which they do not know how to come out of or cope with. In such a case either they have to resolve on their own or become mentally disturbed.

So when we are thinking about death as ultimate parting or ultimate surgery, then are we going to be hesitant again? Because our hesitation is not going to avoid this ultimate act no matter what. Till any difficulty or problem is not faced squarely and analyzed, they remain as festering wound, which cause our existence to be pathological, aimless and purposeless.

Generally we live in beliefs, because of which we become conditioned from our birth. Any belief can be tested or broken by the sure way of meditation. In 1908 King of Kashi was to be operated upon. He was ready to undergo surgery but with the pre-condition that he is not going to be anesthetized. All the concerned doctors were apprehensive, but as the King was undergoing the process of awareness he suggested a way out. He asked the doctors that during the operation he is going to read Bhagwat Gita and at the same time doctors can operate upon him. Then the most amazing thing happened, the surgery was completely successful and the King does not felt any discomfort.

Afterwards doctors asked the King as to how this miracle happened; he told that in Bhagwat Gita when I read that the real self never dies nor any weapon can cut or kill it, then my belief that I am immortal become consolidated and reinforced. And so I do not fear about pain or death. This is the manner in which any belief can be broken, altered or reinforced.

Mahaveer has stated various phases or stages in which we can glimpse our self, of which some are discussed here; sometimes there are very powerful emotions or feelings in our mind when we are less aware of our body and such emotions are of love, joy, happiness, sympathy and compassion. So when we are in any of this feeling then either we can change our old beliefs or reinforce the old one that will make us more understanding in our nature. Generally at the time of sunrise we feel elated without any apparent reason, this happens because one of the basic element of our physical configuration being light, the same light corresponds with the rising sun and we feel that we are suffused with the same glow. On the contrary at the sunset some people of delicate nature feel depressed, the reason behind this depression is the reverse cause of the effect as mentioned in above incidence where the person experiences as if he is suffocating. Water present in the sea and water as integral part of our body contains more or less the same ingredients. Sitting on the seashore we experience profound tranquility just looking at the flowing water, and rise and ebb of the sea. The reason, which is scientifically proven, is water in our body corresponds with the seawater. People of somewhat delicate nature and people, who are facing some psychological maladies, show signs of unease or aggravation of symptoms on full moon nights or on new moon nights. And the same happen in case of sea also; character of its tide and ebb also gets affected due to full moon or absence of the same. Reason behind these changes happen due to effect of the moon on gravitational force of the earth and water present in sea as well as in human starts to flow in accelerated or decelerated manner. And this change in the flow is the reason that disturbed people become more disturbed or gloomy. The same feelings of peacefulness, tranquility and contentedness can be experienced when we are aimlessly wandering in the forest. Seemingly disorderly growth of trees, foliages and vines make us contented only because we remain in the proximity of the nature at its very basic form and this corresponds with our basic nature. All these feelings and emotions we experience at the proximity of natural elements is nothing but inherent affinity of the elements present in our body, which corresponds to the natural elements. When encounter with elemental factors make us sanguine and contented then the same sagacity is to be considered as transition period when we can loosen our association with our gross body or the same can be used to alter our beliefs or assumptions that we think to be troublesome.

For the purpose of deep meditation, period between midnight to early morning is treated as the ideal period. The reason being, position of the sun and its direct effect on our surrounding is at its lowest, which cause total silence in the atmosphere. This total silence and lack of solar stimulation lowers the resistance of our body also and then to concentrate in witnessing manner on our mind becomes easier.

Basically all the states of transition are nothing but middle ground or neutral states, where we are in neither state but are nearer to our real self. According to Mahaveer's Jaini doctrine and all the Hindu religious doctrines, every living being is in the process of evolution. The ultimate destiny of every living being is to reach self-realization and enlightenment. All the cultures accept the existence of God as Supreme Being, so when the living being attains self- realization, the realized self merges with the supreme being i.e. God or Over Self. At this stage duality ceases to exist as our self merges with that of the God. But according to Mahaveer as there is no God, by doing efforts in the manner prescribed by the way of austerity we on our own can gain awareness and then can shed the load of acquired habits, assumptions and beliefs. And then along the way our self starts to integrate and this total integration causes cessation of duality. Cessation of the duality by the grace of God and cessation acquired on our own is one and the same achievement. Mahaveer calls this integrated self as Godliness. Ultimately God as Supreme Being or pure self as Supreme Self, remain as one and only.

At the end of twelfth process of austerity we are going to look at the other part of the formula i.e. Religion is sacred, but which religion? The answer given by Mahaveer is; Ahimsa (Non violence) Sayyam (Tranquility) and Tapa (Austerity) is the first part, and the second part is; Those we come into being by the way of religious austerity, even God bows in front of him. This statement made by Mahaveer is very revolutionary, bold and startling.

According to Vedic doctrine, it is believed that we are mere mortals who have to bow or prostrate in front of the God. But as per Mahaveer there is nothing above or below the human. Humans has such potentials that he can elevate the self to such an extent that he will be above God and with the same potentials he can degrade himself to such an extent that even animals can be above human.

It is the fundamental belief of all the religions and so called Jaini follower also believe that by good deeds as Punya, we will go to heaven and by degrading our self we will be in hell. But as Mahaveer's way is moderate or middle way, for which a synonymous word Samyak is used that means neither extreme, even Mahaveer will not suggest exclusive good deeds and behavior to achieve heaven. The reason is when we choose any one as superior to the other that we have rejected as inferior is the indication that we are still not tranquil enough and further even if we select anything its opposite remains, even if we accept the same or not. To get out of selection and rejection, good or bad, Mahaveer suggests a novel bypass that those who elevate the self above heaven and hell becomes free forever. This state of total freedom is termed as enlightened state or Moksha, after which the self does not have to go into cycle of birth and death. Reaching at this stage is the state of Siddha.

CHAPTER 19

RELIGION: THE ONLY SOLACE

It is opinion of many thinkers that death is the reason because of which advent of religion happened and its practice is advised to humans because death happens to humans only.

Along with us other animates also die, but happening of this phenomenon is considered as much more significant by humans due to certain reasons. Other animates accept death as natural end of the living, but we humans due to inherent qualities like superior intelligence and awareness about self than other animates, create more habits, assume more and believes in anything than intended natural limits set for us. In reality these distinguishing qualities should have to be a redeeming quality for human's further evolution but this very rarely happens. With our increased assumptions and beliefs we start to expect or anticipate more than possible from the total existence with our otherwise limited capability and potentials. Similarly to experience the anticipated or expected we have to be alive, but when we know that death is certain and with it the certainty of loosing our body as experiencing medium also dawns on us, then trepidation, fear and disappointment about death start to increase. Furthermore death like experience leaves very faint impression on the psych of other animates, only because they have very limited intelligence and less awareness than humans. And this is the reason why human being has to practice religion but not the other animates.

We human being try to forget about death and have erected various safeguards to escape from dying. But irrespective of all the safeguards and means at our disposal, somewhere in the remotest recess of our mind we know that death is inevitable. Certainty of death and deep-rooted belief of it's happening, is the basic reason we experience death.

The moment death becomes certainty then religion comes into being. Similarly this certainty cause changes in the meaning of life and living as such. But in most of the cases our all the desires, attitudes and beliefs come under scrutiny and are subjected to reconsideration and some of them cease to exist. To understand and accept death is one thing but the real reason that causes more stress and tension seems to be uncertainty about its happening, as to will it happen now, on the next day or in near future.

To escape or get away from this tension, we create some buffers as beliefs that absorb the uncertainty for time being. Then at least for some time we accept death with the knowledge that every one is going to die, but again we do not include our self in every one. We remain as spectators in the death of others with the belief that we are going to be spectators forever. But when death happens in our immediate family or when we include our self in others who are going to die, then this shock is felt at our very core. And at this stage all the buffers, which we have erected, crumple down.

What happened in case of Buddha happens to very few of us. When Buddha asked his chariot driver that do all the people die, and got the answer in affirmative, this confirmation become the cause for Buddha to renounce the so-called life.

In religious context; when our death is perceived as certainty then we start to look for the answer to an important question as to who I am? Why I have taken birth? And in the quest for self-discovery, the inevitability of death losses its meaning and significance.

Potentials of our mind to believe and assume are infinite. Similarly due to its characteristic nature to accept only immediate and finite, uncertainty about happening of anything and as to what will happen in future are the reasons buffers are created. Faculty of perception of our mind is not as well developed as we think; if we are walking with a candle in darkness we can only see upto limited distance ahead of us, but what is beyond the illuminated area causes doubt and trepidation, which in turn erect buffers. Erection of buffers happens to safeguard our psyche from sudden shock as well as to validate our beliefs and assumptions on which we are banking or dependent upon.

To break the buffer regarding death can happen in two ways; either we accept the death as inevitable, then as to when it will happen becomes immaterial or we have to imagine about the experience of the others who are dying. When this phenomenon is understood in its entirety, then our own perceptions about our mortality becomes clear. The last resort to understand what death is is to go into deep meditation, which will make us well acquainted with deathlike experience, after which actual death remains as mere formality.

In a sense religion is nothing but a scientific way to understand and experience death in proper perspective after which living in true sense starts. Any person is treated as religious person only when he accepts his death. Similarly those who accept death but are not actively practicing any known religion are also considered as religious and the way of their being is accepted as unique way of new but unknown religion.

Acceptance of the hypothesis, that our soul is immortal is also one of the buffers to absorb the shock of inevitability of death. This belief has no substance or validity till we have experienced the immortality of our soul by our own experience, so until our belief becomes fact our old belief will remain as mere belief. We people seek assurance from all the sacred books that our soul is immortal and there is life after death. But again we forget to understand that what the writer has wrote down is his own experience, at the most his way of arriving at the conclusion can be advantageous to us to understand and experience whether the same also happen to us also. But it is collective belief of all of us that when any book is accepted as sacred, we do not verify its authenticity on our own but follow the same as truth. Again this phenomenon happens only because we are very lazy and expect others to give readymade solutions to all our problems. We want to believe in what our forefathers used to believe without any curiosity or inquisitiveness as this belief frees us from individual efforts. Why we want to believe about anything concerning death and our immortality after our death is, we are very much attached to our physical body and do not experiment whether we remain in any other form even after death. And to this kind of beliefs and assumption we attach a label of priceless traditions and precious culture. But to Mahaveer all these beliefs are nothing but buffer to camouflage our uncertainties and fears about death and dying.

Any religion and its doctrine will work for us if we are ready to go through the processes, gain awareness and change wherever it is necessary. When life or living as dynamic flow is understood as birth, aging and death, then religion and its practice takes the meaning as the lighthouse that shows the path of joyous existence. Everything in this existence is ever changing; even our aging is the result of dynamic flow that starts at the time of birth and ends by our death. We never experience the total transformation of our being in integrated manner but divide and look at birth on one end and death on the other end, as our existence. But we forget that the happening between birth and death is the real living. So when we understand and accept that to live in real sense happens only when we exist in integrated manner then the manner in which we change happens due to religion or to live in integrated manner is to be religious.

Our attitude to divide and experience happens because total or integrated picture is generally not perceived as pleasant to look at. In division of joy and sorrow, love and hate, greed and sacrifice and health and illness become manageable; but when the same is looked at in its entirety then the integrated picture seems to be frustrating, trivial and painful, where nothing seems to be desirable or worth pursuing. We want to live without death, have joy without sorrow, but as everything exist with the opposite then our acceptance of the any one causes the presence of the opposite also. A river at its source is the same river till it reaches ocean. River Ganga at its source in Himalayas looks so pristine, the same looks like a mischievous child while flowing down the mountain, but the same Ganga flowing by Kashi and Banares seems to be overflowing sewer. Now which Ganga is true for us? In reality the flow is continuous, what starts in Himalayas and ends in ocean is one and the same. It is our sectional or divided viewing which make the whole picture bearable and convenient. But what we do not understand is that our attitude of division and perceptions create fallacies. We create all the fallacies knowingly or unknowingly, and this mainly happens due to our selective nature and not being aware that as we are part of the existence then its dynamic flow causes changes. No matter what but everything changes and this truth causes inconvenience to live with. In our case also we do not want to change as we are conditioned since long and as we are used to live by the dictates of our habits and beliefs.

Dynamic flow of our existence not only changes our overall appearance but our assumptions, beliefs and expectations also keep on changing. Intensity of our emotions like faith, love, sympathy, compassion, friendship as well as hatred also keeps on changing. We expect our partner, parents and children should have same degree of faith and love about us, but again this very rarely happens. The reason is the same dynamic force of the existence of which all of us are part and parcel. Nature of thoughts, intensity of emotions and feelings, beliefs and assumptions about others and us do not remain constant but keep on changing. So if we become aware about these changes then we remain contented but if we expect the same forever then we are bound to become unhappy. For this phenomenon we have coined a proverb that appearances can be deceptive. But this is not so because outward appearance may take some time to change but emotional make-up goes on changing forever. Then are we to consider that humans are fickle by nature? But again this is not so, as certain emotions remain as they originally are but its intensity keeps changing, which creates the basic personality of the person. Basic reason behind the change of intensity happens because of our anticipations and expectations; either they increase if we are reciprocated more than anticipated or decrease if we are not reciprocated as per our expectations. Radical change happens only when totally diverse action or reaction happens that is not anticipated or expected. If we look at all the emotions we experience and their constant oscillation and as the result become cynical, then contemplative meditation is the best remedy where we will get most of the answers. But this will happen only when we are ready to accept that the way I am is the same way others are, what I feel the others also feel. So if this fact is understood and accepted by us then we may change and this change will help us become more aware and mature.

The way, in which we live, live in anticipatory and expectant manner. Our forefathers, our father, mother, spouse and all the relatives expect something from us and we also expect the same from others. All of us try to fulfill all the expectations and anticipation made on us and vice versa. And in this struggle we literary spend all our life, but most of the time we realize that the degree of satisfaction we expect in return is not even at par. Everyone expect more from the other with the belief that what we are giving is always more than what we are getting. The intention behind this elaboration is not to belittle human relationships, which in certain instances is more than intimate. But to understand the monumental misunderstanding on our part that it is impossible to fulfill everyone's expectations at all the time. The same happens when we try to achieve something impossible, in our everyday life we say that nothing is impossible if we take stock of our potentials and circumstances, then think over it and do more efforts in the right direction so that impossible becomes possible. In fact very rarely such miracles happen but for the same we have to pay very steep price. In religious context, impossible means that which will never happen as it is not in the nature of the existence. At the most we will experience an illusion that with some more efforts impossible is going to happen.

About stability we have some notions, beliefs and thoughts. We do not want to face many changes because of which we also have to change. Changes in environment, surrounding, people, society and culture make us uneasy because to interact with them we have to change and to change means we have to alter, improvise or totally discard our old routine about which we have become assured. It is a psychological fact that even though we are not getting anything worthwhile from our set routine, we do not want to change the old routine because any routine creates security and stability, and setting the new routine causes uncertainty about outcomes. To gain stability when we have to practice religion then this do not mean that we have to become conditioned in rigid manner, but intention behind the whole process is to arrive at an understanding that in ever changing existence, what is happening is going to happen as it is the law of nature or existence. As every thing has its own nature, the same applies to human also. To be in our own nature is called as religious. Then our ever changing existence and surrounding becomes fact and this awareness frees us from needless tensions and stresses. In the summer afternoon we have to take shelter under a tree to escape from the sun. But as the time passes the shadow of the tree shifts and we have to again face the heat of the sun. Then to save ourselves from the heat either we have to close our eyes and pretend that we are still under the shadow or shift our position according to shifting shadow. In this incidence the sun and its heat is reality, the tree and its shadow is also reality, but our closing of eyes is creation of illusion because of which we have to face the heat. In this incidence to be religious is to understand that what is happening is going to happen, but what we have to do is assess and choose from the alternatives that whether we can change the situation then we have to change it, or if it not possible then we are going to change ourselves but if any of the options is not available then we have to bare the situation.

When we understand that as existence is dynamic flow and as we are also the part of this existence and are not stationary, so we are also changing as everything is ever changing, then this realization becomes fact and restores peace. As this is not belief but fact, its refusal or acceptance become immaterial but this understanding saves us from needless struggle. There is no possibility of stability in dynamic force of existence as there is no chance to hold our position in the fast flowing river. To maintain our balance we have to struggle forever. In such a case expectation from other as well as our assurance to the other about anything become meaningless. And acceptance of this understanding is known as religion.

Human relationship becomes satisfactory and enduring to both the parties only when it is based on mutual understanding. Ownership based on erroneous understanding between mother and child, and between child and his wife, cause great miseries to all concerned. The reason being, what can be expected and given by the mother and the same from the wife, are different things. But when both try for the exclusive attention with the intention of sole ownership then it becomes the cause of rivalry. A statement made by Freud, that human being could not be happy ever, is half-truth in the sense that he has not considered the element and importance of religion in the existence of human.

We hope for happiness and joy, only because in our limited experience we have experienced nothing but sorrow and disappointments. Hope is the assurance for future, which still has to happen, but which is nothing but a buffer to absorb current sorrow. As to live in fulfilling manner is to live in present. Most of the time hope becomes mirage, and manifestation of hoped for may or may not happen. To Mahaveer our unconscious existence is the reason that hopes are created and as its manifestation is going to happen in future, about which no one is sure then they are considered as mirage.

Freud stated that expectations of human are impossible to fulfill; if what is expected happens every time, then now or later we will be bored and may feel revulsion about our existence. But if anticipated does not happen then we become unhappy. So in both the cases we are unhappy. Mahaveer states that to be religious is the mainstay in the dynamic flow of existence, and to be in self or to be in our original nature is religion.

All the doctrines of all the religions are trying to point at the same way i.e. realization of the self. This is the way by which Mahaveer, Buddha, Jesus, Mohammad and Krishna reached and by the same we may also reach. At our core is our own nature and where nothing ever changes. To remain at our core or to encounter our core means we have arrived at our destination then we do not have to face any disappointments as well as impossible desires. We are not aware or we do not know but to encounter our core is to face our nature at its basic and when this phenomenon happens then we become wise in true sense. Then the mad quest to achieve anything looses the meaning and we become aware that what is to be achieved is already with us.

CHAPTER 20

ABOUT RELIGION AND TRUTH

To die is very personal experience. To observe while any one is passing away may happen due to curiosity but with some trepidation. But if the other is struggling to remain alive then the curiosity turns into fear of unknown. Loosely defined, fear of unknown is the direct outcome of emotion of fear where our capacity to imagine the outcome falls short of the mark.

All encompassing emotion of love and death are compared as equal in experience. Unless and until we are ready to totally let go or merge in the object of our love, all encompassing love do not manifest. In consummate love our identity do not remain separate from the other as only the other remains. The same happens at the time of death; only self remains and any association with the body ceases to exist. The willingness to experience the cessation of the association with our self or to let go of the self, is the basic characteristic because of which a person in true love loose the fear of death.

In Hindu religion, total theosophical and emotional shift towards Master as God or Guru happens by the way of prayer and faith, which are pre-requisite of an acolyte or the follower. And this type of surrender is called as the death of the acolyte or follower, in the sense that his self do not remain as his, his will is totally surrendered to the master in the faith that whatever has to happen to me is dependent on the will of the master, and the acolyte resolves that herein after the master is going to shape my being as I have accepted him as my sole benefactor.

How do we know that as human we have realized our full

potentials? When we sow a seed, it sprouts and starts to grow in stages towards a full-blown tree. Manifestation of leaves, branches, flowers or fruits of the anticipated quality is the ultimate test, which shows that the tree is fully developed. Any shortcoming in the intended or anticipated form of the tree is considered as short of total realization or being of the tree. The same is applicable to human being when full realization of the inherent potentials does not happen. In reality total realization should happen, but somewhere the human deviates and the onward progress halts.

According to Mahaveer the way in which we live is the way in which we also die. If our existence till the time of our death is of peaceful nature, then we meet our death in the same manner, which become cause of celebration. On the other hand if we exist in violent manner till our death, then our death happens in violent manner. There are saying that, those who wield the sword will die by the sword or as you sow so shall you reap. The meaning is very simple; the manner in which we live is the manner in which we die.

Aggressive way of living becomes cause of much tearing and rending at the time of death for the simple reason, that in death we are going to loose the instrument i.e. our body, which was the means through which we were capable to be aggressive. Any person nurturing attitudes of violence, hatred, greed and ill will towards other experiences death as painful. Meeting death in tranquil state denotes the fulfilled existence till the happening of partition of the self from the body. In such a case death is treated as inherent process of living. Facing death in cowering or unconscious manner is like unread book to be returned to the library on the date of expiry. In this state, the seed and its potentials remain dormant or without realization.

Idiocies or foolishness do not happen due to ignorance, but so called knowledgeable behave in the manner of idiots. We do not call an erring child as idiot because the child is innocent in the sense he is still fresh and cannot differentiate between good or bad. Idiot is the person who knows what will happen and still behave knowingly, even though he has gone through the same exercise with the same results in past. The reason behind this kind of behavior happens due to our ego. To put our hand in fire knowing that fire burns happens to show the others how brave or fearless we are and how superior we are than others. This behavior and thought behind is called as idiocy. General behavior of the people happens as per the prevailing norms of the immediate society. But in this manner there is no novelty and we do not stand out as someone special. To break this mold and to show that we are someone to be noted, people behave in bizarre manner. This behavior inflates their ego and such people try to become exception to the rule.

What do people achieve who climb Everest, where oxygen is scarce, climatic conditions are of extreme nature, the way upward is treacherous and slippery and where a wrong step is guarantees instant death. What they are trying to prove is that they are somewhat special. They challenge us to do the same thing. This behavior is nothing but a very subtle form of boasting, which happens due to inflated ego. To top this kind of behavior, they are acclaimed and are given medals in recognizance of their bravery. As this kind of conduct is not possible to everyone then we have to accept him or her as superior to us. Then shall we award the same medals to the mountain goats that behave in this manner every day, and reach such heights where no human has reached as yet? Psychology accepts this kind of behavior on the part of human, as a desire or drive to do something different than the masses to show that human potentials are boundless. The same desire or drive is treated as search of unknown in religion, which is nothing but search of self.

People like to live dangerously or act in daring manner for the reason that they become bored due to routine and secondly to showoff to others that they are different than the average. But in all of this conduct appeasement of ego remain as the basic motive. At the same that such people are those who crave attention of the others, which is lacking in their otherwise mundane existence.

In every day routine we do not have to exert much energy or strength. In such a case if the excess energy is not used then the residual energy makes us heavy and restless. As most of us do not know or understand as how to be creative, then this excess energy turns into bizarre or odd behavior or become destructive. To Mahaveer cause of idiotic behavior happens mainly because of our ego.

In traditional religious following also we behave in senseless manner. But as mentioned at the start of this discussion, any following without understanding of significance of the concept in proper perspective causes distortion of the concept. It is mentioned that in total of 12 years of austerity Mahaveer had taken food on 365 occasions only, the average comes down to once in every 11 days. This information is inferred as that for 10 days Mahaveer used to fast. But in reality he was so immersed in meditation that he was not aware about the surrounding as well as about his body and its hunger.

People choose treacherous and hard ways, as well as most inopportune circumstances where we have to struggle harder and where chances of success are minimum. This phenomenon does not happen due to ignorance but knowingly. The reason being our ego, which goad us to deviate so that the ego can be satisfied and we can stand out as someone special then the masses. At the same time if there is more resistance from the outside then we have to exert more energy to complete the task and here we use the residual energy which otherwise make us restless. According to Mahaveer more egoistic a person then more idiots he is. To win at any cost is the mindset of the egoistic person, and so if there are more difficulties to complete the task then the task is worth doing which is perceived as livening experience.

Mahaveer and all the pioneers are of the opinion that to exist in our basic nature is the easiest in this existence. By nature fire is hot, water does flow but wherever its flow is interrupted, then it maintains its level. At the same time water by nature is cool. These are the basic characteristics as well as nature of the water. With the same token human are meant to remain in their basic nature. But again due to the conditioning we form habits, which are superimposed on our basic nature and this imposition of the habit in our nature is the cause of our deviation from the basic nature. As human we should be loving, compassionate and sympathetic not only with other human but with all the animate and inanimate who exist in this existence.

A very simple definition of the religion is to exist in our self or to exist as per our basic nature. But even in religious practice the more intricate the process becomes then more attractive it felt. All the mysterious rituals and difficulties in its following basically attract people. Then most adapt person become religious leader and start to control the naïve masses. Then to maintain the position of leadership bizarre behavior like to stand naked, standing indefinitely or to stand on one leg for extended periods, abnormal fasting, walking on the burning coals, laying down on the bed of nails, self-flagellation etc. also starts. Since long ritualistic behavior is believed to be of religious nature or is perceived as practice of religion. And further, this type of behavior is sanctioned by our constitution as an individual right.

To Mahaveer intelligent people are those who understand the reason behind any process or thought, compare the same with the prevailing circumstances and then act. But those to whom Mahaveer term as idiots are so-called learned, who draw inferences, which are to their liking or are perceived as tailor-made to their behavior. These inferences are not related to any religion or to any doctrine, but are taken as a sanction to camouflage very personal motives.

In passing, reference to the now-a-days mass medium as television and its effect on general populace is to be mentioned. Let us leave aside average serials, but the serials of epic nature in which characters from ancient incidences in reference to various religions are shown, the presentation happens in such a distorted manner that average people take the depiction as true or factual. Similarly at the end of the serial the books referred to are listed and it is also mentioned that fabrication of the incidences is based on the text of the same books. Then such books become sacred and are followed verbatim, which most of the times causes in the mind of viewers erroneous assumptions and beliefs. Some examples of distortion of the concepts do show that the character do not eat anything but is living on the air only, standing all the time in every season, getting out of a palatial mansion and living in a straw-hut and all of this is nothing but the other extreme, and this extremity is called as sacrifice. People of average awareness and intelligence get influenced by this humbug, and become more unhappy and disenchanted about life than before. It should be understood once forever that hunger, thirst, sleep etc. are all the natural processes and are meant for betterment of our being, but their suppression with erroneous beliefs will make us more pathetic by which nothing creative will ever happen.

Any fallacy on our part could not stand on its own so we have to strengthen and spice it up with more such stories. The chain thus created is the reason behind our restrained behavior, otherwise an accidental wrong move by us and we get exposed as hypocrite. To create fallacies without any reason and then to behave in restrained manner to cover them causes escalation in further tensions and stress on our mind and such behavior becomes cause of division of our mind. Divided mind due to any reason directly reduces our mental peace and we may have to face various psychological problems in future.

Along with us everyone is desirous to be acquainted with truth and this quest for truth goes on. To think, talk, act and behave in truthful manner has a distinct advantage; we do not have to remember what we have talked as what we are doing corresponds with our talk. In such a case our mind remains calm and tranquil but escapes from the burden various fallacies. Similarly truth about anything stands on its own.

We say that we have experienced the power of truth and its effects on our mind and behavior. But we fail to behave in the consistent truthful manner only because of our self-image and ego. To show what we are not or to pretend what we are, we behave in false manner and to continue the sa ne pretension we have to pile the basic fallacy with other fallacies. Application of fallacy also happens due to fear of criticism. But at the same time we forget that the way in which we are behaving, the other is also behaving in the same manner. And this mutual pattern of behavior is the foundation on which the society exists. In our fallacy we expect to get genuine response from the other and in absence of which we get hurt and disenchanted. Continuous feeling of hurt, disappointment and disenchantment is the main reason because of which people start to behave in abnormal fashion. Division between what we call as normal and abnormal is very vague. To save ourselves from mental anguish and to maintain the balance of normalcy we move ahead and step back again and again. But we consider this type of behavior as practical way of living, but in reality this is the vicious circle from which we very rarely come out.

This precarious balancing acts of ours as actual living breaks to pieces when death becomes imminent. Then we realize that till now what we have thought about life and living was in reality a wasteful existence, and we have achieved nothing of substance. We will never be remembered as a person who has achieved something significant. Realization of wastage of our potentials frustrates us to such an extent that we become depressed. To Mahaveer this type of living is non-religious existence. To bolster our ego and our image we become non-religious.

Mahaveer says that comparison with other and to compete with the other happens due to our ego. As each one of us is unique with inherent potentials, achievements of any two people cannot be evaluated in satisfactory manner. To compare and compete we have to behave outside of our potentials, but if we have no capacity to complete the task then we experience frustration. Basic reason behind comparison and competition seems as no one is happy with his self and has no faith in him self. In such a case we do not face our self but rather we pitch our potential against the other. In the opinion of Mahaveer, ignorance is not the catalyst but intention is. Ignorance can be eradicated by way of awareness and learning from past experiences. But with the intention to win at any cost, we go with both eyes wide open as well as with total disregard to our potentials.

Freud says that humans do not act after due deliberation, but most of the acts happen due to subconscious mind. According to Freud, to be human is to err and there is very little we can do about it. In this statement there is some truth but it is not complete truth. Partial truths are potentially more dangerous for those who are looking for an easy way out for their irresponsible behavior. At the same time when we start to accept these partial truths as whole truth, then we become resigned and helpless due to belief, that as we are basically unconscious there is very little in our power to change. Mahaveer denied existence of the God for various reasons, but one prominent reason being acceptance of the concept that the God is ultimate creator. Because if God is accepted as the ultimate creator, then whatever man proposes, but if the proposed do not corresponds with the tenets of the

God, then it will be disposed off. Similarly if God has created the man as puppets with all the desires and attitudes, then do we mortals have power to challenge the supreme creator? Firm belief that it is God's will that even though human should have all the desires & attitudes but very few are going to be fulfilled, then this belief caused untold miseries to humans, and made him accept his present predicament helplessly and with resignation that he has to be as he is, as his being is predestined so on his own he can not change anything.

Mahaveer is of the opinion that every one of us is responsible to our self and there is no one who is going to help us. So if we have to be happy and joyous then we have to change our self in positive and creative manner with our own efforts. And so to make desired changes in ourselves we have to become religious and become aware as to how this existence functions and how we have to adopt our self in relation to functioning of this existence. Only then we can be masters of our destiny and will achieve in substantial manner.

Mahaveer was aware about psychology of human 2500 years back; that whatever support we are given then due to our attitudes we would cling to the support. Similarly due to the same acquired attitudes we are bound to walk with the help of crutches even though we have potentials to walk on our own. Due to our conditioning and nature we hold and cling to others as if they are responsible for our follies, our acts and our behavior. This blaming the other is the main characteristic feature of egoistic mind of human in which even God is not spared, as God also remains as the other. In this regard Mahaveer seems to be more practical because of his understanding about human psychology.

Mahaveer says you are responsible only upto your self; however you are, good or bad is of your own doing. There is no superior court above you where you can plead your case. You yourself is your judge, jury and counsel, so if at all you have to plead then plead in front of your self, and then to acquit or to punish is upto you. With the understanding of this concept the division of our mind automatically stops and much coveted integrated personality come into being. There is no one to be blamed, not even God, because all of us are living with the same emotions, expectations and thoughts, albeit with the degree of intensity and perception. So whatever changes are to be made they have to be made in our self.

Most of the Hindu religions are of the same opinion regarding concept of God and its existence, in the sense that they accept that God is neutral, formless and without substance. For the same concept the Veda's uses a word as Nirguna and Nirakara, the word Nirguna means the God is beyond any merits and the devotee has freedom to perceive and attach the merits to the God. The word Nirakara means the God is formless, and again the devotee has freedom to create the image as per his choice and imagination. The belief that whatever we send towards it the same comes back to us; if we love God then love comes to us. Now let us look at the total nature of this existence as the basis of creation; there are certain laws and rules of this nature out of which nothing ever happens. The basic rule of our nature is; to every action there happens corresponding reaction. Any reaction happens only when action happens in correspondence with the inherent laws of nature; due to heat of sun water turns into vapor, which in turn becomes cloud and when this condensed cloud comes into contact with the cool air and lighting from the atmosphere, then falls down as rain. In this happening, water is natural element and sun is also a natural element. When the Sun cause transformation of water then rain falls, which is reaction to the action of evaporation of the water. Our not knowing laws of nature or basic laws of physics, and when the ways of happening are perceived as unpredictable, then the happening is termed as act of God or of Supreme Being. The same happens in human element. Action happens by and due to us, but we forget that every action has corresponding reaction. But as far as human is concerned, every action do not cause corresponding reaction for the reason that, if the other human is of the same mental makeup as we are then expected reaction happens but if the perceptions of the other are more developed or under developed than us, then happening of reaction may be different than expected or anticipated. For this matter let us leave the God aside and let us verify the same action-reaction theory on very basic level, we have to hold a piece of bread and will call a stray dog, then if the dog is hungry it will come to us but if it is not hungry then it will ignore us. As mentioned before, except human every animate exists as per his inherent nature, and act or react to any external stimulation only at that time when the action or reaction is perceived as necessary for its being.

Only we humans because of our conditioning, formation of our conditioned nature and ego anticipate many things. But when all the others are of the same nature and are as conditioned and habit formed, then the same action-reaction theory does not happen in corresponding proportions. Some may react in corresponding manner, others may do not react at all and still some others may react in such a manner that this kind of reaction was not at all expected. In such circumstances who is responsible? Basically our desires and attitudes goad us to act, but when anticipated reaction does not happen then we become unhappy and feel disappointed. Now to whom we are going to blame? What Krishna mentioned in Bhagwat Gita is the same as what mentioned by Mahaveer; *you can act and are master of your acts, but what will come back, in which form it will come back and when it will come back is beyond your power and expectations. So whatever happens due to your action, its reaction is to be accepted.* For those who believe in God, the same thing happens when God is understood and accepted as neutral. Its being is like a sounding board, whatever is sent to it as act is reciprocated by counteract.

So for the time being let us be honest and accept that if the superior intelligence is the priceless gift from the God, then the way in which we humans are behaving and using the same is wasted gift, which is further cause of despair even to the God because the way in which we human are behaving is nothing superior.

When Darwin put down the theory that humans are direct descendents of monkey and this happened due to process of evolution; monkeys must have uttered a sigh of relief in declaring that now human has no right to criticize us. The antics of humans are more bizarre compared to monkey. But Darwin's theory was the cause of despair to human, because till then human were of the belief that they were made in the image of God.

The warnings, jitters or unease we feel before any act we are going to initiate is the indication that our basic core is not in agreement with the intended action. This feeling or experiences of these kinds of feelings, is the sign that irrespective of these jitters or unease if we intend to go through the act then what we expect to happen is not going to happen as we anticipate but we will experience sorrow or disappointment. We label this phenomenon as our sixth sense or control of our conscious mind over our unconscious mind that restrain us from behaving in the intended manner. Mahaveer says that whether we are aware or not, but our basic nature or our core always intervenes if the intended act or behavior is not compatible to us or in correspondence with our basic nature. But as we are habit bound and conditioned, we do not pay due attention to the feelings of unease or jitters. Similarly whatever takes form from within us by way of thought or emotion, and when the same passes through our mind, then our mind influences the thought or emotion with its collective data i.e. memory or Smriti, so that whatever comes out come out in altered form. That whatever starts as the truth from our core and when the same passes through our mind then the initial becomes contaminated and may comes out as fallacy. Our pure nature or core or being always remain integrated. Discord in our personality or abnormalities in behavior happen due to clashes of our emotions or thoughts and manifestation of these emotions are related to our attitudes and habits, which directly affect our core being. All the thoughts and emotions of ours are the forces, which induces us towards action. If our emotions are not in correspondence with our basic nature, then mental turmoil happens. If this mental turmoil goes on for extended period of time or if the same is not analyzed by us with the intention of purging the mind from the constant pressure, then chemical changes in the brain sets in, which is the cause of mental and behavioral abnormalities. As our basic nature is not subject to change then we have to change our habits and attitudes to arrive at the accord of our original being. As psychology is the science of study of the human mind then psychotherapy is the way to mold, alter or change the habits and attitudes of the person under advisement as per his basic nature. Awareness gained by way of religion is the remedy for self-analysis that increases the understanding about mind and its way of functioning.

Cause of formation of human relationship happens due to compatibility between basic natures of two or more humans. Development of intimacies in any relationship happens only when both the parties perceive and experience that anticipations and expectations are going to be fulfilled in direct proportion to the demands made. Whether these intimacies remain constant in intensity depends on various aspects, but primary or basic aspect remains as one and that is dynamic force or flow of the existence. So, as we are part of whole existence and as total existence is ever changing then consistency in human thought and emotion also change, and this change may manifest in the form of increased or decreased intensity or it may totally wither away. Appearance of any person may not change in perceptible manner but make-up of his beliefs, assumptions, thoughts and emotions changes with passage of time and due to the same values also change. Understanding that these changes are bound to take place and to know that the cause is dynamic force and flow of our existence but not the person with whom we are intimate, will help us towards tranquility and stop us from blaming others and becoming depressed. Awareness of this nature helps us to become more mature person. Those people who believe in God and believe in their faith in steadfast manner may sometimes feel that they are losing their faith. In this case also the dynamic force of existence causes oscillation in the intensity of faith, but due to which if we think that the God is rejecting or deserting us then the assumption is quite erroneous. In this case also we have to understand that it is not God that is changing, but it is we who are changing.

In all these changes there do not seems to be any firm anchor to which we may hold as constant and which may never change. But in this regards Mahaveer says that our self is the only anchor, which never changes, and to validate its truancy all the religions have come into being and its doctrines are the blueprints that will help us to realize the same.

Honesty in thought and honesty in deeds is deemed to be a virtue in human that makes our personality an integrated personality. If we behave in dishonest manner in relation to others then there is a possibility that others may suffer or not, similarly if the other is more intelligent than us then chances of his suffering may not happen at all. But it is to be appreciated that whenever we behave or act in dishonest manner then our core weakens and then we start to disintegrate mentally also.

Regarding practice of religion, views of Vedic theosophies and theosophy of Mahaveer is different. Religious practices based on Vedic concept accept importance of religious practice and suggests that every human should start to practice religious doctrine by the time he reaches middle age. The thought behind this observation and the reason being, up to middle age the person becomes mature and starts to appreciate and understand that the way in which he used to exist are to be reconsidered. Again, the reason is given that he becomes aware about as all the experiences he has gone through and comes to know that some ways are not upto the mark, so they are to be totally cast away and some ways are to be altered so that expected can be gained. Religions under Vedic system divided human life span in four segments: the first part is intended to be used by any person to remain as celibate and to learn with the intention to earn for the self, second part consists to get married and raise own family. In this part the person should remain with the family till he reaches the age of 50 years. Then the same person is expected to handover the leadership position of his family to his eldest one and then should remain as advisor only. Fourth segment starts at the ripe old age of around 65 years and the same is expected to renounce the family and all the worldly possessions and should start active religious practice with the intention to realize his self. In general this practice is quite good and is also easy to follow as major situations in every persons life are adequately considered. But Mahaveer is of the opinion that human life style do not adhere to mathematical precision and unforeseen incidences like sudden death of the person and other circumstantial incidences, on which we can not have any control, may cause this system to derail in midstream. Further, practice of any religion at the middle age generally do not become effective and may not bear fruits in the intended manner because till the middle age people become more set in their habits, attitudes and beliefs, and to change any of them causes more expenditure of energy and time. About our energy source and its active functioning period was discussed before and further elaboration is coming in the next chapters. But we have to understand that such energy reservoirs may not be available to us at our advanced age. So Mahaveer suggests that it is prudent to start the practice of religion at younger age, only because energies at our disposal are abundant in quantity. Similarly younger people do not become set in habitual ways and so diversion in proper direction becomes easy and following also happens easily.

We have to remember that there is no other power or energy other than our regenerative energy and manipulation of the same helps us to get up or down. By nature it is neutral, but how we manipulate it make us either an ordinary being or a creative being. If directed towards baser inclination, we will become lecherous and if directed towards upper inclination, we will be creative. In Vedic parlance manipulation of the same energy in the above-mentioned manner leads us towards the state of either Yogi or Bhogi. While meditating when we start to gather momentum the cause behind the acceleration is the same energy. Why Mahaveer stresses the important point of early induction in religion happens due to the same energy. At the younger age we have the energy in vast quantity and its source continues to produce the same easily but in advanced or old age its reservoirs depletes and generation starts to slow down. To start religious practice at middle or old age generally happens as last resort or final means of salvation. Realization of the self at the younger age not only increases our intelligence potentials but create rare wisdom in the person which cause total creative flowering of an ideal personality.

In reality the older we become the wiser, more mature and more understanding we should have to be. Nothing should be perceived as troublesome and nothing should cause mental unease or pain. Whatever has to happen has happened, whatever has to be experience is experienced, and ways of world are become known to us and are understood fully. In this manner whatever life we have to live we have lived and so all the water under the bridge should make us tranquil, peaceful and mature in our deportment and behavior. But it is very unfortunate that very rarely, if at all, wisdom by the elderly is experienced. On the contrary we become more set in our ways, not only that but rigidity of mind also happens because of which we just wither away and become more pathetic and senile. A child of six and a person of sixty are said to be of the same mentality, but only difference seems to be a child of six is still innocent whereas a person of sixty is not, which in reality should happen. Gold become more pure by frequent heating and the same should happen in case of human being also. People bend forward at the old age, for which degeneration of skeletal frame can be one of the reasons but other powerful reason seems that at the advanced age there do not remain any hope for future, as there is very limited energy remains with us. Similarly at our core we start to believe that in our lifetime we have not achieved anything of substance worth mentioning, but we have lost a golden opportunity. This emotion and preoccupation as its outcome weighs heavily on our mind and make us despondent and brooding, and is considered as one of the reason why people bend down at the old age.

CHAPTER 21

TRUTH FOREVER

Theosophical outlook of Jainism is warrior based and as energy, power and strength of the body and mind are prerequisites of a warrior, the same strength of the body and power of the mind is used in austerity with an intention to reach self-realization. All the 24 tirthnkaras of Janie's were from warrior class and Mahaveer was last of them.

Any power, if left unchecked or without harness then either it turns towards destruction of the others or of the self or is spent senselessly. So Jaini's tried to harness the same power and strength in such a way, that this natural source should be directed to attain ultimate expression i.e. self-realization and the process so laid down is known as Doctrine of Jainism.

To Mahaveer, as young ones are full of power and strength, it becomes easy to direct the same power in any desired direction. As we have seen in the last chapter, conditioned human mind is prone to acquire habits and causes habit bound behavior. Similarly the same habits and attitudes take much strength and time to nullify, and the power to be applied to make the desired changes take its toll and so our reservoir also depletes. So the logic of Mahaveer to start the practice of any religion and its doctrine at younger age seems to be very sensible. The reason is before any habits and attitudes become firm in our psyche we have to direct the total energy of the individual towards austerity. As young ones are like wet clay, pliant and flexible, they can be molded in desired direction.

Any transformation requires power and energy as driving

force to change and religious way of being requires more energy, as in this endeavor total transformation happens. Then do we think that this task will bare fruit in our advanced age, when our energy is at the lower ebb? If any old person says that now I can practice celibacy, then this phenomenon do not manifest due to austerity but due to natural decline in power, energy and degeneration of related faculty. When total potential is at our disposal with the capability to express it in natural manner and when any person decides to use the same potential to transform the self, then what happens is true transformation and realization of potentials.

Practice of any religious doctrine and following of any religious doctrine are different concepts. Following of any religion and its doctrine may happen in the manner as successive or inherited following that is happening in our society since long. And this phenomenon happen due to prevalent systems ingrained in the society in which we exist. In reality it is erroneous to accept that any following is to be considered as religious following. In its place the following should be considered as cultural following. In this light it is to be understood that practice of religion happens with the intention to realize our potentials and cultural following is the way that guides us towards those doctrines, which in turn lead towards religion.

Vedic culture believes that ego and egoistic nature of human mind is the characteristic feature because of which people are restrained from becoming religious and the same restrain causes hindrance between ultimate fusion of human and Supreme God as creator. Most of the religions based on Vedic culture are of the opinion that our egoistic state of mind is to be purified to such an extent that total dissolution of ego will manifest and our mind will become crystal clear. But Mahaveer says that this process is very time consuming and our whole lifetime may be spent in this task but still we may not purify it completely. Instead of purification, Mahaveer suggests that however and whenever we encounter our ego or egoistic nature, we have to elevate our self above the ego. In this case we ignore its existence or bypass it's being. As any person of average intelligence and honesty can practice analysis of self, this process bears fruits in relatively less time and by spending less energy.

About truth and concepts on which truths are based, Mahaveer laid down certain parameters. Similarly how truth should be presented is also mentioned. Presentation of truth should happen without malice and with awareness. Generally truth is used as weapon with intention to harm the other emotionally, mentally, physically in most of the circumstances as well as in insulting manner also. When we accuse or criticize any one about anything and even if the information on which our accusation or criticism is based are factual, but if our intention is malicious to show the other as how superior we are than him, then this presentation of truth is very subtle kind of violence. Before presentation of truth we are advised to look at our motive, as our motive is the driving force behind our act and behavior. It is further stated that we must anticipate the effect our presentation is going to cause on the other. Presentation of the truth should be beneficial to the other. We know that truth begets benefits and we have availed of such benefits in various circumstances on countless occasions. But Mahaveer seems to be mocking us or pulling our leg; this condition of Mahaveer relates to our conditioning and habit nature, so when it is convenient and when immediate profits are going to be ours, then only truth becomes significant to us. But still benefiting someone other than us is an idea alien to our being. As we are cleverer than Mahaveer we use truth that will benefit the other but benefits we are going to reap due to our ulterior motive will be more beneficial to us than to the other. How to present truth is the reason because of which Mahaveer remained mute for the total period of his austerity.

Realization of truth in relation to us is personal experience and the same happens to of all the others. Experiences may vary from person to person as every individual is unique and capacity to comprehend also varies as per individual wisdom and perceptions. Sugar is sweet for us but degree of its sweetness as experience may happen in various forms from person to person. So sugar is sweet is truth for me and collective or universal truth will be, sugar is generally sweet. In this manner truth becomes personal as well as universal.

Further condition of Mahaveer is, we should not be insistent about truth or its validity. After completion of his austerity if anyone asked Mahaveer about his opinion then Mahaveer started to use the prefix 'perhaps' before his opinion. The reason being, after realization Mahaveer understood the enormity of the whole truth as well as its personal versions, so to save himself from becoming opinionated and answer truthfully he has to prefix 'perhaps' before answering to anyone. It is noted that even in fallacy an iota of truth remains, because without truth nothing ever exists.

The reason we have to experience difference of opinions because we exist in conflict and duality, so our opinions are bound to vary from incidence to incidence and the same applies to others. But when we become insistent that what we are saying is absolute truth then our statement is correct up to certain extent as we are adhering to our version but its experience by the others may not correspond with us. Mental makeup by the way of beliefs, assumptions and perceptions are the factors that are unique to everyone but due to these factors meaning of the same thing is inferred by everyone in the individual manner. We know the tale of five blind people who for the first time encountered an elephant and tried to understand its shape by touching it from various angles. To the one it was cylindrical, to the other it was very broad and to the next it was tapered at one end and became broad as he went up. Now the experience of each was truth in itself but at the same time the truth was very personal as per everyone's perception. If these people were not blind then they could have seen the elephant in total perceptive and their experience about its being would have been total. The same happens with all of us and because of our limited vision and understanding, what we experience become true for us but does not happen to be total truth.

This is how enlightened person experiences the truth because of his total awareness, but at the same time he could not explain it to anyone, for the simple reason that all of us are not as yet aware enough as the enlightened person is.

Let us leave aside truth and our insistence that everyone should accept it, but even in fallacy we are insistent and most of the time we have to be more insistent for the simple reason that no fallacy stands on its own. Our arguments become heated, we bang on the table and our body movement happens to be exaggerated. In reality this kind of behavior happens only to get our point across. Even in court of law, a counsel who is sure about his stand in a case presents his argument in sedate manner, but if there is ambiguity about his stand and when he has to muddle the issues further, he carries stack of law books and argues very vehemently. This kind of behavior supports the fact that for every fallacy support is must, as it never stands on its own.

In case of truth, we expect assurance and guarantee from the master or pioneer that once disclosed the truth must remain as it is. As mentioned before people expect readymade solutions to their problems without doing anything on their own. And Mahaveer is not capable to provide any answers only because to him what he has experienced is his achievement and what we are going to experience will be our achievement. No pioneer has the power or capacity to make us enlightened without our going into due process. So we must understand that doctrines are the pointers and may become way also for us, if we are intelligent and wise enough, then we will also reach where the pioneer has reached. When anyone reaches in this manner then his experience will be unique but will be different than the other, and for this reason it is stated that the way is same for everyone but realization happens as per potentials of the individual.

CHAPTER 22

SEXUALITY: SEARCH FOR THE OTHER

At the outset it has to be stated that the nature of this chapter is going to be in the form of debate upto certain extent for the sake of explanation. Even though the concepts in practice are in various forms but in reality all the forms are outcome of only two basically accepted concepts. They are Tantric and Jaini concepts. Practical presentations of these concepts and its understanding by way of expressions is based on individual perceptions of the practitioner.

Basic energy in every individual is the energy of sex or energy of regeneration. By nature it is neutral and can flow in any of the two directions only. When the cause of flow happens due to influence of the other then the occurrence is called sexual expression and when the flow is directed towards self the expression is called as yogic expression.

Water boiled upto 100 degrees and above turns into vapor, which in turn become light in the sense of weight and evaporates into air. But if the water is kept below 1 degree then it condenses and become ice as solid mass. As happens in case of any solid object, ice due to gravitational force comes down to earth. In both the cases water is the common element but its transformation happens in two ways and in the same way the energy of regeneration can be transformed and can flow in either direction.

Sexual expression is the downward flow of the energy, which is released in sexual intercourse and its upward flow is termed as yogic expression, which is the cause of self-realization. So as happens with the water vapor, the energy flowing in upward direction is the phenomena where the law of gravity of the earth losses its hold and the pull becomes null and void. Manner in which the conversion of energy happens is termed as swimming against the flow. To swim against the flow is to be understood as to behave or express in diverse manner than accepted way of behavior or expression. How we manipulate and use this energy marks our achievement and destination.

As our sexual faculty is neutral energy and as various emotions influence our mind then this influence is the causal drive that causes arousal. When this arousal is felt then we are induced to express the same by way of relevant act. Religious doctrine related to sexual expressions make us aware as to how we can consciously manipulate the ultimate expression of our sexuality, as we are responsible for ultimate expression. When our mind is not regimented and not analyzed in proper way, then it takes control of our sexual faculty and we habitually express the emotions felt in stereotyped manner. So if we will it to flow downwards then we experience pleasure, pain or frustration and when we will it to flow upwards, then we glimpse our self and become aware about our basic potentials. What we have to understand and accept at least once is however we express our sexuality, no matter what but we are responsible.

Transformation of our sexual potentials can happen in two ways but the destination remains to be the same, and even though the destination remains as one, the processes and its procedures are different from each other.

Tantra, a branch of Vedic culture, is of the opinion that unless and until we experience the sexual act in its totality, transformation of the same is not possible. As per Tantric doctrine, any experience in full is the only way to cast away any act, behavior and its repetition, and only then the related faculty can be used in creative manner. At the same time if the casting away do not happen even after going through the act and its related experience, then the act related to the faculty is to be considered as reciprocal to our basic nature. In Tantric parlance, that which can be severed or cast away, is to be understood as acquired attitude, which we know as conditioning or conditioned behavior. Tantric definition of attitude is; any act, which happens in repetitive form but which always or most of the time, causes frustration or sorrow. But when the same act happens in its totality with awareness and when the intention behind the act is to check whether the experience corresponds with the anticipation but do not cause frustration, then the said act is to be treated as reciprocal to our nature. Tantric doctrine stresses the issue that our every act has to be checked and gone through with total awareness, for the simple reason that, whatever is not necessary or against our nature, has to be dropped or cast away as its practice causes dissipation of vital energy, and then the remaining is our nature with the help of which we can go into austerity.

Tantra compares and identifies notions behind repetitive sexual acts with phobic behavior and is of the opinion that when any emotion is experienced at its extremity, then it either causes behavior of avoidance if the experience is perceived as emotionally fearful and frustrating or if the experience is felt pleasurable to senses and to the body, then to feel same pleasure again, repetition of the same act continues. When a piece of rope is perceived as snake in the darkness and when any reasoning on our own or by others fails to assure us that the notion or belief is erroneous, then Tantra suggests that we must face the situation in conscious manner with the intention to verify whether our fear is justifiable or just our imagination. These willing encounters with situations, incidences and objects, which cause feelings of fear or drive us towards avoidance of the situation, may purge us forever from erroneous notions and help us to stop behaving in phobic manner. Similarly to believe and assume that the manner in which the person of opposite sex is behaving is a call or cue to us and expects from us acts related to sexual nature, can be our notion but not reality. But when we believe in these kinds of notions then our acts and behavior starts to happen as per our notions and we start to spend our energy on the notional concepts that may not be reality. This is how total experience with awareness about anything purges us from phobic behavior as well as repetitive acts that sap our energy and causes sorrow and frustration. It is observation of the Tantric doctrine that, repetitive sexual act causes nothing but frustration and is the reason of senseless wastage of precious energy. But on the contrary, if the same act cause profound satisfaction as well as rejuvenation of mind and body, then the same act is to be understood to be one of the aspects of our nature. At the same time insistence to cast away the act or behavior as wrong, is nothing but a erroneous belief will cause suppression of the emotion and will make us pathetic. Any act, which has to be repeated but when each repetition cause frustration, then it is to be understood as acquired attitude and the attitude is against our basic nature.

Way of Mahaveer is basically yogic way. He says whatever experience we go into, it causes formation of habit and most of the acquired habits are hard to do away. In our habitual behavior, we tend to become mechanical and as habits create second nature our habit nature shrouds our basic nature. The meaning as to repeat, is implicit in the word habit, so once habits are formed then repetition starts to happen but most of the times the same repetition cause frustration. When due to frustration we try to restrain our behavior, then our mind provoke us to repeat the same act again and again, as habit forming is the attribute of our mind. But in this case, our nature and our mind clashes and again we experience frustration. And this phenomenon is known as vicious circle. When acts and behavior happens due to habits but do not correspond with the biological demands, then either we have to repeat or become frustrated. Unless and until we are not sure or aware as to what our biological demands are, then we become frustrated due to non-fulfillment or due to repetition of the same acts.

Most of the acts happen by us due to notions, assumptions and unawareness, but the intention remains to have experience of the anticipated. But when what we anticipate or expect do not happen as per the notion, then we go into the same act again and again till the anticipated happens as per our expectations. And this is one of the reason because of which repetition starts. To solve this riddle of habitual behavior and repetition of acts, Tantric doctrine stresses the concept of going into any act in totality and with awareness.

Even psychology accepts, that most of the habits and traits of personality takes firm root by the age of 7 years, after which any change becomes impossible and the same traits remain with us till the end of life. So Mahaveer is of the opinion that stop before habits form; but if at all possible stop before going into experience in the first place, because once the seed is planted it will sprout and grow and will become full fledged tree and will bear fruits. And this is the reason why Mahaveer is of the opinion that induction and ordination should happen at the younger age. When the younger one comes to age then the faculty of regeneration or sexuality becomes potent then the same can be directed towards creative realization of our potentials. In such a case potentials of every faculty also remain potent and the person enjoys good mental and physical health throughout his natural life.

Our breast fixation starts with our mother as source of food, love and feeling of assurance that in time of need we will be taken care of. Then the same association remains with us till death with varying degrees of values attached at various age stages. Then the same organ of the female is perceived not only as symbol of the appeasement of biological hunger but to fulfill and express hunger of love on physical level also. Most of the movies, paintings, sculptures and songs are related to this fixation.

For this reason Mahaveer says that when habits are formed and then become central to our existence, then it is better if we do not go into experience in the first place. When the young ones experience the sexual stirrings for the first time then the phenomena is indication of natural changes taking place and means that the youth is attaining adulthood and is on the threshold of becoming a full-fledged man or woman. As reasons behind this happenings are biological and natural then it is proper to let the children know as to how this powerful faculty of ours can be used and directed towards fulfilling creativity. Similarly they are to be taught as to how they can create heaven in their life by developing healthy intimacies based on mutual understanding and trust. Any way can be paved at any time; provided the territory is virgin or generally accepted forms of behavior are not learned. And the opposite happens in the cases where habits are formed, and then such habits take inordinately long time and energy to alter or to be totally cast away. In a nutshell habits are like well-worn shirt; its touch to our body soothes due to long association.

In the opinion of Mahaveer basic habits of eating, sleeping, going about everyday activities to earn for living etc. are considered as biological and sustaining activities. But to create new ones, which are going to sap our precious energy is where Mahaveer asks us to be aware. As it is, in our basic habits also we are unconscious in the sense that our behavior happens in mechanical fashion. In mechanical activities our self is not behind our mind, our mind is not behind our activity but still we go on doing what we are doing. And this manner of doing anything is termed as unconscious behavior that is the cause of formation of habits.

Most of the theosopher, thinkers and other religious leaders are of the opinion that the ways of Mahaveer are ways of suppression, suicidal and against human race. But to people like us, who are learning about the working of human mind and are going to be psychotherapist, we know the meaning of the concept of suppression. Suppression is to restrain by all the means and by every angle, not to express or to stop from manifestation of the emotion that is going to be an act. But Mahaveer is not asking us to suppress anything; on the contrary he is asking us to stop for some time before expressing or acting. To take stock and consider should not be deemed as suppression, but in this exercise when we are sure that the way in which we are used to behave is fruitless, then we have to garner our strength so that the energy can be redirected in creative manner. Our restrain from acting or expression is the time that is initial stage of transformation, after which we are going to leave old and fruitless ways behind and will behave in creative manner. An archer puts the arrow on the string of the bow and stops for some time when he pulls the string; but this does not mean that he is restraining the arrow from flying or letting go. To stop before letting the arrow go, is the pre-condition to gather the strength and concentrate so that the arrow can reach the intended mark. And this is how Mahaveer asks us to act, that before we commit ourselves to any act we have to analyze our emotion and then act.

Tantric doctrine and doctrine of Mahaveer aims and arrives at the same conclusion. Both use traits of human mind that are known as interest and desire. But the ways of both are diametrically different and opposite to each other. Tantra asks us to go into any experience with total concentration and with all the energy, so that the resulting experience will stop the repetition or if the experience is nearer to our basic nature, then we will know what we are, which is the intention of the doctrine i.e. to know the self. But Mahaveer is aware of frailty of human mind and unconscious nature of human being. Unless and until awareness of the self is not realized and our intelligence is not master of our mind, then every emotion of ours will turn into act and every act of ours will form habits. This heedless way of going on committing acts and formation of various habits which cause further repetition of the same acts and further dissipation of energy, is considered by Mahaveer as deviation from the self.

Way of Tantra is way for intelligent people who are basically practicing the doctrine of awareness. No doubt people has inherent intelligence, but when our intelligence is eclipsed by our mind, then only mind rules and intelligence withers away. Majority of populace falls under the category of mind over intelligence class. And for this reason Mahaveer stresses the issue of awareness and understanding first and then act and experience.

Those cultures, which are liberal in sexual expressions and where all the emotions relating to sexual behavior are no more taboo, are fast loosing interest in sexuality. At the same time the cultures, which are somewhat orthodox and prudish, are more interested in sexuality. The reason being, those who are liberals have reached saturation point due to which they lost all the interest and those of orthodox outlook are more curious so are speeding towards gathering of more experiences. Basically human race is more prone to satiate two primary hungers only; first is hunger of food and the other is hunger of love, which is directly related to the sexual faculty. At the same time both are dependent on and related to each other. When both can be satisfied to the utmost, then both loose the drive behind the interest. And this kind of behavior of the average people is the cause of advent and existence of religious doctrine and its practice. All the pioneers of all the religious doctrines are of the opinion, that the reason of human existence has much more importance than just to satisfy basic hungers.

This world is treated as illusion by so called religious figureheads for the reason that they consider existence of the human race at the hub of this existence, and that everything is because of and for humans only. But the discussion we have till now is an effort to show that many things were in existence before the present evolution of the human race and much more are going to remain as they are, even after extinction of human race. But the importance given to the human race is nothing but a belief and because of this belief human mind functions on the same line. As once any belief becomes firm, then to change the belief become a tedious job. The doctrine presented by Mahaveer is very much related to human mind. He knows the working and nature of human mind, and is of the opinion that unless and until we become masters of our mind, our mind on its own is going to lead us. Our association with our mind and its use as medium of all the experiences is the reason the existence is understood as an illusion. In reality our mind is also an organ and as its primary function happens to be in our brain, then whole brain is to be treated as mind. Some functions of the body, which are involuntary, like breathing, functioning of our heart, some reflexes which happen when our body or any part of it is in danger of injury, are the ingrained features which are common to all the humans as the basic features of our brain. Even these basic and involuntary functions of our brain can be controlled or manipulated through some regimentation of mind. The said regimentation of our mind happens only when we understand as to what our mind is, how it works, how to use its vast reservoirs of accumulated data we have acquired by way of various experiences etc. Ultimate end result is to gain total awareness about our mind and this awareness helps us to use our mind in desired manner. The tool we use to harness vast potentials of our mind is our willpower. At the same time all the thoughts and emotions we experience are chemical actions and reactions that also happen in various parts of our brain. All of our sense organs gather information by way of direct experience or feelings which are passed on to our memory for further use in future as well as all the commands from the brain are passed on to all the sense organs as and when necessary. All these collective functions of the brain should be treated as working of mind. When every action and reaction happens mechanically due to function of our brain through medium of our mind, then routine sets in which is nothing but habit and these habits are the cause of creation of our subconscious mind. Even at this stage we can control or totally negate the dictates of our mind and the instrument at our disposal is our intelligence & our willpower.

To analyze and understand the working of our mind, and the relationship between mind and brain, and between brain and all the sense organs through the mind, is the process towards awareness. Mahaveer names this concept as fusion of brain and mind as one and the same. So when he realized how intricate this working is and how impossible it is to change the old ways, he warns us before going into any act to imagine about the outcome happening due to our act. And so he asks us to refer to our mind as reference library, as to what we have learned from the past experience of the same kind of acts, what were the thoughts at that time and what were the emotions, what was the stimulation and what were the cues at that time. Because if all the thoughts, emotions, stimuli's and cues are same now as they were in the past, then what we are going to experience now, is also going to be same.

Alcohol causes trouble to many people, in such case Tantra suggests that to kickoff the habit, go into drinking binge with total awareness. Increase the awareness as we go on drinking, then feeling of intoxication will not happen. But again Tantric doctrine accepts that the people practicing this mode of awareness are somewhat more intelligent and are more aware than average people.

In Mahaveer's opinion, we have seen countless people who were under the influence of alcohol and the manner in which they behave. Then it is wise to abstain from going into the experiment in the first place. We know that poison causes death, so no person in his right mind will swallow poison to verify the validity of the statement. Only thing is, alcohol is slow poisoning and it takes longer to kill and generally the process of dying is very painful.

Addiction to any drug, alcohol and tobacco may be happening due to contents of the substance, but have we ever thought that our own habit nature is more addictive than the substances mentioned above? Addiction of the substance can be left or cast away with the help of counselor, by using medicines or when our body on its own, starts to reject the substance when it can no more tolerate its administration. The same happens in our sexual expression and behavior. Even psychology in general accepts the hunger of food and sex is inevitable, but hunger of food cannot be postponed or neglected for indefinite period, which cause death due to malnutrition. On the other hand sexual function and relation with other does not fall under the category of inevitable, as it do not cause the death of any person if the said person do not have sexual relations. But as so many traits of personality are passed from generation to generation by way of genes, to function sexually, is also passed down genetically. Our birth is the result of our parent's sexual union, so not only personality traits but also sexual traits are passed down. It is the opinion of the Mahaveer, that our genetic trait of sexuality is the root cause because of which most of the habits are formed.

People due to their morbid curiosity and surface understanding are getting attracted towards Tantric doctrine, where sanction to express sexuality at its basic and primitive form is allowed or this is how the concept is understood. But it is to be understood that there are very stringent pre-requisites which are to be followed & fulfilled, where all the old habits & beliefs are to be discarded and only then when we become like a clean slate then the master of the doctrine allows the disciple to go into the experience. In Tantra male and female are considered to be Shiva and Shakti, as basic creator of the universe. Till every female is considered as source of Shakti or basic form of mother, no disciple is allowed to co-habit with the female and is only allowed to go into actual act with the most sacred and pious emotions. Half-hearted practice of the doctrine or bypassing of any process will very definitely result in totally shattered psyche of the person whose remaining existence will be very pathetic.

Mahaveer presents the easy way out by not going into the experience in the first place. He says that when the energy starts to accumulate and when the accumulated energy starts to stir for the way out, then direct the same in desired direction. To him male-female coupling is release of the energy on the outside but to redirect the energy on our self will help in the realization of the self.

Mahaveer is not against male-female sexual relations, but at the same time habit of the same relations is the cause of spending of the energy, which is useful to know our self. And for this reason i.e. to seek the other for the release of the energy is considered as non-religious behavior. Behind 99 percent of the goals, that are to be achieved in our life, energy of our regeneration or faculty of our sexuality is used. Materialistic accumulation, higher designation or to be successful in any field, are some of the forms which are nothing but forms and expressions of our dormant sexuality.

At the start of this chapter two hungers of the humans were mentioned and was stated that both are dependent on each other. Food is considered as fuel or energy generation source of the human being and sexual activity is for procreation of the human race. Energy created by food also provides fuel to our regenerative faculty and when we spend the same energy in sexual activity, the depleted energy level of the faculty start to demand more fuel and automatically food intake also increases. This is how both the hungers are dependent as well as reciprocal to each other.

According to Mahaveer potentials of human sexual faculty should applied in two ways; one is re-creative and the other is self-creative. And according to him the latter option is the bane of real creativity and realization of our true potentials. Human sperm has potentials to cause numerous births at any one ejection out of which only one is sufficient to impregnate an ovum of the female and then the remaining sperms are flushed out as useless. Very few people know and understand this process and the potential they have. In spite of these potentials we die like a pauper. If at all there are no humans in this existence, it is not going to make any difference but on the contrary the existence sans human will be heaven on earth, as everything barring human exist in its basic nature.

The ways in which we human behave happen due to importance given to the physical body as our original form. We are very much attached to the body so in whichever way we act or react; the effects as good or bad are felt and experienced by body. Then all the objects that are supposed to be for the betterment of body, for its safety, its adornment as well as to appease it's all the hungers and thirst become important. Then hoarding of money and the objects which money can buy starts to happen. And in this fashion money become more important, so much so that even other human who has less money than us can be bought, provided the other is attaching the same value to money as we are. At the same time hoarding of anything, money or objects, cause shortage of the same, which deprive others, who may be more needy than the person who is hoarding; this cause social unrest, which is felt at psychological level. This unrest is not only felt by the deprived but by the hoarder also; former thinks that as he is poor so he is helpless to do anything, but at the same time starts to find the ways by which this disparity can be overcome. But when the proper ways are not found, then other ways that are not so proper are brought in to application. And the possibility that those who are facing privations are going to snatch what we have accumulated is the cause of unrest the hoarder is feeling all the time. And the irony is, at the end both die the same way without accomplishing anything of substance.

To accumulate, to collect or to hoard is result of the belief that the more we have then less deprived we will be or we feel secure in numbers. More money make us feel more secure, that in any eventuality or in any unforeseen circumstances, money is the means by which we may come out unscathed. The same happens with all the things like foot wares, cloths, ornaments, vehicles etc. At the same time we also know that after us all that is accumulated is not going to end with us, but some one else is going to use them as before our acquisition it was with some other. Why accumulation of anything after certain extent cause preoccupation or unrest is; in the first place we strive very hard to accumulate, but the number of which to be accumulated goes on increasing as we go on accumulating, then in the second place we have to be on our guard as to how to safeguard whatever we have accumulated. There is a story about a poor person who prays to the God that he is desirous to own vast tract of farming land. The God materializes and grants his wish with a provision that till the end of the day whatever land the poor person may cover will be his. In the morning the poor person starts to walk but prior to afternoon thinks that what he has covered is not sufficient, so he starts to run and as the day advances runs very fast. By the end of the day he falls down with total exhaustion and death becomes imminent. Then the God materializes and tells him that at the end every person needs land measuring 3′ by 6′. This story may be perceived as cynical but the moral is applicable to every one of us.

Projection of sexuality towards other is bondage, slavery or dependency. Faculty applied through the medium of mind bind us or make us dependent on the other either animate or inanimate. Again this dependency causes sorrow when the other ceases to exist or when the other is no more interested to continue the relationship. There is a good and meaningful word for sexual intercourse in Sanskrit i.e. Sambhog; the meaning is equal indulgence by the way of emotions, readiness and reciprocal activity. Even psychology accepts the outcome of satisfying sexual activity to be ideal union when both are equally aroused, should reciprocate needs of each other's and both should arrive at mutual orgasm. How many times people experience this ideal union, why women are more frustrated in matters concerned to sexual activity? How many times males are tolerant to the woman's willingness and desire? Why there are so many depraving expressions to human sexuality and deviations? Why male experience impotence some times and why women are termed as frigid? These and so many questions are the root cause of various abnormal behaviors of the human that are presented before family physicians, sexologists and psychologists. Whenever any person takes the other for granted and where there is no intelligent deliberation before the act but only dictates of mind are followed, then more questions are bound to arise along with the old ones.

Have we ever thought that every type of intimacy is the basic cause of enmity? In intimate relationships we become vulnerable and as we open-up more in front of the other, then more vulnerable we become. Some times this kind of relationship is called as love-hate relationship. Either of the two thinks that the other is too much dependent on me or is trying to cling in every situation, which cause emotional suffocation as well as cause drainage of the energies of the person on whom the other is dependent. Then to gain the breathing space, the dependable one either batters the dependent emotionally or starts to neglect the other. Then the dependent one feel let down and become hurt, and out of this hurt emerges enmity towards the other and then the dependent tries to get even when the shoe is on the other foot or as the opportunity arises. This behavior like a seesaw goes on till either one ends the relationship. According to Mahaveer every relationship, either intimate or casual, remain intact till such time that both are getting what they expect in equal measures and in ratio, which is never even. What Mahaveer means by ' in ratio, which is never even' is every one always thinks that what he is getting is not in proportion to what he is giving. This disparity of perception in any give and take situation happens only because of our exaggerated worth as our ego and our mind's involvement where our mind never feel satisfied, no matter how much the other is giving. As mentioned earlier, it is the basic characteristic of our mind that it will never be satisfied; as there is no way in which it accepts the logical end as true and real end. And this is the reason of slavery and dependence on the other; it may relate to our faculty of sexuality, taste, vision, auditory etc.

We believe, that what we are depends on the acceptance of and appreciation by the others. This belief happens due to our image about our self. At the same time our projection of our image confirms when others accept us as we are, but if we are not accepted, then with the aid of other outside sources we try to enhance and reinforce our personage. This dependency on others to be appreciated and accepted is the sign that we are not so sure about our worth or our self, or we are not ready to accept our self as we are. Similarly the way we are conditioned since birth and learning from the way other family members are behaving and attaching the value to the appreciation and acceptance by the others, reinforces our own belief that to be accepted and appreciated by the other is of primary importance. The other side of this kind of behavior is called as narcissism, where the person become obsessively aware about his own looks and become self-centered and beyond his looks and appearance does not care for anyone. According to Mahaveer, without understanding our basic nature and appreciating our true self-worth means to deviate from the self that will not help us in the end.

We generally adorn or beautify our body to attract the attention of the other. Behind this beautification our intentions are varying and manifold, for which we have to use other items or objects i.e. cosmetics or ornaments. Dependence on such outside props make us habit bound and at the same time we start to become preoccupied which is the cause of distancing ourselves from our basic self. Intention of Mahaveer behind this condition is to live and appear in regular manner, at the same time do not waste time on outside props but to use the same time to understand our own nature. He says that any person may attract attention of the others for very short time by way of outside beautification, but if there are not human like qualities inside, then this kind of adornment is of no use to anyone. Similarly the subtle intention behind beautification is also a form of libidinous projection to attract the opposite. As our faculty of regeneration is the only faculty we have that is going to be rundown as our aging is bound to happen, and as the energy of the same faculty is the source, with the help of which we are going to realize our self or potentials, then we are warned not to spend it in heedless manner.

About our food intake, he suggests that the food we should eat must be simple in preparation and light for the sake of digestion. Considering our day-to-day activities, our diet should be such that we must get the required amount of energy, which will help us do our work and at the same time our body must be recouped so that it can prevent any illness form manifesting. Food of rich contents generates more energy, which after our general consumption remains as surplus. And this surplus energy is automatically passed on to our regenerative faculty, which become active and starts to stir to vent or empty the fullness of the faculty. So he suggests moderate quantity, moderate taste and moderate in contents.

Our food must be vegetarian and about milk as one of the forms of food, his observations are worth considering. Basic need of milk as dietary intake is must for every mammal. And by natural process this demand is met and fulfilled naturally. Including human every mammal gets sufficient milk from its mother. This milk is important to form basic structure like skeleton, musculature, and permanent immunization from certain diseases and to develop various organs of the body as well as blood. At the time of infancy certain enzymes are formed due to mother's milk, which form our basic constitution and remain with us till our end. After some time the secretion of the milk stops, which is nature's way of indication that the baby is capable to take other food for its sustenance. Except human and its young, all the infants of the mammals shift to natural food. One more basic attribute of milk is it creates natural sexual potential in the consumer, because of which the creature becomes sexually active in certain seasons only. This seasonal activation of the sexual faculty is intended for procreation of the species.

Naturally the same should happen to human also and will happen, if the human stops the consumption of the milk derived from other animals like cow, buffalo, goat, camel etc. Milk of other animals is intended for its young ones, but when humans consume the same then the potentials of the same are passed through the milk to humans also, which affect basic faculty of the human's regeneration, and is further influenced by the potentials inherent in the milk of the other animals, which cause disturbance as well as distortion in human arousal pattern and behavior. It is suggested by Mahaveer that the person who is intending to be on the way of self-realization should avoid milk of other animals as well as products made from the same.

About human food habits, Mahaveer says that ideal dietary intake is vegetarian and should remain as such. It is proved that the length of human gastro-intestinal canal is lengthier than those animals that are non-vegetarian. The juices or acids, which secrete in human digestive system, are meant to digest simple veg food, which passes through various internal organs and various nutrients are separated along the way. On the other hand meat or flesh of other animals is ready-made food, which require more potent digestive acids, which are present in non-vegetarian animal's digestive system. Process of digestion takes long time in human being; a good square meal takes 6 to 8 hours to digest. But non-veg diet takes much more time to digest, only because necessary digestive acids are not present in human system. We have heard that the way in which we eat influences our thoughts and emotions, the explanation is very simple; if we eat food heavily laced with various spices and oils, then this kind of food takes more time to digest and the energy expended in this manner is also vast. So till the food is totally digested the energy supply to our brain as well as blood flow to various organs and to the extremities of our body happens to be at reduced rate, so we feel total lethargy and slowing down of thoughts and mental concentration. Further if the food is of non-vegetarian variety, our digestive system has to secrete more digestive acids in more concentrated form, so that the contents can be broken down and can be assimilated fully. Most of the time due to our regular eating habits we go on eating without giving time to our digestive system to recoup and before prior food is fully digested. This type of constant flow of food cause constant secretion of digestive acids, which require constant blood supply and this cause sapping of our vital energy, which make us listless. At the same time on full stomach we are unable to drink sufficient water, which is the best medium of breaking down of the food contents. The cumulative effect we experience is heavy stomach, labored breathing, acidity, indigestion, irregular bowel movement and total lethargy. Any one symptom or collective effects of all the symptoms is less supply of blood to our brain, which affect our mind. Excess of acid just do not remain in our stomach but mixes in our blood also and when the blood so laden with acids reach our brain it cause alteration of chemicals in our brain which cause either alteration in its structure or alter the chemical configuration which affect our behavioral pattern. Even if we know or not, understand or not the way we eat and what we eat is the cause of our behavior, and above are some suggestions and insight given by Mahaveer. Further more Mahaveer says that behavioral traits of the animals of whose flesh we eat become apparent in us after some time.

All the suggestions given by Mahaveer are proven scientifically as well as medically. Basic energy of our regeneration or sexuality becomes charged as per what we eat. And when the same is brimming, then it stirs and starts to vent by natural means, but if this energy is redirected at the time of its stirring then creation of self manifests. To express the energy towards other is the way of sexual behavior, which requires the other and aggressiveness on our part, but to come back to the original source or our self, just tranquility requires. When we are tranquil, energy can be directed towards self but when the same energy becomes power then we have to look for the other to vent it on.

CHAPTER 23

CELIBACY/BRAMHACHARYA-WHY?

As discussed in the last chapter to behave in sexual manner is biological and natural for animals and humans alike. But most of the times in human being its expressions and manifestations happen due to habit nature.

Existence of animal and human depends on biological expression of sexuality, as both are the outcome of its natural process. But in animal world sexual perversity never happens; barring those animals that are removed from their natural habitat and placed at zoos, circus and some domesticated variety known as pets and this happening cause deprivation from their natural mates. But perversion in human happens only because human are evolved with more analytical mind and superior intelligence and are by habit learned to live with instincts. Male to male and female to female sexual relation has no place in animal existence as they exist naturally and can perform with opposite only.

A report of Kinsey shows the results of an exhaustive study that 60% people have experienced homosexual relationship once in a lifetime (both sexes are considered), and 25% of the people from the same category remain as homosexuals or lesbians. Attraction between opposite is biological and natural but attraction for the same is considered as abnormal or perversion. As humans are more potent in mind they have capacity to elevate above basic and natural attitude of sexual expression, so the abnormality is not considered as abnormality at all. But at the same time no animal is capable to practice celibacy as they are biologically anchored to the faculty and they have no potent mental faculties beyond what is natural to their existence.

Intention to shift or transform may take some time by way of deliberation, but once decided, the happening is always sudden. At the same time shifting or transformation is to be considered as one of the extreme end of behavioral pattern. In this light the doctrine of Tantra is one of the extreme and doctrine laid down by Mahaveer is the other extreme. Both doctrines let the faculty of human sexuality to fill upto the brim, and then the former goes into the experience in totality and the latter redirects the generated energy in intended direction.

People who are obsessed with their own libidinous mindset, perceive the Tantric way as sanction by religious doctrine to follow the same for personal reasons and people who are by nature masochists, follow doctrine of Mahaveer under the erroneous understanding to suppress the faculty. Both loose the essence of the basics and reach nowhere and this happens when following happens by traditional way where meaning of the concept is not understood at all or when the same is misunderstood. We have to understand the subtlety of the doctrine and have to go through the preliminaries, without which no perceptible realization will ever dawn. The way, in which we are used to function and perform, happens due to formation of our habits. The moment our faculty starts to stir and nudge, then we hastily go in to its expression i.e. intercourse. Then what we experience is very lukewarm than our expectations. This is the manner in which most of the people behave and function. Basic problem is, we have no understanding and we are not patient or bold enough to look at the stirring and at the phenomenon of arousal in totally detached manner. Because this looking at in detached manner is nothing but witnessing on our part. The more aroused we become then more energy starts to gather at our sexual center and this activation of our faculty make us heavy and restless. Then if the gathered energy is not released immediately, we think that we are going to be mad but this is the moment when either we can go in to experience in totality or redirect its flow towards our self. Many of us has to face this type of experience in our life but we loose to take advantage of the situation only because we are conditioned or not aware about any other way to express and experience its results. Because if we are ready to be witness to the arousal then we will come to know that emotional arousal and the gap between actual happening of the act, is the window or the period in which it becomes possible to glimpse our basic being. If we are capable to be a witness to this activation of the faculty to the highest pitch without intervention of our mind, then we can either go into experience or redirect the energy. And happening of any of the two will help us to overcome all the previous beliefs as well as mad running behind the mental preoccupations forever. It is to be understood that wherever and whenever our mind intervenes or is involved, and when our intelligence is under the control of our mind, then to castaway old habits or to break any routine is not possible. It is the innate nature of our mind that it cannot be made satisfied at any time and anywhere, as it is superimposition of the mind on the faculty and not the basic faculty that is going through the experience.

We have to choose and have to adopt any doctrine as per our capacity and understanding with the precondition that, are we willing to change? People are not ready to change only because all the habits form routines and every routine create safety due to familiarity. But to go into any new direction we have to leave aside old habits and routines, and this shift from old to new cause uncertainty and doubts about possibility of our reaching anywhere. But if we are honest enough and aware enough to understand that our old habits and routines have not given us what we have expected, then this shifting from old to new become possible.

Not in psychology but in any religion practice also, to change is the process that happens only when we are ready to analyze our self. We have to look at and understand our active mind as well as our subconscious mind, and for witnessing of the thoughts we have to go in to how and why such thoughts materialize in our mind. Do we think over the thoughts present in our mind; if the answer is yes, then it is the sign that by way of thinking what we are doing is deliberating whether to act or not, but if we are not deliberating then our action due to basic thought is going to be impulsive action. And this is the reason for which Mahaveer has suggested that our mind should be refereed to as reference library, where every action of ours along with related thoughts and every experience of the said action is stored. When we use these past performance for future acts then either we act or do not act at all. At the same time in this process we have capacity to alter the way in which we can act when the previous act of the same nature and the resultant experience was not as per our expectations. It is always easy to deceive the other but to deceive the self is not easy and those who try to deceive the self have to exist with divided psyche. When we start to analyze all the processes of our mind, initially we are going to experience more restlessness for the simple reason that till now we have never tried to delve in our mind in any orderly manner and our analytical approach is going to stir our mind to its depth. Very few people know that all the conscious or unconscious thoughts are stored in our mind forever, whether we intend to act or not. So as we start to analyze our mind all these stored thoughts come to surface of our conscious mind for the first time and their volume and presence causes much restlessness. To experience peace is not to search for peace at all, but to resolve our chaotic mind in logical manner, which is self-analysis, and is the key to reinstate peace. Let us understand once forever that absence of chaos is peace, to exist in non-duality or to exist without conflicting thoughts and emotions is peace; basic nature of our being happens to be peaceful nature.

To be celibate or virtue of celibacy is not to be decided by way of act or expression on physical plane. As we know, behind every act there is thought, insistence of thought create emotion to act and act or outward expression is termed as actual act or behavior and in this manner only our thoughts take form. Mahaveer says that condensation of the emotion is to be considered as actual act; even if actual happening do not manifest, then absence of non-manifestation is of no importance, because there are chances that at the last minute we have to restrain ourselves due to various reasons. But this non-fulfilled emotion remains dormant in our mind and its willful suppression is the cause of various psychological abnormalities and illnesses. Any person will be celibate only when he analyses the thought regarding sexual expression at formative stages only and before the thought becomes emotion.

As mentioned at frequent intervals, we are still living at the state of conflict and because of this type of existence we try to rationalize all our emotions. We erect all kinds of logical barriers around our emotions to show others how logically behaving person we are. But most of the time this rationalization is the disguise of our powerful mind, which does not want to change its old ways.

Every thought of our is the seed which may create or give birth to an emotion, the emotion in turn is the driving force behind the intended act, then every act happening in this manner creates basic attitude and every attitude is the reason of emergence of habit because of which we behave in habitual manner and then go on repeating the same act again and again. Behind this entire circus our mind is the faculty which is basically passive and when all the experiences are taken through our mind, then the original faculty due to whose drive we initially has to go into the experience do not experience the fulfillment of the act and again the repetition starts. In reality our mind is the faculty that is to be used for contemplation or deliberation only, under the command of our intelligence before we commit our self to any act. As mentioned before, our mind is the organ or faculty, which has enormous capacity to store each and every thought we have in the past as well as every emotion which has induced us to act and end results of the act as experience or impressions is also stored. And Mahaveer is asking us to tap this data stored in our mind with the help of our intelligence to save our self from futile and needless repetition of any act. This is a very common phenomenon in our family that whenever we have to decide on any course of action of monumental nature, we consult the elders of the family and verify the intended course we are considering to take; the intention behind this consultation is not only to verify the way in which we are going to act but we are looking for confirmation of the results which we are going to encounter after the commission of the act. In this regards elders are looked upon as people of wisdom who have gone through the experience before us and may guide us in our intended action whether the course we are considering is proper or not. The said elder in our self is our mind and our intelligence is the pointer which shows us the way whether the intended action is going to bring back results we are expecting or not. For this reason Mahaveer says that every habit and attitude of ours can be resolved and changed at any time, and the way is honest self-analysis. Mahaveer define intelligence as; when any person applies the accumulated knowledge in logical manner in any situation, is the person of intelligence.

Mahaveer further suggests that we must be aware of the impressions caused and inferences drawn through word, form, smell, interest and touch. All these characteristics are related with our basic sense organs and some of the resulting experiences are gross and some are very subtle. Similarly all the sense organs are channels that are linked to our faculty of regeneration and send all the data collected from the out side environment to the said faculty. The collected data is inferred and experienced as stimulants or cues in psychology.

Our touching the other body with our hand is gross experience and looking through the eyes and experiencing the same feeling of 'touch' is inferred as subtle experience. The way, in which we hear and draw the inference, the manner in which we perceive the smell and what the smell make us feel are the causes of arousal of emotions which create interest to go through the experience. And this is the manner in which all the sense faculties are treated as collection centers on behalf of our faculty of regeneration. To Mahaveer this reciprocation of the various stimulations and cues that cause arousal of baser instincts from all the sense faculties happens due to involvement of our mind and all the inferences are conclusions of our mind and not of the sense faculty that is going into experience. At the same time the involvement of the mind is the cause of distraction as well as driving force, which make us dependent on the other. To verify the authenticity of this statement Mahaveer suggests us to apply process of witnessing to our emotions.

Every animate in our existence has its basic scent which includes humans also. Excepting human, all the animals perceive the presence of any other animate by smell of this distinctive scent only. Humans have lost this faculty to the larger extent only because of its intervening mind. Biology as a branch of pure science accepts the fact that smelling of any scent is the cause of stimulation and has potential to drive the recipient towards action. Most of the animals exude typical scent at the time of mating season, which attracts the opposite of the same species, similarly some animals give voice signals that again are perceived as call to mate. Even humans have typical body scents, but most of the time the chemicals, which cause the manifestation of the scent, are altered due to the food we consume. At the same time our mental activity is also one of the factor, which alter the scent we exude. The reason behind the alteration by way of mental activity is perceived as stimulant and commands given by our brain change the chemistry of our body also.

Naturally all the sense organs we have are for clear-cut perception about our surrounding, to understand the exact significance of the surrounding and to save us from harm. But with the intervention of our mind they are used to tantalize our thoughts and emotions. To become tantalized is the preliminary before the actual act or to be tantalized has action potentials; it causes in us lust for the other or cause us to be greedy to acquire the other. And this phenomenon is more powerful stimulation that alters our perception in manifold than the actual experience if gone through in straightforward manner. And for this reason it is sometimes better to directly go for experience, than to let our mind gloat and contemplate. When a man and woman hug each other they close their eyes; the reason being our mind goes into overdrive to compare the anticipated feelings and emotions while the actual proximity is maintained. Similarly with closed eyes it become easy to fantasies about the anticipatory feelings that we do not experience in reality.

Freud says that male and female are compatible to each other, because male by his innate nature is voyeuristic and female is exhibitionist; when one is ready to show the other is willing to see. And for this reason male desire intimacy in well lighted atmosphere and female prefer darkness; because if the female let the male see all that there is to see, then the element of tantalizing ceases to exist because of which the hold female have over the male start to taper off. Mahaveer says that when we look at something in starkness, then its titillating effect on our psyche looses the hold and most of the fruitless repetition stops. To be tantalized is nothing but subtle form of vibrations, which stimulate our mind, and then our mind stimulates our brain, which in turn stimulate our faculty. With the advancement now available in medical science, if we fit some electrodes in the human brain which can stimulate our sexual center, then the resulting satisfaction in place of physical intercourse will be so profound that the same person will never desire any female, however alluring and willing she may be. This technique will give the same results as happens in Tantric doctrine of experiencing the act in totality. At the same time when any faculty directly experience the result of any related act, then the same intensity is not felt with the other, however reciprocating the other may be. And this is the secret that Tantra and Mahaveer are trying to tell us, as to how we can separate our self from the dependency on the other which is deviation and the cause of repetitive acts and behavior. To Mahaveer those who can be tantalized easily about anything are of weak psyche and are bound to behave in obsessed manner because if they act they become frustrated and if they restrain they feel empty.

When people are obsessed with other person or objects and when the association with the person or object does not cause the desired and anticipated satisfaction, then out of frustration and to save face, they disassociate themselves from the person or object under the guise of sacrifice. But this is not sacrifice at all; on the contrary it is an avoidant or extremist behavior. Sacrifice as the word mean and in truer sense very seldom happens. Association with any other person or object with total awareness and to understand that without such assistance it is not possible to fulfill the desired or anticipated result is the sign of mature person. But to depend on the same person or object with the same anticipation to fulfill all the other wishes of ours is the cause of sorrow. As we have seen in previous chapters every person and every object has its own unique nature and they can be of assistance to us only when what we expect from them falls within their scope of nature, potential or capability. Sacrifice of anything on outside happens only when the process to cast away or leave aside the person or object to which we are attached or dependent on, takes place on the inner plane of faculty to which our intelligence is applied. Repetition of any act due to habit is the key factor that causes dissipation of energy and to understand with awareness, that this kind of behavior is not necessary, and then to consciously leave aside the same repetition is to be understood as sacrifice. In this process the person on whom we used to depend or the object without whose possession our being used to be empty, stops bothering us. In this process all the others; persons or objects, remain as they are but our association is terminated and this is called as sacrifice. We can sacrifice only when we are masters of our faculties and this process happens in our inner realm but its manifestation is seen on the outside.

Sexual relations between male and female primarily happens to procreate, but its repetition for momentary sense satisfaction is considered as deviation, only because it is the cause of depletion of the only energy source we have and its senseless and careless expenditure halt our progress towards flowering of our potentials. Mahaveer is not against sexual expression between male and female, but warns us that excess indulgence of the faculty is going to cause formation of the habit and any habit once formed takes more time and energy to change. Similarly the energy generated at the center of the faculty has limitations and generation of the same energy starts to ebb as we start to age.

Till now we have experienced joy or happiness through our sense organs only. But this happens very rarely, only because we desire to experience and form our attitudes accordingly. But according to Mahaveer our desires are the basic hurdles because of which we do not experience joy. To him experience of joy or happiness through sense organs is but an illusion and experience of pain and sorrow is reality. What seems good today is experienced as better, but when the same starts to happen everyday we experience boredom and has to look out for other means to experience the same happiness. At the same time if we do not experience anything then we experience sorrow. Sorrow is also of two types; when we get what we anticipate then we start to anticipate some more, but when this does not happen then we experience sorrow. At the same time when we anticipate pleasure primarily but nothing happens, then this phenomenon also causes sorrow.

According to Mahaveer cause of every sorrow happens to be of organic nature. At the outset we have to remember that this statement is made because of the habits and attitudes we have formed around our sense organs and not because of the existence of the sense organs, which are considered as enemy by the so-called followers. As mentioned before, we are creating habits and attitudes that are superimposed on our basic faculties, which is the cause of formation of the second nature. And this phenomenon happens due to our not being masters of our mind and due to absence of intelligent deliberation on our part. At the same time it has to be understood and accepted, that in all the existence only humans are miserable because of our conditioned nature to experience everything through the medium of our mind, which cause formation of habits and attitudes and for this no one is responsible other than us.

In general, all the religious pioneers are of the opinion that the cause of our rebirth happens due to our unmet desires.

CHAPTER 24

GLIMPSE OF INNER GREED- ATTITUDE OF ACCUMULATION

To reshuffle or refocus the attention from interest and to totally cast away anything of interest may be perceived as two different concepts. But in reality both are reciprocal halves of the same concept and the application of the former cause manifestation of the latter, and then what remains after the completion of the process is of substance.

Formation of interest in any thing happens due to intervention of mind between actual act and the related faculty for which the act is basically intended. Initial intervention of mind happens due to our unawareness; we are not aware that the faculty for which the act is intended can be felt or experienced at the level of faculty only, as primarily we are conditioned since birth to experience everything through the medium of mind. So once our mind becomes involved in any experience, then formation of the habit start to take shape, after which repetition of the act starts. In such a case any act happens in the same manner and whether the faculty wants the act to happen or not, becomes immaterial. But at the same time our mind on its own starts to dictate our faculty that the experience is necessary and act must happen. So basic state of our unawareness, poor understanding about the working of our basic faculties, and our basic conditioned nature to experience everything at the level of our mind are causes of formation of habits and attitudes.

As mentioned before, every faculty of ours causes the drive for reciprocal action to happen, the action happens when the said faculty becomes charged with residual energy and to release this energy as its natural expression the act has to happen. Our feeling of hunger for food happens because food as the fuel for workings of various organs of our body is essential. The same happens with all the sense organs, which are basically safety measures to save our body from inadvertent harm and dangers to our being. In such cases mind should work as medium of warning between our brain and our body, and no more than that. This is the basic intention behind self-analysis, to cast away those habits and attitudes that make us wary and perceived as troublesome that cause blockages in our realizations of our goals and achievements.

Constant intervention of our mind and its dictates on all the organs is the reason why we experience stress and unease. Dictates of the mind continuously keep our faculties on alert, which generate drive potentials which most of the time were not required. And this is the reason that in reality the stress does not happen on the level of mind but on the level of organs, but as we live by instincts and not in natural manner the stress and restlessness is felt in our mind. In such instances we consciously try to restrain our behavior by avoiding to act, in which case our mind start to contemplate as to how the experience would have been pleasant, what we are loosing by not going into the act etc., which is commonly known as daydreaming or tug of war of emotions. Most of the time such daydreaming become so alluring and powerful, that the same act happening in reality will not cause the same degree of satisfaction. Similarly contemplative mode of our mind about any emotion or thought goes on to such an extent, that basic interest of the concept becomes distorted, for this reason it is better to act than just to think.

To the people like us who are not sufficiently aware, our

nights are experienced as more eventful than our days. In the sleep our subconscious takes full advantage of our total unconsciousness and takes form in vivid details by way of dreams. Whatever we suppress in our waking, materializes with redoubled force in our dreams, details of which seems bizarre to us in the morning.

Once it is understood that because of involvement of our mind, interest in all and sundry is formed, then casting away of the same interest becomes easy when we shift our focus of attention towards our mind. All the sense organs are data collection centers that stimulate our brain and at the command of our brain further action or reaction happens. In reality involvement of our mind is not necessary to execute the commands of our brain, but the way in which we are conditioned, this involvement happens. Then through our mind, incoming stimulation and outgoing commands undergo some changes due to our past memories and these subtle changes cause formation of interest. When sense organs start to function under the dictates of mind, our mind through these organs become master of our pure intelligence or self. On the contrary when we become aware, then the same mind is bypassed and sacrifice happens. It is to be understood that all the sense organs are nothing but instruments and when our self remain present, then the sense organs function only when their functioning is necessary and in this manner they function to the their capacity in creative and useful manner. So when we would like to hear music then our ears are the instruments and when we would like to look at something then our eyes are the instruments. This is the manner in which our sense organs must function because for this reason only they are attached to and incorporated in our body.

The relationship between our sense organs and our self determine who is the master; if our mind is driving force behind our sense organs then these organs become our masters and this way of our existence where our mind remain dominant, is termed as sinful existence. Our mind never becomes satisfied, no matter how many times we go through the acts and its experience; for the simple reason that the intended act related to any sense organ never releases the energy generated on the center of the organ to the fullest. Then the residual energy starts to nudge our being again and again, which cause the repetition of the act again. So when self is present then the act happens in totality, the energy generated at any center is released to the fullest and in this manner the cause of interest loose the hold and casting away of the interest about anything becomes easy. Casting away of interest related to any sense organ do not make any faculty obsolete but on the contrary they start to work in more efficient manner which was not happening till now. We know the meaning of the concept of concerted performance. When each organ starts to function at its fullest capacity in its intended manner and when all the organs starts to function in the same manner, then our being and behavior becomes harmonious where nothing causes discord. When our self is present as conductor and our senses as individual performers, the harmony between the two create integrated personality.

We have to appreciate the meaning of each sense organ, understand their purpose & functioning to our being, why they are useful to our existence, knowingly limit their use to their intended capacity, then nothing of any interest will cause stress and tension, but at the same time those interest which are cause of needless energy expenditures will automatically stop. We do not have to take any special efforts to leave any thing, but only have to be aware as to what we are doing and why.

We have heard about the chariot that is drawn by five horses and the driver of the chariot has reins of all the horses in his hand. This metaphor is used to denote our basic sense organs and command of our intelligence as mind as its true driver. If every horse tries to draw the chariot as per its will in different direction, then the chariot will not reach the intended destination but at the same time the vehicle is going to be damaged. Some times the damage is so profound that to repair the same is not possible. In religious parlance the horses are considered as our sense organ and the driver is our wisdom. Till our self in the form of our wisdom or intelligence, is not present at the helm as the master of the vehicle, we are going to exist in chaotic manner. What appeals to eye will not appeal to ear, in that case our ear is going to assert itself and we will experience tension. And in this manner when every sense organ tries to assert itself in absence of our intelligence, then we have to face mental disorders. And this is the reason why we experience mood swings and emotional turmoil. To remain in this type of turmoil for extended period causes brooding on the same thoughts and emotions, which is considered as vicious circle. We oscillate between one extreme to other and when to get out of this condition becomes impossible people become depressed, preoccupied and appear to be rundown.

Whatever we see, hear, smell happens in very subtle manner. Even while passing, what we see is getting stored in our subconscious mind and this happen due to our peripheral vision. In this manner whatever we store is like junkyard or scrap collection. So when we have to think or contemplate about any specific difficulty or problem, our mind empty all the information collected till now and we become confused. This confusion cause fragmented concentration and we have to sort out as to what is relevant and what is useless, which again takes more time and cause lose of precious energy. To avoid this cluttering of mind, Mahaveer has laid down the technique of remembering, returning and reliving, in which we can retain only that much which is going to be of substance and the remaining is purged from our mind.

Awareness of this phenomenon will make us adapt to look at what is necessary, hear only that much that is necessary and talk only when it is imperative to talk. This is the way of energy conservation and is also the way that saves our faculties from excessive ware and tear. Why our eyesight is becoming impaired at the early age; the reason seems to be excessive visual stimulation we are exposed to since our early age, on top of this the abnormal viewing of television as the medium of entertainment which cause damage to the nerves before the faculty is fully developed. The same happens to our auditory faculty. Constant bombarding of various voices and noises are damaging the delicate mechanism of our faculty of hearing and the resultant impairment causes poor understanding and attention span. Both the impairments mentioned above play significant role in any developing child and its repercussions are felt at psychological level also.

Television as a major medium of entertainment and its role as medium of educational and general awareness are very questionable. No doubt it is one of the powerful medium of audio-visual display of various concepts. But the advantage taken by purely entertainment industry and advertising agencies is great cause of concern not only to psychologists but to social reformers and workers as well as to all the educational institutions and parents of school and college going children. Television is the invention of Americans, to which they call as an idiot box, but to the same we call as status symbol. How this invention has influenced and disrupted their social structure, family relationship and general outlook of the viewers in relation to the values they are attaching to the trivia's than to human beings, is major cause of concern. The same is happening in our society also; the programs broadcasted and the serials shown, the nudity, depraved and distorted concepts of human sexuality, depiction of violence shown as justifiable way of behavior, all these are not only causing undue strain on our eye sight but causing radical changes in our mind by way of thinking which is causing utter degradation of relationships between humans.

How teenagers of India are getting influenced by television and the advertisements shown on it and what is in store for these children in future which is also going to affect the society at large, is presented in an issue of India Today, published in August 2003.

This is how excessive exposure of any sense faculty clouds our mind, thinking process, expression of emotions and attachment of values, personal judgment and overall behavior. If this is to be considered as scientific and modern advancement for the betterment of the human race and if the old pioneers like Jesus, Mohammad, Buddha or Mahaveer take birth in today's environment; then these humanistic people who have tried to taught us how to live joyously and in creative manner, will have to commit suicide because they were not so much advanced.

All the sense faculties has potentials to fulfill intended individual functions like eye to see, ear to hear, nose to smell, tongue to taste and skin to feel. They transmit the data or information to our brain by way of direct stimulation and the brain in turn relays the command to act or react. Upto this point everything is happening very naturally and scientifically, but to act or react or do not act at all, should happen on the say of our self or intelligence. But in reality, at this stage, involvement of our mind changes all the perspectives, then what do not want to happen happens and what has to happen do not happen, and this happening or not happening is considered as deviation. Presence of our self or intelligence at this stage is termed as existence in total awareness.

It is to be understood that our mind is very powerful faculty & this much developed mind is the distinctive characteristic that differentiate human from all the animates in this existence. But to use it properly we have to use it for contemplation, deliberation or as reference library only, and on completion of any one of these functions it has to be switched off and shelved till further notice.

Principle characteristic of attitude to accumulate is the belief that there is safety in numbers. Our attachment with objects and people shows our dependence on others, which happens due to greed as well as due to our belief that on our own we are not going to achieve anything. Any feeling of security causes dependence on the others, which in turn induces us to cling to the others, and this attitude makes us greedy. But to depend on others and to be greedy are states and characteristic features of our mind.

When only aim of our being becomes to earn more and more, then the habit of accumulation starts and when we apply the same notion to all the objects, then it turns into attitude. To Mahaveer this state of being is sign of unconsciousness. Money is medium of exchange, which helps us to live in relative comfort and to have money is not considered as sin. But to attach exaggerated importance to money and to accumulate the same in heedless manner, is the sign that now money is more important than our being or self. When we loose something and even after extensive search do not find it, then the loss causes disturbed state of mind. This shows how we attach exaggerated value to everything and anything. A child becoming disturbed after loss or damage to its toy is justifiable behavior as the child is still young and innocent. But when a grownup behaves in the same manner, then his display of distraught behavior is considered as distortion of the emotion. This out of proportion presentation of emotion happen due to association with the other. At the same time the perception that the other is more valuable than the self, happens due to attitude of accumulation.

According to Ruskin, a person is to be treated as rich only when he is willing to donate. But when this willingness is not present, then even though he is materialistically rich but it is sign of a poor person. Richness and poorness are also attitudes of mind, so to grasp or grab anything is the sign of poor and to donate anything is the sign of rich.

To give away or to donate indicates the attitude, that what is given is less important and less valuable than the self, and its absence or presence is not going to make any difference to my being. This attitude is the indicator that the master is present. When this giving happens with profound joy, then it becomes donation. And when we understand that my being is important in itself, my being is not dependent on anything and when everything becomes secondary, then whatever is cast away or left aside is called as sacrifice. It is a popular misconception that what we can sacrifice has to be precious. Again what we consider as precious is our state of mind and when we consider anything as precious, then at the same time we have to accept our belief that our existence is less precious than the other that is more precious than us. This perception that the other is more precious than our existence or being, is the cause of emergence of dependency on the other and to save the other as precious we have to cling to the other which happen due to greed and insecurity. At the same time preciousness of the other shows how inferior we are and this happens due to balancing act of the nature.

When any person experience feeling of containment or happiness in direct proportion to his acceptance by whatever the other is giving, then he is dependent on the others, and shows that the person do not value his self. Mahaveer calls this state of being as state of unconsciousness.

Ultimate expression of sacrifice means potential to cast away or leave aside even our body. This is the meaning of the statement made by Mahaveer when he renounced general way of existence; that from now onwards I leave myself at the mercy of the environment or existence, it may sustain me or not, is not upto me and I am not going to do anything to sustain myself as I am willing to exist or cease to exist as I am.

After going through the concepts of donation and sacrifice, and after happening the said acts on physical level, Mahaveer explains about a very subtle characteristic of our mind that exists due to our ego, and the said characteristic is nature of clinging of the mind. After donating or sacrificing, if our mind retains the same fact as a special virtue of ours, then even physical partition of the object or attitude thus cast away is not cast away in reality at all. Even mentally clinging to the acts that has happened in reality long back in the form of donation or sacrifice are still important to us and the value we have attached to those objects are still of importance to us, then it shows that by nature our mind is still attached to those objects. As mentioned before willingness to donate or sacrifice primarily happens at the plane of our mind and once the manifestation is happened then there is no need to remember about them. But according to Mahaveer, this kind of donation or sacrifice happens when we have to go through the act to let others know or show, that by nature we are very sympathetic and compassionate.

Our general pattern of our behavior shows that we are very subtly hypnotized by others or objects. To be hypnotized is a state of mind where any object, thought or emotion become so dominant, insistent and attractive or obsessive, that till the object come in our actual possession or till the thought or emotion is not acted upon, we experience emptiness or unhappiness. In this regards our eyesight is the more powerful as well as the most vulnerable sense organ of ours, which can be stimulated from faraway in very subtle manner. Most of the mediums of advertising take advantage of this vulnerability of ours to create artificial demands for the products that are not necessary for our existence. And for this reason only when any person at the time of Mahaveer or Buddha shown inclination to be ordained as a monk, he was used to be kept on probation for at least 3 years with the added condition that in this period his eyesight has to be set in such an angle while walking, that no more than four feet of the path can be seen. Similarly at the end of the day he has to recite where he has been & what he has seen, to the superior monk. The reason being all the external stimulations should not cause undue contemplation in his mind as well as to conserve the energy of the visual faculty.

This is the common day-to-day experience of ours that in spite of our sleeping for 6 to 7 hours we steel feel listless and wary on awaking in the morning. The reason is, all day long we go through all the work in routine manner and at the same time various thoughts go on in our mind that do not form fully & are not expressed in any manner at all. All such thoughts remain stored in our subconscious mind and the moment we go into deep sleep, our conscious or active mind looses its hold and thoughts from our unconscious mind start to surface. Such thoughts take forms of dreams and these dreams disturb our sleeping pattern. Further such expressions of the thoughts by the way of dreams also create tension in our already tired body. When our tired body is not given sufficient time to heal and rejuvenate which should happen in our sleep, then we start to experience listlessness and weariness in the morning. Then continual experience of this nature for extended period of time takes its toll and tolerance system of our body breaks down and we remain in constant fatigue.

Materialistically poor people experience discomfort but not sorrow and rich people experience sorrow and unhappiness. Discomfort is experienced due to privation and sorrow is experienced due to emotions. Poor goes on experiencing discomfort with the hope that in near future the conditions will change for better and then he will be happy. His hopes are still intact. But in the case of rich there do not remain any hope for the simple reason that whatever has to be acquired is already acquired. He becomes frustrated because there is no future and this prospect cancels all the hopes. This is the manner in which dissolution of all the hopes and no discernible future cause sorrow and unhappiness.

Generally extreme materialistic achievement and accumulation leads towards depression. Feelings of sorrow and unhappiness are basic characteristic of materialistically rich people, and privation felt or experienced due to lack of the same materialistic possession is the characteristic of the poor.

Basically, mental attachment with anything and then its absence or loss cause sorrow. At the same time expected possession of any object, till its actual possession, cause the feeling of wanting or emptiness of mind and emptiness in the immediate surrounding, is called as inner greed by Mahaveer. And to him this is the reason of emergence of attitude of accumulation.

Attitude of accumulation is state of mind. As shown in various chapters before this discussion, natural inanimate objects are present due to schematics of the existence and they exist as per their basic nature. The same applies to the objects that are invention of the human, for the reason that such objects make our stay tolerable and easy. As far as humans are concerned, relationship and attachment with other humans remain constant till both are going to benefit, but the major difference happens when either of the two feel or think, that hereinafter this relationship is not going to be beneficial, then severance of the relationship also happens. As all the humans are conditioned to expect and anticipate more or less the same from all the others with whom they are related, and as all have the same will power and unique nature of their own with the same faculty of mind to think with the same emotions, then people go into relationship with others as well as are capable of to brake the same when viable cause for continuity is not felt or experienced. In a nutshell this is the basic tenet of awareness. Nothing is attractive or repulsive; animate or inanimate, but nature of our mind through its thoughts and emotions attach exaggerated values to all and sundry.

Mahaveer states that to experience thirst or hunger are valid feelings of our body and whenever they are experienced they are to be fulfilled, as they are biological and natural. At the same time it is to be understood that such experiences are going to be felt again and again, and every time they have to be fulfilled. But Mahaveer says that when this demand for food and water are felt and supplied with appropriate means, then the matter is to be deemed as closed. But when we attach exaggerated value to these demands and means of its fulfillment, then this type of exaggeration causes dependency and attachment that results into pain and sorrow. Only way out of this predicament is to understand our need and apply the intended object to pacify the same need, which in psychological parlance is called as transactional behavior. All the objects are to be treated as means to an end but not as end in itself.

Mahaveer laid down certain steps by which we can remain aware and save ourselves from pain and sorrow.

1) Every object is to be seen as it is i.e. objectively and is not to be attached with exaggerated value, with the hope that they are more precious than they really are.

2) Every object is to be treated as means and not end in itself at all.

3) Every time we must remain present in awakened capacity as master of our self with the same understanding as mentioned above.

Whatever happens or manifests on the outside, the reasons behind are the thoughts or emotions that are present in our mind. Until we consciously focus our self or intelligence to look at our mind in analytical manner we remain as extrovert. General behavioral tics like movement of our legs as if we are walking while sitting on a chair, wringing of our hands, exaggerated body movements while talking about ordinary subjects, constant change of posture, aimless movement when we are alone; like walking aimlessly, setting or resetting of the objects kept in the room or reading the same newspaper that we have gone through in the morning shows that the thoughts going on in our mind are not subject to analysis or are of such nature that to act on them will cause embarrassment to us or we will be criticized by others. But we readily criticize the same behavioral pattern presented by the other immediately, for the reason that under the influence of our mind our nature remain as extrovert. Mahaveer says that if someone criticizes us, do not neglect the criticism out of hand for the simple reason that most of the time others make us aware about our shortcomings and about ourselves as to what type of person we are in reality. Our ego and our perception about our image and the way in which we behave may not be in correspondence to each other. So the disparity between the two, is the cause of criticism happening by the other which in reality are pointers that can help us to be more introvert about ourselves and may help us towards integrated personality.

Real question is not what we are accumulating and why, but our attaching exaggerated values to others, which most of the times is out of proportion. Basic reason behind this phenomenon happens due to involvement of our mind that causes dependency, which in turn creates greed and lust. If we use objects to pacify the object-related demand at any time and go on our way, then involvement of mind is not necessary. It is the basic characteristic of the mind that its existence is felt only when any extreme emotion or thought is present, otherwise experience of emptiness is experienced. But our perception of our self happens through our mind and we feel alive only when our mind remains active; this happens only because we are not aware as to what our true form is, what our true nature is. Our belief that we are body gives undue importance to our mind. All the religions and this discussion about Mahaveer's doctrine is the way to let us know and understand that the true nature of our being is not what we believe in, but something else. To understand what we really are and to experience the same in firsthand manner is going to change everything. And when this happens then our gestalt about looking towards life and living will also change in radical and creative manner.

Real necessity and necessity felt due to greed are two different phenomenons. And the amazing thing is any greedy person can very rarely fulfill his necessity, the reason being to spend on to fulfill the demand he has to draw from the accumulated which is going to deplete the reservoir which in turn will cause more emptiness. Then feeling of this kind of emptiness is going to cause further stress and tension because now he has to start accumulating again to level or top-up the reservoir. On the contrary, poor also experience privation but mostly they are not misers in relation to the so-called rich only because the poor dares to indulge himself whenever possible only due to his realistic encounter with actual privation. Furthermore he knows and understands perfectly well that whatever he has, the same is not going to be substantial with any stretch of imagination but at the same time if he do not indulge then he is going to experience profound privation. Funny thing about accumulation as basic trait of greed is, it is state of mind and its related behavioral pattern happens in the miserly manner. It is basic law of existence or nature that any emptiness experienced because of the state of mind cannot be filled in any manner anywhere, least of all with the help of any tangible objects.

The so-called emptiness we experience in our being is equal to the vast void we know as sky. And in this void, either we can experience our basic self or being, or this void can be turned in to our active mind. Such mind can be used in the capacity of verification, deliberation or contemplation of our thoughts and emotions under the supervision of our intelligence, which is and should be the way in which we can benefit from our mind. Or we can fillip this void with all the junk with our unconscious being and may face the consequences in the form of various mental illnesses at latter date. This void is our sanctum sanctorum, where we glimpse our basic being, our true nature and to dwell in this void for any period of time is called as state of Samadhi and realization of our self. Any person who experiences this phenomenon at least once in his lifetime, do not remain as he was but he changes in very radical way. The same change is considered as resurrection of the same person or is called as Dwija or twice born. Hereinafter the same person starts to live in harmony with his self that coincides with the whole nature that we know as total existence. This is what is known as enlightened person in every religious context and the same person is appreciated as a person of totally integrated personality in psychological parlance. Any person who has reached this stage becomes capable to realize his full potentials and then he can scale any heights as per his aims. All those people who we know and are recognized as great musicians, painters, towering personalities in all the branches of businesses, enterprises, medicine, scientists from all the walks of various sciences etc. are nothing but enlightened people in their own way and their achievements are equal to what any religion accept as realization of self. An expression of this type of realization is the same ultimate blooming and flowering of the potentials, which is considered as explicit and is recognized in religious context also. We the people of India are very fortunate that our present day President Dr.A.P.J.Abdul Kalam is the one of the persons in this present times who is of the caliber equal to all the known pioneers, who laid down priceless doctrines for the betterment of the mankind.

Let us understand that inner awareness is sign of integrated being and inner unconsciousness is to exist in absentia.

CHAPTER 25

BALANCING ENERGY FORCE AND ITS REASON

Some more explanation about greed as the basic nature of our conditioned and habit bound mind is to be elaborated. Expressions of libido, anger and delusion (i.e. attachment with any object or a person, that is deemed to be of value and its importance to further the cause of emotion implicit in our mind which is termed as Moha in Vedic doctrine) are nothing, compared to the state of mind in the form of greed. At the same time all these expressions are very subtle forms of greed only. Even newborn comes into being with inherent greed.

Expression of the emotion of anger happens due to circumstances, but at the same time any circumstance may become adverse due to greedy state of mind. The mind under the influence of greed expresses itself in various forms. Experience of anger happens when the greedy expression of our mind is blocked or thwarted. Sexual expression by the way of act happens due to greedy state of mind. Biology as a branch of pure science, accepts the fact that death is inevitable and psychology accepts the basic characteristic of the human mind that no one wants to die. In the light of these scientific and psychological statements, emergence of concept of immortality is nothing short of fantasy, but the nature of our conditioned mind to cling to any concept that furthers its beliefs, accepts this phenomenon of immortality due to greed.

Sexual expression by way of act of intercourse happens to procreate part and parcel of our being, with the notion that if I am not going to live forever, then at least some part of me is going to remain in this existence in the form of my children. In this regard to sire offspring's and specifically to have male child is considered as important achievement only because the male child carries the same lineage forward. And this belief is very firmly entrenched in Indian culture and in the minds of all the people.

When expression of the emotion caused by greed is blocked or thwarted by anyone or the circumstances, we experience anger and it is projected. Inability to express emotions cause manifestation or feelings of anger. Attachment to any object or to any person happens when the same helps us to fulfill or achieve the goal desired by us and the said desire is the emotion of greed. To understand what greed is, is to know that to be greedy is the basic reason that causes us to behave in the angry, libidinous or clinging manner. Understanding this state of our mind by way of self-analysis helps us to be free from the greedy nature of our mind. And this awareness, that to be greedy is the characteristic of our mind and emotions of anger, libido and undue attachment with anyone or anything, are also expressions of the greed.

Behind all the human thoughts, emotions, actions and reactions as well as achievements and goals, greed in the form of driving force remains present. In human existence at all the times, greed as the subtle driving force of our mind remains more or less constant. Our emotional oscillation from one extreme to other happens due to the same greed. It is not possible for us to exist without conflicts and contradictions, because we bank heavily on our mind and identify our self with our mind as our true being. Basic nature of our mind is like mercury, never still or constant. People turn towards religion at the advanced age because they have less energy to change themselves and religious practice seems to be only assurance to maintain the sanity in otherwise chaotic existence. Similarly, the belief that anyone practicing religion in traditional manner do not face hardships or gets what he wants at the end, carries much weigh in our society so people starts to follow religion or to become religious at late middle or old age. Furthermore in our younger age possibility of old age and death are perceived too far away or thought about as non-existent and this belief causes the heedless spending of energy on the matters of no substance. The same happens with the monetarily rich who wish to be recognized as a wealthy person, but when the desired appreciation is not awarded then the same person starts to donate like crazy with the same intention to be recognized as donor. His intention to be appreciated by the others and to remain in limelight happens due to greedy nature of his mind.

Renowned psychoanalyst Karl Gustav Jung states that, majority of the patients he came across were of the age group of 40 and above for all the types of abnormal behavior. And the reason he pinpoints is, lack of worthwhile religious practice worth adopting which will give succor to otherwise chaotic mental states. Similarly Jung is of the opinion, that upto the age of forty human sexuality by way of sexual emotions and its corresponding expressions revolve around as pivotal to existence, for which marriage is coveted but after the age of forty religion takes the place of sexual expressions and religious practice is deemed as central to existence. According to Jung, there is no religion of caliber that can touch all the facets of human life in western cultures and this is the reason that more elders from the western culture are prone to madness in their advanced age. On the other hand completely opposite happens in the eastern cultures. The reason being, clinging to puritanical meanings laid down in all the doctrines and strict adherence to the same without any sanction to evaluate the same in relation to current situations and where human sexuality is considered as very baser emotion and its expression in any way is frowned upon. As mentioned from time to time in current narration, all the doctrines can be applied to our present existence in creative manner only when its inferences as to what is of significance can be understood and when the basic principle laid down in the doctrine become practical. And this is the reason why blind following of any religion makes people more frustrated and so they start to distance themselves from anything concerning religion. So when the same religious practice is forced on the younger generation without giving due explanations as to why they have to behave in the stated manner, with the added list of behaviors termed as sinful, then the young ones become more frustrated and their creative energy atrophy and cause various mental illnesses. But when the same younger generation becomes old, then out of resignation and as a last resort, cling to religion as the only main stay in otherwise bleak existence and become pathetic and more rigid but not mad. Young ones are to be given opportunities to express their thoughts and emotions, because they have boundless energy and corresponding drives are also very powerful which if not channeled at the right time in creative manners, then the same energy cause havoc in their psych and this is the reason Mahaveer is interested to introduce religious practice in the young ones. According to Mahaveer our faculty of reproduction is the same faculty that can lead us towards realization or Moksha.

According to Mahaveer desire to experience realization of self or desire to experience our faculty of regeneration are two sides of a coin and both become driving force due to greed as the basic feature of our mind. The faculty we term as our mind is the emptiness where fusion of our self known as Prana or force of life and our soul happens at the time of realization, which is known as enlightenment and ultimate destination of the human. But till we arrive at this stage we experience jitters and trepidation in our mind due to its emptiness. We perceive our mind only when it is active and this may happen due to thoughts, emotions or while we are contemplating. But momentary glimpses of the inner emptiness cause our mind to create conjunctures and hypothesize as to how this emptiness can be filled, but these conjunctures or hypothesizes are nothing but forms of greed. The same greed is the means or driving force of our mind, which starts to attach values to all, with the intention to fill up the emptiness. But we must understand that it is not possible to fill all the emptiness at all the time. If we look at the desert and its vast emptiness where there is just sky above and sand below, then we will understand the futility of the task to fill such emptiness. The same void or emptiness is our inner realm and this can be experienced only when we can remain as witness and our mind becomes tranquil. As a human being we have the potentials to encounter our basic being or true form, with the help of our superior intelligence and advanced mind at the background of our inner emptiness.

For this reason Mahaveer says that, however powerful greed may be and no matter how many objects we have, but they have no potentials to fill our inner emptiness. In this sense our mind is very naïve and its arithmetic is very simple; collect whatever is handy, accumulate any thing and place it in the empty space so that the emptiness cannot be felt. All the processes of this doctrine are means or pointers to empty ourselves from all that we have accumulated by way of habits and attitudes, so that when we really become free and empty, then the emptiness of our inner will coincided with the emptiness we have achieved by way of austerity and both will merge and this merger, however momentary it may be, causes us to change and then we start to live in positive and creative manner as an enlightened human being for the first time.

Mahaveer not only rejects existence of God but rejects existence of devil also. He says godliness is present in every human and so is devilry in the form of greed, because the same greed is the barrier that blocks us from the realization of godliness i.e. our self.

Nature of the human mind to exist in the perpetual state of GREED is the cause and reason of oscillation of moods, shifts of the emotions from one extreme to other as well as opposite extreme. The same cause abnormalities in behavior when we cling to any one extreme or causes emergence of various relationships and also break the same, causes friendship and enmity also and is one of the powerful causes of degradation of the human being. Generally greed is motivational driving force behind most of our actions and reactions as well as cause of creation of the barriers also. Then the same barriers either block the same actions or reactions from manifesting or become the cause for erection of new and opposite barriers. And this mental state of ours is the cause that we behave in the manner of puppets most of the times.

Mahaveer implores us to look at the empty place in our being as our mind, which denotes the sky as one of the basic elements of our being. A water glass is the object, which we use every day. Till we have to use it for drinking it remains empty and after its usage it again becomes empty. This feature of the water glass to remain empty when not in use is the basic characteristic of the glass and for this reason only, the glass is important to us. Mahaveer says that we have to look at our mind and use it in the same manner as we are using the water glass when the occasion arises to use it. This is how, we as intelligent entity can be masters of all the faculties we have, and will understand that mind is nothing but one of the faculties.

Desire to fill the emptiness makes the other important, but at the same time filling with the help of anything that has no potentials to fillip the same emptiness causes heaviness. Our mind full of thoughts and related emotions cause the same kind of heaviness in our mind. People indiscriminately go on thinking about anything and everything without being aware that by nature thoughts have very subtle forms. But still its existence makes us droop or bow down physically as if very heavy load is placed on our shoulders. When only thoughts has so much potentials which make us experience this much heaviness, then we have to imagine what all the desires and related attitudes will add to the already heavy burden we are carrying. Under this collective heaviness, eventually people crack or break down which in general is termed as abnormal mental conditions or behavioral abnormalities.

It is greed that causes emergence of interest and any thing as interesting is the reason the taste is experienced. The same happens in respect to our eating habit and whatever is experienced as tasty creates more interest in the food. At the same time wherever our mind is involved as the intermediary to any experience, then the repetition to experience the same feeling starts to happen. But in this manner due to repetitive acts, either the energy of the related faculty drains totally or floods the faculty to the overflowing and this kind of draining or overflowing is the cause of the sickness of the faculty. This phenomenon can happen with any of our sense faculty and its related organs. Concept of interest and the taste related to interest is applicable to all the objects of every nature, animate or inanimate.

Mark Twain was very ill and one of his visiting friends asked him where he would like to be after death. Mark Twain replied that I am contemplating on the same issue and my conclusion is; for climatic conditions heaven is the best but for the sake of company hell is better than heaven. Twain is pointing towards conditioned human nature, where either we are not acquainted with our self or not happy with our self and to forget this troublesome existence we covet company, which is hell.

According to Mahaveer, to take food before sunrise and after sunset should be avoided by those, who are on the way of self-realization. This tenet is important not because of religious doctrine but is based on very scientific principles. The energy which is coursing in our body is of the same nature and character as the energy emanating from the Sun and its being in the human form is known as energy force of life or Prana. Naturally the force of energy present in human remain more forceful in the day time, for the simple reason that its most pure form emanating from the Sun is present in the surrounding atmosphere, and thus it reciprocates and coincides with the energy force present in us. The coincidence of both the energy forces is the driving and motivational force; due to which we very easily go about all the tasks we have to do. For humans to generate working energy, food is the means that is used as fuel. The saying that we have to have breakfast as the King, have lunch as the Prince and have dinner as the Pauper has great significance.

In our sleep we do not require food for the reason that; sleep is the resting and rejuvenating phase in our being. Not only our body but all the internal organs as well as our brain and our mind as the part of our brain also take rest and recoup on their own, so that our body should function in energetic manner on the next day also. To have substantial food in the morning called breakfast has literal meaning i.e. to break the fast, as during our sleep we do not experience hunger. This initial intake is used as fuel that generates initial energy, which helps us to start functioning again after daybreak. In the same manner our lunch is also used and the additional energy generated make it possible for us to work till sunset.

Due to our night time abstinence from the food, our breakfast intake undergoes digestion at higher rate but when time coincide with the prior digestion and we add intake by the way of lunch, then generation of the energy goes on till end of the day. Any intake of food in substantial quantity takes upto 6 to 8 hours to digest fully, depending on the nature of work we undertake. The energy generated using food as fuel is not only used for body movements, but the same energy is the energy that helps our digestive system to go about its function of digestion, waste disposal etc. As all the organs are part and parcel of our body, at the end of the day our body as integrated machinery including all the organs experience fatigue and become tired. Similarly, food to be digested and process of energy generation also slows down. This experience of fatigue and tiredness is the indicator shown by our body to notify us, that now we has to take rest. Similarly at the time of sunset and within one hour after the sunset, a chemical called melatonin starts to secrete in our brain that is carried to all the parts of our body through our blood stream. This chemical is of Opiate nature and is natural tranquilizer, which takes us in deep sleep. Effect of this chemical wares off within 5 to 6 hours by metabolic process happening inside of us and is flushed out by natural flushing system. Secretion of this chemical depends on the way the person is, his nature and the type of work he goes throughout the daytime.

Now when we take food after sunset, our digestive system has to work overtime i.e. in the rest period also, with whatever meager energy reserves our body has. In reality this is the basic natural process of the nature that the same reserve is to be used for restoration and rejuvenation of all the organs and its related faculties, so that in their healthy state we could again use them on the next day. But we intervene in this very natural way of working of the nature in our favor, by eating at the nighttime and its adverse effects by way of listlessness, fatigue, heaviness in mind and body, acidity, indigestion and irregular bowel movement are to be experienced. Persistent irregularities of this nature experienced in our body for extended period of time, causes various illnesses and sicknesses we have to experience and fend on physical and mental level. All the branches of medicine including psychiatry, are of the opinion that disturbed cycle of our sleep pattern and its effects on our circadian rhythm that should coincide with our innate biological clock goes haywire which not only affects our body but indirectly affects our mind also. And the primary reason behind this happening is our nighttime eating habit. Similarly cause of most of the people experiencing nightmares and disturbed sleep cycle lies in our general eating habits and specifically our nighttime eating habit.

The way in which Mahaveer suggests and asks us to reconsider our habit to eat after sunset has very scientific significance which reflects on our overall mental and physical well being and is worth considering as well as adapting in our everyday life. Nighttime is for rest only i.e. not for our body but for our psyche also. Further he suggests that by way of witnessing, we can separate our mind from our body also and this will be doubly advantageous to our being. Very few people are capable to sleep the moment they are ready to sleep, and this happens because we are not capable to switch off the thinking process of our mind as to when we are ready to take rest by way of sleep. So Mahaveer suggests that when we think that we are ready for sleep, and then we have to let our self become witness of the working of our mind in detached manner. In this manner, when we consciously look at all the comings and goings of the thoughts and emotions in our mind without thinking on the thoughts or the emotions, then our mind starts to loose momentum and the same starts to disappear from our conscious mind and then we become tranquil. This tranquility of our mind become cause of loosening the hold on the residual energy, which otherwise is to be spent on the antics of our mind, and the same energy then become useful to reset, recharge, regenerate and rejuvenate all the organs and faculties of our body that we have to use on the next day. This is the manner in which meditation in true sense happens and the meaning of the statement made by Shri Krishna will be understood in its true perspective. There is a statement in Bhagwat Gita that true austerite never sleeps and even in sleep he remains awake. Mahaveer says that nighttime is the time when our body reposes in restful manner and we do not have to consciously cater to its demands.

Any person of average intelligence, who is ready to change in positive and creative manner, will have to understand and adapt himself in this doctrine where how to meditate takes more time and possibility of his arriving at the stage of self realization may happen or not. But if we accept that average life span of an individual is to be 60 years, then 17 to 19 years are spent in sleep and if the sleep is used in the manner suggested by Mahaveer, then his chances of realization of self are guaranteed.

About meditation people have various beliefs that to meditate we have to spend more energy and have to concentrate willfully, have to empty our mind of all the thoughts and emotions, but all the beliefs are erroneous. Even to contemplate or to deliberate is the process of our mind, and to go about this functioning of our mind is to become clinical about the thoughts going on in our mind and to apply our intelligence as to which thoughts and emotions are going to be helpful and proper to the future course of action also cause energy dissipation. But to meditate in proper perspective, our pure intelligence or our self remains as witness to the proceedings of our mind in the capacity as overseer, but we do not have to think on the thoughts or emotions present in our mind. To meditate is to just remain as we are and this witnessing is the process that leads us towards awareness of the self. And this phenomenon is possible and its advantages are twofold; our body goes in to rest as our mind is disconnected from our body in this process and our mind becomes tranquil and experience of peacefulness consolidates.

The chain of events that happens in our daily life and their effects on our health and our mind, are elaborated by Mahaveer in some details and are worth considering. As mentioned before, night is for rest not only for our body but our mind also. But when we eat at night, our digestive system has to work overtime.

But we forget that our digestive system is also part of our body and the same system also needs rest to work efficiently on the next day. Any substantial intake takes at least 6 to 8 hours to digest fully and necessary digestive juices are to be secreted as per the intake. People eat at night and due to heaviness of stomach either experience drowsiness and go to sleep or for the same reason remain awake till such time that the sensation of heaviness becomes tolerable and then go to sleep. In both the cases digestive process slows down in which case on the next day we experience either indigestion or acidity. For indigestion our system has to secrete more juices so that the residual food is processed adequately. We experience acidity when due to sleep our body also relaxes and the same juices remain in our system. These juices very rarely remain as dormant but they mix in our blood stream, as our blood is the medium which not only carries all that is of nourishing value to all the organs but carries the toxins as wastage to appropriate flushing organs so that they are thrown out at regular intervals. When residual acid mixes with our blood in its concentrated form, then purification of the blood happening in our lungs takes more time. But till total purification happens, the same blood with all the impurities remain in circulation and its contents are deposited in all the organs along with nourishing elements. High blood acid level of various types and its being deposited at various organic sites is the reason of malfunction of various organs and at the sites of various joints is the cause of stiffening of joints as well as it's deposit in our muscles causes inelasticity in our musculature, which cause spasms and muscle arrests, which impose restriction on our movement. The same blood when reaches our brain cause irritation in our brain function, which not only cause all types of headaches but become cause of change in chemical composition of our brain. When all these changes are considered and understood in medical terms, then what these changes are capable of manifesting can be understood.

This is how Mahaveer looks at the relationship of food with night, food with human and night with human being. Also in this manner it becomes clear that how deep Mahaveer has gone as far as human psyche and human biology is concerned and how both are related to each other. To understand this relationship and to change our self accordingly is the reason Mahaveer laid down this process, which is called as process of awareness.

Not only Mahaveer but also all the pioneers of all the religions are of the opinion, that at the most two moderate intakes a day is sufficient food for any person who desires to realize his full potentials in any walk of life. But as we are people who behave in instinctive manner because of intervention of our mind, we are bound to be eccentric. Our organs can be satisfied in the manner of direct experience between organic demand and concerned act, but as our mind is not organ per se, it is not only difficult but also downright impossible to satisfy our mind in any way about any thing. And to understand this enigma as to this is how our mind is, is awareness.

Further Mahaveer says that we have to shun not only from actual food at the nighttime but even about thought of food. We know how our mind goes in to contemplative mode when we restrain our self from any act from manifesting. And most of the times mere contemplation is more interesting than actual act that cause more wastage of energy, so in such case it is better to act than to just think Even in Vedic branch of Yogic practice, it is stated that those who meditate regularly, nighttime food intake is restricted which is called as Upwas- the meaning of the word being Up stands for secondary and Was stands for stay; secondary stay near our being.

As to how we can manipulate our force of life in the way of control and redirection it, Mahaveer suggested certain hints as to how we can verify the movement of our force of life in desired manner. It is suggested that initially we have to start from our extremities i.e. hands and legs. We must stand in relaxed manner and concentrate all of energies on the desired site and experience the surge of energy coursing and enhanced sensations at the intended site. When we become capable in this manner then we can shift the energy on the other site and go through the experience again. It is further suggested that until this phenomenon is not experimented upon our extremities and till we are not capable to experience the energy surge with awareness, we are not going to will the same on our heart or brain. When we experience and understand the energy surge, then it becomes easy to direct the same on the site of our heart and brain in controlled intensity, so that these delicate organs are not inadvertently damaged. And this technique is the key which become handy when we start to meditate, at the end of which we have to direct the same surge at our core and experience for the first time the inner glow and integration of our total being.

When we start to experience this energy surge at our core and remain at this state for any length of time, then this is the moment when we become totally innocent; where nothing bothers us or pulls us anywhere and for the first time we experience the true nature of our self that is perfect peace and tranquility. Innocence experienced at this state has such quality that innocence we see in young infants seems pale in comparison; happening of this phenomenon is like a being, which was lost in an alien land where the being has to flounder just to maintain itself to survive and to remain sane, but when the same being comes back to its original source then what it feels is peace and tranquility. This state, to come back in to our true nature is considered as to discover us but not to innovate ourselves.

CHAPTER 26

DISCIPLE AND HUMBLENESS

Hindu culture is of the opinion that there are two types of people; first type are those who look and search for that which they desire to posses and second type are those who search that which is of substance. Former is interested in objective and latter is interested in subjective.

What mostly happens in the first category is, people think that when they have in their possession what they covet for then they will be contented. And this thought or belief to possess becomes their aim or goal and they direct all their energies towards those efforts that will help them to achieve what they wanted. Till the manifestation of the achievement their hope remains intact, but after actual manifestation, some of the people do not experience desired satisfaction or do not feel the expected satisfaction they were hoping to experience. According to Mahaveer, such people mostly follow dictates of their mind that are related to sense faculties and people feel disillusioned at the end of manifestation, which cause sorrow and pain.

People of the second category pay scant attention towards desirable or otherwise, but their overriding desire is to achieve that which will never part from them at any time and should be of substantial nature. And such people pursue this concept steadfastly and it ultimately manifests as realization of the truth. People falling under this category are primarily well aware that what they are thinking to achieve is very hazy and cannot be described in our everyday language. But they believe in their gut feelings and go for the search of unknown. Mahaveer says that the persons of the second category are the people who invariably follow path of the religious austerity and may reach the state of self-realization.

It is our experience till now whatever we try to achieve or ultimately achieve in materialistic sense cause pain, sorrow and disillusionment afterwards. Cause of this type of disappointment happens due to involvement of our conditioned mind behind every thought and emotion. When our mind dictates its desire to any sense faculty, the faculty thus driven causes happening of act and this phenomena is known as behavior. As we have seen before, organic demands happens due to biological reasons, which when appeased in proper manner cause satiety in very natural way. But as we are not so adept to differentiate between demands of organ naturally or biologically and demands created by our mind due to habit or routine, we go on fulfilling each and every demand as and when they are experienced. This type of behavior is termed by Mahaveer as unconscious behavior.

In this regards it is opinion of Mahaveer, that people from second category experience more sorrow and pain initially when they start the quest for unknown as such efforts are known as austerity. The reason of initial experience of sorrow and pain happens because we have to look at all the organs and its related faculties as well as our mind in critical manner with the intention to understand and realize that are we acting due to motivation of our mind or due to legitimate demand of the concerned faculty. This critical analysis is the process, where for the first time we as masters are going to be at helm but not our mind. Till such point our mind was at the controls and we have to dance to the tune of our mind. This assertion between our self and our mind, as to who is master, causes all the pain and sorrow. In this process of assertion, our mind create various doubts; that the way on which we are going to walk is not reaching anywhere, that what we are going to experience is not going to be pleasant, that the goal we have set is not going to be realized as it is not realistic etc. And this tug of war between our own mind and our self, literally shot up our body temperature, which is the meaning of Tapa in Vedic parlance and to the same we have given the name as the process of austerity. This process is equal to purification of gold, as gold is to be placed in fire again and again to purge all the inherent impurities out of it.

People erroneously believe that it is our faculties of senses and all the related organs that are our enemies and they are to be purified or suppressed, so that they will not torment us with constant demands. Similarly this belief gather further strength when we are repeatedly told that it is our senses which are our enemies, due to which we are not experiencing God's grace. Whenever any doctrine is accepted in traditional manner without taken into consideration period of its emergence and social conditions at those times, then misinterpretations of its concepts and intended meaning are drawn in erroneous manner. No doubt the words used at that time are still in practice but its meanings change in very subtle manner over the period of time due to continual changes in all the aspects of existence. It remains as our duty to look at the same concepts according to current conditions and then apply them in our everyday life so that we can gain from them. Basically we are intelligent and after some experiments even we come to know the difference between faculty/organ (biological) generated demands and demands made by our mind.

Mahaveer says self-analysis is the only way where we can understand reason or cause of wanting as against desire. We have to understand that genuine wanting is the direct experience of the emptiness of the related organ, which happens due to natural and biological reasons, but most of our desires are related to our mind and are experienced due to our habit nature. Mahaveer suggests that even though initially we have to experience discomfort, we are not going to deviate from the chosen path because along the way when our mind come to know that we are serious and are resolved, then it starts to become amicable, mellow and stops creating barriers. And this is the stage after which we start to become integrated.

Mahaveer says that, seeker of the self or seeker of the truth about self, initially experience sorrow and pain but ultimately experience joy of being in the same lifetime. But on the contrary seeker of the happiness experience illusion of joy initially but has to ultimately experience sorrow and pain. This latter phenomenon happens due to manifestations that in no way corresponds with the anticipated and when this is experienced then sorrow and pain become imminent.

Why we have to experience these contradictory manifestations between these two categories? And why we do not get what we expect to get? By any other rule, we must get or have, what we want or expect. But when our mind is the cause and driving or motivational force behind every action and reaction, then all the sensory faculties and its related organs make their presence felt and start to make demands, which most of the time are not genuine demands. Similarly demands made by our mind are based on the experiences and inferences stored in our mind by way of memory are related to our past. But what we do not realize is as circumstances of the past as well as we ourselves are also ever changing, the degree of the experiences and its outcome also changes but invariably do not correspond with our previous experiences. Then potentials of our eyes to look at what is necessary turns into just an instrument of our mind, which orders our eyes to look at that which is interesting to our mind but may not be necessary to our being. Not only looking at anything, but also our way of looking becomes so twisted and bizarre, that our mind starts to draw inferences of its own, where nothing remain as substantial from which any inference can be drawn. In this manner, when looking at the same become routine, then novelty of the looking as such wares off and we have to shift the attention towards something new. It is the basic characteristic of our mind, that it never remains fixed on any thing and it become bored very easily when it has to follow any routine and look at the same thing for any extended period of time, so it likes to look at something new every time. And the same happens with all the faculties; touch of the same body, hearing of the same voices, tasting the same food, all the sensory inputs create boredom, then to break the monotony our mind lures us towards that which is not yet experienced and which is perceived as novel.

Our way of looking gives different meanings to different things, even though the object of our focus is not projecting what we perceive. And this characteristic of our mind to draw inferences where nothing is to be interred is called as illusion or visual hallucination. And when the same phenomenon is applied to all the faculties, then what we should experience in reality and what we are experiencing, happens in different perspectives and the way in which we start to behave become abnormal behavior. This is how gestalt changes. Mahaveer says that people do not understand and are not aware enough, as to how our mind is capable of to change the intended meaning into the meaning of what our mind wanted to believe or infer. We have to understand that our sensory faculties and its related organs are not to be blamed at all, but we have to understand that it is our mind that changes the meaning. In this manner whatever we experience may satisfy us for time being but the satisfaction is not going to be fulfilling. And when this phenomenon of momentary satisfaction but not of perpetual fulfillment happens again and again, then this is the cause of sorrowing existence where pain and disappointment are our constant companions. But ultimately this sorry state of affairs is the force that drives us to change. Then person of intelligence starts to check his conscious with the intention as to is he existing in fault, are his notions based on illusions. And this search within is nothing but analysis of the self and at the same time such person resolves to change on his own and starts to accept responsibilities of his acts.

But for most of the people, this search within do not happen easily and they have to have help of the person who has gone through all the phases and has ultimately realized how to exist in peaceful and contented manner in the present. Such a person is called as Master or Guru in every type of religion.

In our previous discussions we have gone through the difference between Master and Teacher. When any person is to be recognized as Master then to be a Master is an achievement in itself and such persons are considered as unique phenomenon in the class of his own. Qualities of the master can be compared with the person placed at the third rung in the first chapter, who is named as Acharya. Master or Acharya is a person who behaves as per his thoughts, whose deeds and thoughts are well synchronized and he talks only when his pure intelligence allows him to talk and he talks in the manner that is beneficial to others. Master is the embodiment of realized self and exists in total awareness.

According to Mahaveer, if at all we have to be disciple to any such Master then to be humble is the only virtue we must have and this precondition makes the relationship worthy. To be humble is the sign that now we have totally cast away our ego. With ego and our image as its byproduct, we have not achieved any thing of substance; we have experienced many setbacks, pain, disappointments and sorrow. So when these realities become glaringly clear to us, then we become humble and start to search such person who will help us to realize our own potentials. And such person is Master or Guru. It is to be understood that Master does not do any thing mysterious or spectacular but he takes the form of mirror and shows us what we really are and what we can be. At the most, he gives us hypothesis or concept on the basis of which we may arrive at our rightful destination.

As a disciple, why we have to be humble and why humbleness is accepted as basic virtue of a disciple has psychological significance. When all the experiences we have gone through and when the knowledge acquired by way of such experiences do not make us mature and creative personality, then the frustration and emptiness we feel cause us to look for counsel from such other person who will help us to overcome the shortcomings of ours and direct us towards right path. This willingness on our part to seek assistance from the other is the indicator of humbleness. If absence or dissolution of ego is to be taken as sign of humbleness, then this analogy is correct.

Humbleness as a virtue makes us open mentally, which never happens when we are egoistic. Master is like water laden monsoon cloud; when we become humble, then like an empty vessel we become ready to collect the water falling from the cloud. And in Master-disciple relationship the disciple sits at the feet of Master or bow at the feet of the master, is the sign of total surrender as well as acceptance of the Master as the only anchor or succor for the disciple in otherwise chaotic existence. It is very common and everyday gesture we have followed and seen in our life that to those who has to receive has to open his hands from below and the giver gives from above.

Master does not expect anything from disciple, except open mind and heart, and then the Master just pours down. According to Mahaveer, this exchange between Master and disciple is the purest form of love. This exchange between Master and disciple, and the relationship between them is completely different than what happens in the exchange between teacher and pupil. In the case of teacher and pupil exchange we come back as better informed and well learned. In case of Master-disciple relationship, we come back as mature and totally transformed person. It will be appropriate to say that the person who went to Master do not come back at all, but a new person comes back who is now more enlightened and aware. And for this reason it is said that, at the feet of Master we have to willingly die from our old ways and only then total transformation happens, and then we come back as a new person. This transformation is termed as resurrection, twice born or Dwija state of being.

Faith in the cause or faith in the Master is the key that helps us to go into the kind of relationship that happens in the Master-disciple relations. Emotion of faith stems from our heart but is not related to our intelligence. We know about Sage Kabir and there is a legend that happened at the time of his realization. When Lord Krishna along with Kabir's Guru manifested in front of him, Kabir first bowed down in front of his Guru and then in front of Krishna. Krishna smiles and asks Kabir as to why he prostrated initially in front of Guru. Kabir says that it is due to this Guru that I realized you; otherwise it was not possible for me on my own and in my Guru I see Lord Krishna. Every religion places the same value in Master or Guru and it is stated that Master is the reincarnation of God on this earth.

To be positive and creative, every human and disciple must have faith in self, faith in the cause and faith in Master or Guru. Faith is commitment on our part that now onwards I am ready to accept without reservation whatever happens, I am not going to deviate from my faith. Even at this stage Mahaveer has given liberty to us, that we have every right to check the person we are going to accept as Guru in any way, but once we accept, then we are not going to deviate from the resolution. Any person, if and when resolves to follow his own dictates or of his Masters', but do not sticks to the same and breaks the same and then go through the same exercise again and again, starts to becomes more pathetic after breaking of each resolve. Such a person is considered as fickle by nature and will never reach anywhere in his life. And for this reason, Mahaveer says that we are going to consider all the options we have, and then we will consider our capability and all the resources at our disposal, then decide the goal and follow it to the end. This behavioral regimentation is for our mind and in this way only, we can elevate above the dictates of our mind, which most of the times are mere whims as the outcome of our habit nature.

Further Mahaveer states that a disciple should obey his Master, should remain near his Master, and should understand the meanings of the gestures and body language of his Master. We accept or go to the Master only when we think that he will direct us in proper manner that is going to be beneficial to our existence, so when we on our part are willing, then not to obey and not to follow his dictates is foolhardy on our part. In a sense, Master is more of a psychotherapist of the disciple than guide and when he understands the nature of the disciple, then with his understanding he orders in such a way that those traits of ours, which are causing barriers, are pulled down. When this weeding of trivial and unwanted is sorted through and discarded, then new orders towards creative are instated and the disciple goes onto the path of realization of his potentials.

Further it is expected from the disciple, that he should not talk about his feelings and experiences with any other than Master. This condition is laid down for the simple reason that when we talk with anyone who is not conversant about our relationship with our Master, may unknowingly pass on such thoughts or criticize about the way in which we are following the Master. Such thoughts and criticism can be contradictory and can become cause of doubt in our mind about the Master and about the way on which we are progressing. In reality such doubts hamper our efforts and slow the drive towards fulfillment of our goal. Next Mahaveer says that the disciple should become adapt in deciphering the gestures and expressions of the Master. As the bond between Master-disciples become firm, day-to-day language as medium of communication becomes obsolete. Most of the times verbal communication may not convey subtleties of emotions or may be perceived erroneously, so to save the disciple from deviating from the proper course this condition is laid down.

We have unfortunately lost the faculty to read body language in which we were quite adept at the time of our infancy. Any infant, till he develops the faculty of speech, very well understands the emotion of love, sympathy and anger of its mother by her expressions or by way of her touch. Mahaveer says that Master or Guru is nothing but, or more than, mother to the disciple as mother gives biological birth and Master causes theosophical birth. Next condition is disciple should be humble. Humbleness as a virtue is necessary to listen to the Master without letting our ego or our limited intelligence intervening in the process of hearing and imposing our old impressions to draw the inferences or conclusions. When the Master is talking to us, the words may be familiar to us but meaning to the context may be altogether different and to understand this different meaning we have to listen with concentration but not to just hear. Due to our conditioned nature, most of the time we listen selectively or listen to only that much that we think is advantageous to us. To be humble in front of the Master is to clean our slate totally of all the old impressions and to start to listen attentively. This manner of attentive listening helps to open our core, so that what we take in as instructions of the Master can help us to change in creative and positive way.

Mark Twain, in his lighter mood told that whenever he was asked to criticize any book by the publisher, he used to write the criticism before the said book was read by him. He told that he wanted to save himself from getting influenced by the book after which to criticize the same may become hard. All of us behave in the same fashion. We label people as per our beliefs and this labeling is our safety measure to safeguard ourselves from getting influenced. In this manner whenever the other talks then it become easy to draw impressions and inferences as per our own parameters, otherwise we experience unease.

Mahaveer says that the disciple must not be insolent. Insolence is also a state of mind as well as a weapon of violence or retaliation. When we are on shaky ground and are challenged, then we become insolent rather than accept our shortcoming. Insolence is opposite to receptive state of mind. Further, disciple should not be overactive physically as well as mentally. Overactive behavior is the cause of loosening of concentration on any subject or concept. Let us experiment this phenomena in very ordinary manner; we have to pinpoint any thought or emotion and concentrate on the same, then we are going to jump on the spot for ten seconds and will again look at the thought or emotion. In this exercise we will realize that the said thought or emotion do not remain as it was or totally dissolves as the result of the jumping activity. The disciple should be steady in mind and body, should not be of deceptive nature but straightforward and open. Disciple should be of enquiring nature but should not be of unduly curious nature. Enquiry happens when genuine solution to genuine problem is sought but curiosity is applied to hedge the central issue. Most of the small children fire question after question out of curiosity but are not interested in answers.

Disciple should not hate anyone, for the excellent reason that to hate anyone, we have to step down to the level of whomsoever we have to hate, which is considered as degradation of the self as well as of mind. Even our force of life plummets downwards. There is a saying that we may choose friends easily but has to choose our enemies after much deliberation. Try to praise others irrespective of his status or even if he is not praiseworthy; when we praise anyone we expand mentally and our force of life also elevates

Emotion of anger should not linger; Mahaveer says that the disciple, if experience feeling of anger, must become witness to the emotion, in which case one of the two things will happen; due to witnessing either the emotion will subside if the manifestation happened due to our non-awareness or express the same in controlled and justifiable manner. Mahaveer accepts that emotion of anger is ingrained in our basic nature and by way of witnessing only it can be totally eradicated as we gain more awareness. But lingering emotion of anger is the cause of downright fall of any human and its manifestation and expression at all the times will cause nothing but misery to the person expressing the emotion as well as to all those who are in his vicinity. Lingering anger is the byproduct of repression of the thoughts or emotions and can be resolved only through self-analysis.

Disciple is expected to maintain goodwill towards his friends. We consider anyone as friend only when both are compatible by nature to each other. But after long acquaintances some traits of the person as the friend come to fore which create unease and doubt in our mind, due to which, the emotion to criticize the person behind his back become strong. Mahaveer says that do not criticize any friend and this non-critical set of our mind will give birth to the virtue of goodwill and equanimity towards all and sundry. Disciple must not feel proud after reading the relevant scriptures and books of religious doctrine, which may create illusion that we have more knowledge than others and is bound to inflate our ego. To understand the meaning of such books and because of that to feel that we are more knowledgeable is nothing but illusion. But when we apply the same knowledge in our practice then nothing remains as illusion and so there do not remain any cause for ego also. To have more information is not sign of true knowledge but to apply the same in practical manner increases our awareness and this awareness takes the form of knowledge.

Disciple is warned not to discuss the faults of others. Basic psychology behind this dictate is to show how superior we are than others and in this manner our faults seem as insignificant compared to others. But the pitfall in this process causes our downfall, as our faults remain dormant. At the same time our criticizing the other is not going to help others but on the contrary there is a possibility that the other may become more set in his manners just to spite us.

Mahaveer says disciple must be intelligent. Mahaveer's concept of intelligence is not related to disciple's IQ level but the intended meaning is to go on the chosen path ignoring all the outside stimulations and cues. Mahaveer says that before becoming disciple we have gone through the day-to-day life with all the experiences of every thought, emotions and expectations known to us and has achieved nothing of substance and has arrived nowhere. But now we become wise and mature, and are not going to be snared in the same rigmarole again in the role of disciple. Any person who understands this phenomenon is called as intelligent person.

Last quality of the disciple is the disciple should be aristocratic. By aristocratic Mahaveer means, a person who is gentle, polite and unassuming, and who perceive only good in everyone but not interested in any trivialities.

CHAPTER 27

FLOWERING OF AWARENESS-TO BE HUMAN

In this last chapter Mahaveer gives some more instruction about selection of Master and about mentality of disciple.

Mahaveer says we consider and contemplate on our capabilities in relation to current atmosphere and arrive at the stage where we decide whether to act or not act at all. And this phase is termed as commitment. When we think that we are ready to stick to the commitment then it is the time when the said commitment becomes as aim or goal to be achieved and then the journey towards achievement starts.

The same process is undertaken in selection of Master. Even when Lord Krishna told Arjuna to surrender to him i.e. to Krishna, Arjuna did not surrender immediately but asked many questions, enquired about all the possibilities and their possible outcomes. When Arjuna was convinced that the completion of the course of action would manifest only after his surrender to Krishna, then Arjuna surrendered. Bhagwat Gita is nothing but questions and answers, all the deliberations, explanations and discussions between Lord Krishna and Arjuna.

Most important issue is how long we should take to deliberate and contemplate? Is model master is in existence for whom we are searching? In this regard Mahaveer gave us two choices; either go on the search till we meet someone who seems to be ideal master, then accept him in entirety with the resolution that hereinafter what the master says to us, does to us and asks us to do is upto him and we are going to do as he dictates. But if we are not successful in our search but still feel that our cause is important enough to be pursued, then we have to go through the contemplation and deliberation phase with our self & on its satisfactory conclusion have to commit to our self, with the resolution that no matter what will be the outcome, we are not going to deviate.

Now whenever we decide to do anything, what happens as far as our mind is concerned is we accept the majority decision of our mind. According to Mahaveer this majority decision happen with about 70% of our mind, either for or against. And we arrive at this conclusion due to our intelligent deliberation and in these deliberations, reservoirs of our mind under the heads of all types of memories is considered and used. Why we have to accept 70% capacity of the mind and not just 50%? If we finalize at 50% of the mind then chances of our taking and finalizing any decision and pursuing the same becomes very hard or rather non-existent, because both sides of our mind will start the tug of war and both will try to attract our attention, which state is known as halfhearted decision or to exist in doldrums. Then 60% is somewhat better than 50% but extra 10% are spent to equalize the balance between both the sides and again any decisive commitment do not happen and then we experience stagnation. But when we decide at 70% then 10% more than 60% will be useful as push towards decisive action against remaining pull of 30% at which state we arrive at commitment level and to act towards fulfillment of the commitment gather momentum. So once we arrive at this stage then some part of the remaining 30% leaves the middle fence and joins forces with basic 70%. In such a case the balance percentile either dissolves or joins to the cause of commitment. And this is the stage where the decision to act or do not act becomes final which is known as resolution.

So when we say that I have arrived at a conclusion or made a decision is the time when 70% of our mind is made. But we have to remember that we do not take any decision with 100% mind, because no matter what or how, some percentile of our mind always remains as neutral or divided or against our commitment. Total integration of our mind always happens at the time of realization of the goal for which we have decided to act. Basically we experience the presence of our mind even after commitment to act, due to absence of that portion of our mind that remains as neutral or against our commitment. Total integration of the mind happens only at the conclusion of deep meditation but at that time our mind do not exist as mind, but becomes like boiling water that reaches 100° temperature mark and evaporates in the form of vapor.

For this reason Mahaveer says that, unless asked for, do not interfere in other people's deliberation or influence others when they are deliberating, or criticize the decisions of the others, because our intervention may muddle their mind and this inadvertent meddling of ours is considered as subtle form of violence.

This characteristic of our mind to commit and decide, is not known to or understood by many people, because of which people stall or postpone from taking any firm decision and this phenomena is known as lack of capacity to arrive at any conclusion. People wait till such time that when their mind is made 100% then they will decide and act. But 100% involvement of mind in anything never happens.

Why there is much more failure in human life, the reason happens to be our beliefs and attitudes, and our attachment to and association with our mind as the essence of our true nature. In reality beliefs and attitudes are characteristic features of our mind and mind is one of the faculty of our being but not vice versa. So when we give benefit of doubt to the negative 30%, then failure is bound to materialize. When we perceive our being through our mind, then our mind due to its settled ways of habits and routines resist any change. Then however intelligent deliberation we go through but our old ways gained by way of experience prevail. In such a case even our attitude to stall does not happen to gain time for further deliberations but we deliberate to stall. In this manner we as separate entity do not remain as central aspect to anything, but our mind becomes focal point, and as our mind could not remain at any one place or state for any length of time as it constantly oscillates, then we exist at either extremes. The process of any and every religion and its doctrine is nothing but way that teaches us how to be central in every thing.

If at all we have to grow in positive and creative manner, then to exist in any extreme is not going to help us but if we can jettison our self in the middle, then there is possibility of our moving either up or down. In materialistic sense going up is considered as progress and in religious sense going deep towards our core is considered as progress. But to move from side to side is hedging and not considered as movement in any direction at all. At the same time any person, however unconscious he may be, do not want to slide down at any time. To be spiritual or to be aware is where religion comes in to play.

Every decision becomes powerful because it is ours and its acceptance generates the necessary power that is considered as motivational force or strength behind the drive. Every decision is the threshold that is considered as crossroad and whatever way we choose becomes cause for further choices and next batch of decisions. At this junction what we choose or do not choose, turns in to opportunities or lost opportunities. And Mahaveer says that to exploit these opportunities to our advantage happens only when we keep our mind open and use our intelligence for deliberation. As a metaphor Mahaveer tells that as a vessel if we close our lid tightly and ask the river will it give us water? Then what is the meaning of this question? River is always flowing and is ready to give at anytime, but we have to open the lid. This is how open we have to be and the disciple has to be. Opportunities are always happening all around us, but unless and until we are open we are not going to benefit from a single opportunity.

We are used exist in our surrounding in either fully open or fully closed manner. In Vedic philosophy an example is given of the royal bird known as swan, which has capability to separate milk from water, and takes only milk when the bowl is placed in front of the bird. And this phenomenon is described as " nirskhir vivek". The moral behind this myth is we have to accept only that much which is useful to us and helps to develop us according to our basic nature. So when we are fully open mentally then we take everything inside of us, in which hazardous as well as beneficial to our being is also accepted. Now or later this hazardous or unwanted create many problems in our psyche as well in our body and due to which we have to pay dearly in the form of psychological abnormalities and physical disabilities. Exactly opposite happens when we remain totally closed mentally. We loose opportunities to grow in positive and creative manner and our potentials atrophy without any kind of realization. It is a law of nature that whatever we are given, if it is not used or exploited properly then the potential to use the given or inherent, withers away and falls from us.

Only human race has freedom of choice, but most of times more choices than necessary create confusion and stress, and to shield the self from this confusion and stress, people remain mentally closed. And at this junction religion as means to develop our awareness become useful. We have to remain open to such an extent that we can control the traffic of what is to be taken in and what is to be left aside. This is how person of awakened nature behaves.

There is an engraving of a tortoise going towards sanctum sanctorum in every temple. What is the significance of this engraving in relation to human for whom these temples are built? Four legs and a head are five sense organs and faculties of human's that retract into the shell the moment we are near the

God. Tortoise is just a metaphor denoting human potentials and capabilities. When we study and understand the significance of every sense faculty and its related organ in relation to our being and existence, by way of experience we gain knowledge and the knowledge gained in this manner frees us from all the false notions, which is awareness. Manifestation of awareness is the cause of enhanced intelligence and our intelligence is shown as our head. When we become aware, is the stage that now we are ready to surrender ourselves in front of the chosen deity or God and in the manner of tortoise our sense organs and our intelligence retracts in the shell as our physical body and we surrender our self to the God.

All the things are reciprocatory and are instrumental to our journey, the goal of which is but only one i.e. realization of self. The same happens in the presence of master or guru. He is also instrumental to help us to achieve realization of our self, where he has reached before us and is aware of all the pitfalls on the way about which he can warn us. But even master or guru part from us once we achieve self-realization, because after happening of this phenomenon there remain nothing of significance to achieve.

We have limitless potentials and how we use or exploit them depends on us. Krishna is as valid today as Mahaveer is, as Mohemad is as is Buddha and Jesus. No doubt circumstances are drastically different in relation to all the pioneers mentioned above. But due to whom and for whom these circumstances are different, is the same since and now or later i.e. us as human beings.

Evolution from monkey to human being is monumental in itself, but this evolution is not the end of evolutionary process as far as we humans are concerned. The possibility remains largly because humans have vast potentials to develope in more creative manner and to help in this endavour superior intelligence is accorded to us as an instrument. But it is our ego and to the larger extent our notion of our selfworth, which cause restraint in our creative development and maturity.

Until now and on various occasions names of the most of the pioneers of every religion are stated, who were towering personalities before us. At the same time in present also, there are numerous personalities who has evovled upto the same extent. Their being, their way of life and their thoughts are still known to us, but it seems that very few of us can take advantage of this knowledge. Generally we absolve ourself by telling each other that those people were chosen ones and it was God's will. This defeatist attitude of ours is the cause of not realizing our full potentials.

Is being of God is reality or not is immaterial. Mahaveer, Buddha, Mohemad, Jesus or Krishna may or may not have experienced the presence of God. But what difference this phenomenon is going to make in our being or living is importent. At the begining of this discussion it is stated that Mahaveer denied presence of the God or the concept that the God is supreme creator, only because Mahaveer knows the conditioned nature of human being as well as psychology of the humans. Even we, as grown-up looks for assistence in everything we intend to do. Till we are supported and proped-up from all the sides, we do not act. We have become so sullen by nature, that any peception of imaginary or actual insult or criticism by other's moves us to the core. For this reason Mahaveer has to rudly awaken us, that we are responsible for our being and the state in which we exist is our doing and no one else is responsible for us. There is no God that will help or assist us anywhere and at any time, till we are ready to take responsibility of our self. We have choices and we may choose to behave like animal and die like one, or behave like humans as we are intended to be and then die like humans after realizing our potentials. Even as dotting parents we do not carry our young ones for indefinite period but we set them down so they can walk on their own; otherwise they start to cling to anyone and everyone or look for assistence at all the times.

Egoistic personalities face very chronic problem namely adamance and insolence because of which they do not learn new and creative ways or acquire new knowledge. So when we set our ego in ivory tower and when we have to face any difficulty or barrier then the moorings and foundation of the same tower become loose and we start to shake. Mahaveer points towards the fact that why there are so many psychological abnormalities? Why people behave in bizzare manner? When any person from otherwise sane and sober family and society, starts to behave in abnormal fashion, to whom we are going to blame; the individual or his family or society at large? In psychology, general surrounding and circumstances are also considered as stressers, which is one of the causes because of which the perosn is deemed to be affected. But if the family has to take responsibility and society has to take resposibility, then the affected person seems to be victim of a large scale conspiracy. Then how come a person from slums become successful in all the wordly manner and accrue fame and riches, irrespective of all the letent privations he has to face since birth? Mahaveer says this happens only because of our unconscious nature. When people start to build castles of future in the present without taking stock of their own capabilities, then now or latter they are going to experience shocking and shattering surprises. Compassionate and sympathatic approch is a good virtue, but how much sympathy is optimum; sympathy in constant supply also causes dependency on others, and this dependency cause anger, frustration and revulsion in the mind of the compassionate helper. So if and when we are really willing to change then there is possibility of change, but if we are going to be adament and pigheaded in our set ways, then even presence of Mahaveer is not going to be of much help. Mahaveer says that if we meet any master that is near to our ideal, then totally accept him and be a good disciple or if we are sure of our self then we have to be our own master.

Way of Mahaveer is way of male psychology; it is aggressive by nature. By nature male is always aggressive and female is always passive and submissive. To resolve is characteristic of aggressive nature and to surrender is characteristic of submissive nature. Meerabai is the epitome of total surrender towards Lord Krishna. Resolute person is like an arrow; going straight towards intended mark, without paying any attention to all that lies in its trajectory or surrounding.

In resolution, resolving person realizes his potentials on his own and retains his entity and individuality, but in surrender, the merger with idol or concept happens where the surrendering person ceases to exist but only idol remains. Both reach the same destination but ways of journey are different. What is to be unerstood is that even in resolution, the mind of the person resolving do not agree cent percent, so what remains as undecided is to be turned into surrender towards the cause for resolution. And the same happens in total surrender but what remains as undecided is to be turned into resolve to stick with surrender.

At the conclusion Mahaveer says that to take birth as human is not end in itself, but evolution is still happening. Only thing is to be human we have to acquire the qualities like we have to be humane, should practice riligion, should have faith in our self and have to be tranquil. To realize our self is also implicit part and parcel of evolution. In evolutionary process, changes in everything at all the times happens. In case of humans, process of evolution stops and comes to fruition only when the person realizes his self, after which the person completely goes out of the loop of rebirth and death.

Basic difference between Mahaveer's doctrine and other religious doctrines is; all the doctrines believe that a supreme creator has created every thing. But Mahaveer says that if this is the case, then there is no possibility of further evolution. Then what we are is limit bound, and when very few enjoy and others suffer, then the creator is very much biased. Similarly if the human is made in the image of God, then what this image is suffring today and doing to each other directly reflects on the God; that God has created very inferior product in the human form, which is not happy as it is. Then why we humans are bestowed with superior intelligence? In this regard Mahaveer says that there is no supreme creator that is omnipotent, omnipresent or omniscient. But what we are is part of evolution that is happening in nature continuously and it is our responsibility to evolve further, for which we have a faculty called superior intelligence and keen mind.

Even theory of Darwin is pointing to the same evolutionary process and not towards creation by any superior power. In his research Darwin found that we have basically evolved from acquatic origines. When scientists checked the validity of Darwinian theory, they found many similarities in animal and human anotomy. Even today in some basic acts, functioning and baser expressions we act and behave like animals, for eg. characteristic similarities of locomation between human and animals are same; animals walk on four legs and humans walks with the help of two legs but our one foot and one arm move at the same time in the same direction, in anger we clench our jaw and grind our teeth as animal clenches its jaw and bares its teeth before attack.

But Mahaveer says that as humans we have not only developed physically but our force of life is also developed. And because of this developed force of life and superior intelligence, Mahaveer incorporated concept of Ahimsa/ non-violence, in his doctrine. From a tiny bacteria to human being every one moves because of force of life or Prana or Chaitanya, and its coursing through our body is the reason we are alive, and the same force of life also courses through all the animates. Similarly we may have passed through in various forms of organisms and animals, but as all the organisms except human's are not so much awakened and intelligent, we may have died without due awareness and so we do not have any past recollection as to what we were. Mahaveer says that even animals we are seeing today are going through evolution process and they may evolve as humans in future. So when each and every organism is happening due to evolution, we do not have any right to harm anyone knowingly or unknowingly, and doing so is called as basic sin and pure violence. Similarly as a human being we do not have any right to harm or kill any one, as we do not have capability to bring back a life in the first place.

For the last time we have to understand that advent, existence and development of religion and its doctrine is meant only for humans. In other words religion is nothing but code of conduct for the humans, as only humans have very developed mind and matching intelligence. And this developed faculty of mind and intelligence is the reson that humans can and may go out of law of nature or can transcend the same. Religion is not for any other living organism because such organisms exist as per their intended natural nature. Religious practice is not senseless ritual; religion is not for those who are totally destitute or for those who have lost everything and as a last resort should become religious. Similarly religious practice is not last duty of the aged for whom nothing of significance is possible to do. To be humane human and to live and exist like human is true religion. Religion is the basic norm of humanity. Any person transgressing the bounds of norm either go to jail or behave in abnormal manner. Cause of behavioral abnormalities of all the types happen due to repeated deviations from the norms set down for humans by the nature and surrounding existence.

Mahaveer says to be humane, we have to be compassionate and sympathatic towards all and sundry. What we have to understand is all these characteristics can be acquired by way of inner change only. We appear like human, but are we really are? What about Hitler, Stalin, Aurangzeb, Rawana, serial killers, mass murderers, caste aginst caste, cult against cult, minority against majority. Then are we devil in the guise of human? Emminent thinkers tell that Hitler is to be explained as human attitude and as attitudes are acquired by humans, then we or someone like us are collectively responsible. To proclaim any race as superior is sign of megalomaniac mindset and a person and his cohorts of this mindset were people who were ignorents with tunnel vision but were heedlessly ambitious.

Humane human is the person who has expanded mind and his mind functions under the rule of his intelligence with awareness. Then such a person is considered as fully bloomed personality with total awareness. Flowring or blooming of a person is journey towards total awareness, which when totally blooms is the moment of realization of self; like all the patels are fully opened and scent emanating from it is making the surrounding fregerant and then whoever comes in its contact experiences joy and happiness. This manifestation is called as Punya or most sacred being of any person.

Let all of us make a commitment with our self that as intelligent persons and as future psychothearapists, we will strive to realize our basic self and our full potentials and try to help all those people who are going to need our help and help those people to realize the same potentials as we have realized. Let us start to live and exist as we are intended to be– as humans.